RUNNING ALONE

RUNNING ALONE

Presidential Leadership—
JFK TO BUSH II

Why It Has Failed

AND

How We Can Fix It

JAMES MACGREGOR BURNS

A Member of the Perseus Books Group
New York

Published by Basic Books
A Member of the Perseus Books Group

Designed by BackStory Design

Library of Congress Cataloging-in-Publication Data
Burns, James MacGregor.
   Running alone : presidential leadership from JFK to Bush II : why it
has failed and how we can fix it / James MacGregor Burns.
      p.   cm.
   ISBN-13: 978-0-465-00832-2 (hardcover : alk. paper)
   ISBN-10: 0-465-00832-1 (hardcover : alk. paper)
   1. Presidents—United States—History—20th century.   2. Presidents—
United States—History—21st century.   3. Presidents—United States—Biography.
4. Political leadership—United States—Case studies.   5. Isolation (Philosophy)—
Case studies.   6. United States—Politics and government—1945-1989—
Case studies.   7. United States—Politics and government—1989- —Case studies.
8. Political participation—United States.   I. Title.

   E176.1.B9345 2006
   973.92092'2—dc22

                                                                2006021680

10 9 8 7 6 5 4 3 2 1

For Susan

Contents

"I THINK YOU
UNDERESTIMATE HIM"

One day, when John Kennedy was still in the U.S. Senate, I asked him how he looked back on his days in the House of Representatives. "Oh," he said, "we were just worms there." Curious, I thought, but typical Jack Kennedy humor. A few years later, though, when I asked him in the White House how he remembered his life in the Senate, he made exactly the same comment about the upper chamber.

Worms? What could he possibly mean? Later, as I reflected on my conversations with him and studied his character, I concluded that he harbored a deep, perhaps unconscious, even hubristic, desire for personal and intellectual independence—a distaste for being part of the pack. This often meant keeping his distance from the "worms," with their petty quarrels and artifices. Some of this doubtless showed the influence of his father, Joe Kennedy, who was famous for his financial and political self-assertiveness. Neither father nor son had any sympathy for worms or losers.

Still, Jack Kennedy's disdain for politicos surprised me because he himself was such a natural politician, so attractive and gregarious, though without any effusive glad-handing. He was the most engaging "great man" I ever met—bright, funny, utterly lacking in pomp. It was like meeting an old college friend. Not that he didn't know the score. He had a fascination with the mechanics and minutiae of politics that rivaled that of a ward boss. On one occasion, he greeted me right off with, "How are you doing in Boston?" I thought for a moment he had forgotten I lived at the farther end of the state; then I realized he was bringing up a

1

political scrape of mine in the Hub so trivial that no newspaper had reported it.

I MET Kennedy early in his career, through my involvement in Massachusetts Democratic politics, and we became better acquainted in 1958, when we were on the same ticket—he running for reelection to the Senate and I for a first term in the House of Representatives. He won and I lost. He had been helpful to my effort, campaigning alongside me through my western Massachusetts district. He appeared with me on the radio in Boston; as we were leaving the station, he slipped a small wad of bills into my coat pocket as a contribution to my meager store of campaign funds (I only feebly resisted). But I was one of the rare candidates with whom he campaigned together. Other Democrats were disappointed that he would not share his coattails with them—that in effect he ran alone.

Not, of course, that he had run alone in any literal sense. Far from it. I had had a firsthand glimpse of the extent to which his 1958 campaign had relied on his large family and a tight political clan of loyalists, on a powerful and efficient statewide political organization that worked apart from and sometimes in conflict with the Democratic party.

This style of politics heightened my interest in Kennedy. In 1959, as he was beginning his race for the presidency, I decided to write a book about him. He agreed to open up his Senate files; asked his family to talk with me; and endured being tape-recorded for hours. It was understood that I had no obligation except to write as complete, truthful, and revealing a study as that access would allow.

As it turned out, Jack and his family were enormously disappointed when the book was published early in election year 1960, especially by its final judgmental sentences. My conclusion had emerged from an examination of Kennedy's relationship with the Democratic party, particularly his conflicts with its activist, impassioned, ideas-driven liberal wing, to which I myself belonged. To the real issue of our age, I wrote, the issue of survival, "Kennedy could bring bravery and wisdom; whether he would bring passion and power would depend on his making a commitment not only of mind, but of heart, that until now he has never been required to make."

The most moving comments came from Jacqueline Kennedy in a hand-written letter from Hyannisport:

"I think you underestimate him. Anyone sees he has the intelligence—magnetism and drive it takes to succeed in politics. I see, every succeeding week I am married to him, that he has what may be the single most important quality for a leader—an imperturbable self confidence and sureness of his powers." What other candidate, she asked, had talked with Chamberlain and Churchill in his twenties, known Nehru and Ben-Gurion in his thirties, and visited Stalin's Russia? Who else had friends and colleagues in the French and British parliaments?

"You are like him in many ways," she added beguilingly, "—an intellectual who has gone into politics. You know the hard parts and the pitfalls. Can't you see that he is exceptional?" Her critique struck home: Had I badly underestimated a potential leader?

IN THE 1960 campaign, Jack Kennedy proved, as his wife had predicted he would, that he had the drive to succeed, first winning the Democratic presidential nomination and then the presidency itself. To an astonishing degree, he ran nationally as he had in Massachusetts, apart from—and sometimes against—the Democratic party. The personal organization he built for 1960—reaching down to the grass roots in counties across the country—was so powerful and efficient that it became a campaign issue itself, especially among the party rivals he had beaten for the nomination.

With his startling success in 1960, Kennedy invented a new brand of political campaigning. He engineered a new route to the presidency. After him, most candidates would no longer see party leadership as essential to their ambitions. While wearing party labels, they would follow Kennedy's example by hunting for votes wherever they could be found—not only in the swelling ranks of independents but also in the opposition party. Like Kennedy, they would ignore party platforms when it suited them and tailor messages narrowly to reach vulnerable constituencies. Like Kennedy, they would piece together personal, transient electoral coalitions whose one purpose was to get them into office. They would take what they could from their parties, of course, but they would give them limited leadership in return. Their proudest boast was not that they were Republicans or Democrats but that they were independent—of party bosses, party ideas and ideals, and party commitments.

Why then did JFK adopt personal leadership as his basic strategy? Partly because it suited his enormously competitive instincts and his drive for distinction from the herd, as well as his skepticism toward ideological commitments, toward the dogmas and doctrines that unify and vitalize political parties. Partly because his main experience with Democratic politics was among the factional "pols" of Boston. He took their personalistic politics to a new—and ultimately national—level. But his separation from—even antagonism toward—the Democratic party had profound implications for his leadership style when he entered the White House.

As Kennedy knew well from his history and government courses at Harvard, most presidential candidates in the end had run as loyal Democrats or Republicans. And the greatest presidents in American history had succeeded in office because they were great party leaders. Their transforming leadership—the deep, comprehensive, and enduring change they achieved—was grounded in the collaborative action of government, which in turn was based on party mobilization and cohesion from the grass roots up.

These lessons were lost on John Kennedy. In the White House, though, JFK discovered that the "Kennedy brand" had its limitations. To lead, he needed the help of all the Democrats in Congress. Efficient and creative government calls for strongly collective government. Historically, that has been achieved through presidential party leadership. But when Kennedy sought to put through his major reforms in areas such as health care and education, he found that many of the Democrats in Congress with whom he had refused to run together in the 1960 campaign did not feel obliged to help him govern in the presidency. They would leave him to govern alone.

RUNNING ALONE has become the dominant political strategy in the forty years since Kennedy's death, with grave consequences for American government. Presidential candidates who have run alone successfully have tried to bring that style of leadership with them into the Oval Office. The attempt to govern alone has taken various forms through successive administrations, but it has been the defining principle of presidential politics since Kennedy and a crucial factor in the failure of so many presidents to lead.

Richard Nixon put personal loyalty to him far above any allegiances to party or ideology. As president, he viewed government bureaucrats and even his own Cabinet secretaries and White House staffers as potential enemies instead of as collaborators. Desperately lonely at the top, Nixon shifted left and right in politics and policy, picking up support opportunistically even among liberal and especially conservative Democrats. Unlike Republican presidents of the past, he was unable to build and govern with stable party backing.

As Southern governors, Jimmy Carter and Bill Clinton both ran "against Washington," opposing even their own party's national leadership. Both men slighted the liberal base of the Democratic party in an effort to appeal to the middle ground, the uncommitted constituents who came to be known as "swing voters." In the White House, their centrist strategies, which left them governing alone, apart from their party, defeated their efforts to offer transforming leadership.

Ronald Reagan, one of two Kennedy successors—the other was Lyndon Johnson—to reject JFK's brand of leadership and to forge, at least for a time, a true collective leadership, bequeathed to the first George Bush a Republican party revitalized around a new and conservative core. But, lacking Reagan's strong ideological partisanship, Bush I* abandoned the right for the center and lost the GOP's fervent base.

Unlike his father, Bush II ran together with the right-wing base of the Republican party, but unlike Reagan, he has failed to fashion a true collective leadership. Instead of broadening the GOP, Bush II has narrowed it, creating a disciplined, hard-right organization that has barely won elections and barely wins votes in Congress. It has become the vehicle for the personalistic presidency of George W. Bush.

The Bush presidency shows the dangers of the Kennedy brand of personal leadership when practiced by aggressive power seekers. True collective leadership, which combines the power to lead with accountability, means that a president governs together with a broad and united coalition of Americans.

---

*These designations are not invidious but result from perusing too many books that do not make clear which Bush is being referred to. Alternative designations are either condescending (Bush Junior) or confusing (Bush 41 or 43).

Resting on his narrow base of right-wing militants, Bush II has consolidated personal power to an extent unprecedented in American history, and he has used that power to evade accountability. In the White House today, a tight little band of leaders—president and vice president bottomed by a fiercely political staff of right-wing ideologues—runs the most conservative regime in the last century. Lacking a wider mandate, they govern by stealth and deception, by usurping the functions of Congress and the courts. In effect, they govern alone, producing the outcome the Framers of the Constitution most feared: unaccountable presidential power.

EVEN FROM within the highly disciplined ranks of George W. Bush's Republican party, we are hearing the voices of dissent. America needs better leaders. Since Thomas Jefferson, great leadership has emerged from strong parties, from leaders who have run together with such parties and presented Americans with genuine alternatives. These leaders have won broad mandates from voters, with a winning party team that has united president and legislature in a government with both responsibility and power.

We need such vital and creative collective leadership as we confront the daunting challenges of the twenty-first century, but to get it we must reverse nearly a half century of decline. We need a new and compelling leadership that speaks to the real needs of Americans, that will mobilize them behind a drive for deep and enduring change. We need a leadership that will run and govern together with Americans, a leadership rivaling that of the Framers, who fashioned a constitutional and party transformation two centuries ago.

Chapter 1

THE TRIBAL THRUST

Reporters who interviewed Jack Kennedy were often captivated by his ready bonhomie and even more by his occasional candor. This openness might have been a carryover from Kennedy's earlier days, when he had taken a stab at journalism and interviewed tight-lipped European politicians and diplomats. Of course, he was aware of the image he wanted to project and guard, but he also understood reporters' needs—and he needed their goodwill. Certainly when I interviewed him for my biography in 1959, he was forthcoming about his early life, to the extent that he could recall it. Only very occasionally did he ask that I not mention some indiscretion in "your book." Although he was a bit hazy about where he had lived as a child, he recalled his first home in a "third rate district" in Boston, and then moves to better neighborhoods—Brookline, Bronxville in New York—as his father's wealth grew.

Talking with me about his father, Joe, John Kennedy was both revealing and reticent. Where did his own drive come from? "A lot of that was my father, I think, who was always rather harsh, not harsh but more harsh years ago. I don't think his health was good, he was always living in a nervous pitch, he was speculating and all the rest so he was always somewhat peremptory, but he was always emphasizing [competitive] racing and all the rest, that we always do well. He's more mellow now, but then he was quite. . . he set rather a standard for action."

Joe's own drive—his fierce ambition and stubborn self-reliance—fueled his feverish rise in the business world. After apprenticeships in banking and shipbuilding, he made fortunes in liquor and motion pictures, in stock and real-estate speculation. Still, his real hunger was for political power and prestige. Though his pro-business conservatism and fierce nationalism were more in line with the Republicanism of his era, Joe was a lifelong Democrat, loyal to the party of his birth. In 1932, realizing that in the circumstances of the Depression the country needed "a leader who could lead," he became an early supporter of Franklin Roosevelt, who named him the first chairman of the Securities and Exchange Commission and then ambassador to Britain. But Joe infuriated FDR in the late 1930s with what Roosevelt considered his defeatism in the face of Nazi aggression, while Joe chafed at his subordination to "the boss" and his State Department. Their close alliance descended into bitter rivalry, an enmity that destroyed Joe's chances to realize his ultimate ambition—winning the presidency for himself.

The father's drive set the standard for his children. It defined what it meant to be a Kennedy. The siblings were ferociously competitive among themselves—warring at games like football and swimming as well as in dinner talk of current events, where Joe himself could be challenged, though guardedly. But they were united and disciplined in their competition with the world, absorbing Joe's hard lesson that life was a struggle for survival and achievement. They created a circle of mutual dependence and trust that even close friends—and, later, spouses—found difficult to penetrate.

The eldest son, Joe Jr., was the focus of the father's ambition for his children. According to *New York Times* reporter and family friend Arthur Krock, Joe intended for him to be "the political leader in the next generation." Physically aggressive, the mirror of his father's conservative ideas, startlingly self-assured, Joe Jr. confided to friends even before he went to college that he was going to be the first Catholic president of the United States. Jack, the second son, was different. Often ill as a child—among his many ailments was a serious bout of scarlet fever at age three and a debilitating but undiagnosed condition that persisted through his teens—Jack was frailer, shier, and more self-contained. Long confinements to bed made him more bookish than his siblings. He was drawn to biographies and histories featuring Great Men and plenty of "flair, action, and color," as his mother Rose Kennedy remembered.

But Jack too shared the family's competitive thrust. "He played for keeps," a Harvard football coach would recall. Bullied by his older brother, Jack fought back. "Physically we used to have some fights," he told me in 1959, "which, of course, he always won." One time, "we ran a [bicycle] race against each other around the block" in opposite directions and collided. "I really tore this all up and got, I guess, 28 stitches and he emerged unscathed."

The Kennedy spirit of distinctiveness, as well as Joe's wealth and power, insulated the children from the discrimination he himself had known as a young Irish Catholic struggling to penetrate Boston's WASP establishment. Joe's father, P. J. Kennedy, a prosperous saloon keeper and political boss, lived quite separately from the "drunken Irishmen" down near the wharves. More prominent families, like Rose Kennedy's parents, the Fitzgeralds, lived even farther out from the Irish ghettos, in handsome houses in the suburbs. Still, in Brahmin Boston, Jack's parents felt marked. But, talking with me, Jack himself couldn't say that he was highly conscious of being an Irish Catholic boy at the elite private schools he attended. His experience wasn't "comparable to the usual one, like someone growing up and going to a Boston school as Irish Catholic, where the social barriers between racial groups—Irish and Italian, between so-called Yankee and Irish—are extremely sharp." At Harvard, Kennedy made strong and lasting friendships with Catholics and Protestants alike. It wasn't so much his religion as his independence—his resistance to the insularity of the college's social and political clubs—that kept him, as he told me, "somewhat outside the numerically small but most cohesive group in the class."

But then, despite his closeness to leaders of the Church, piety was no part of Joe's creed, at least not where his sons were concerned. Jack remembered his mother as the Catholic he was most aware of in his life, partly because his father "was away a lot" on business. But also, "she was terribly religious," and "he's not so religious," Jack said. All the boys went to secular schools and colleges, but Joe sent the girls to religious schools because "he felt that the development of personal qualities was more important for the girls, and the development of the abilities to maintain yourself in a difficult environment" was more important for the sons.

JOE KENNEDY expected less of his second son than of his first-born, but that didn't give Jack a pass. The pressure was direct, insistent, and consistent. When Jack, a 17-year-old senior at Choate, promised to stop "bluffing myself about how much real work I have been doing," Joe replied sternly. "Now Jack, I don't want to give the impression that I am a nagger, for goodness knows I think that is the worst thing any parent can be, and I also feel that you know if I didn't really feel you had the goods I would be most charitable in my attitude toward your failings. After long experience in sizing up people I definitely know you have the goods and you can go a long way. Now aren't you foolish not to get all there is out of what God has given you and what you can do with it yourself." Joe didn't expect Jack to be a "real genius," but, he wrote, "I think you can be a really worthwhile citizen with good judgment and good understanding."

And Joe was ready and able to give his son's talents a shove in the right direction. When Jack finished his Harvard undergraduate thesis on Britain's failure to re-arm in the 1930s as the Nazi threat mounted, Joe enlisted Arthur Krock to edit the manuscript and acquire an agent. Krock even came up with the title, *Why England Slept*. Published in 1940, the book was mightily promoted by Joe and became a surprising success, selling 80,000 copies in the United States and Britain and winning praise from reviewers. Jack became a minor celebrity, and to Joe that was the point. "You would be surprised," he wrote to his son before dispatching copies to London's political elite, "how a book that really makes the grade with high-class people stands you in good stead for years to come."

Would Joe's bottomless paternalism spoil Jack Kennedy? Some close to the family feared that he would become as dependent on his father's ideas as he was on Joe's money. But this did not happen, partly because Joe did not wish it. Rather, he encouraged Jack to shape his own views, even urging him in his book not to whitewash the British leaders whose appeasement of Hitler the ambassador had supported. Like Joe, Jack was pessimistic about the capacity of democratic societies to compete in military might with dictatorships, but the son recognized better than the father that "the great advantage" of democracy was that "ability and not brute force" was the "qual-ification for leadership." The challenge was to produce able leaders in times of crisis. He warned Americans to learn from the British example and pre-pare for conflict with dictators—a stark contrast to the advice Joe had given both British and American officials.

Jack distanced himself from his father's political views in other ways as well. His travels across Europe in the 1930s and war experiences in the Navy produced an internationalist, even interventionist outlook that clashed with Joe's angry isolationism. His Harvard teachers fostered in Jack political ideas distinct from Joe's strong pro-business conservatism. Talking with me in 1959, Jack reflected that, confronted with the overbearing influence of a man like his father, you do one of two things—"You just do nothing or you move out from under."

But not for many years did young Kennedy "move out from under." It was a determined Joe Kennedy Sr. who pushed Jack into politics. The fa-ther's hopes for his eldest son died in 1944 when the plane Joe Jr. was flying on a mission to the Belgian coast exploded. Devastated, the father shifted the focus of his ambition to Jack, who himself had been seriously wounded in the Pacific when a Japanese destroyer rammed his PT boat. Only a few months after his eldest son's death, Joe gave Jack his marching orders. Jack didn't want a political career, Joe remembered a dozen years later. "He felt he didn't have the ability. . . . But I told him he had to."

For a while, Jack resisted his father's pressure. He had always wanted to be a writer. The success of *Why England Slept* had roused hopes of a brilliant literary or journalistic career. Indeed, after the war, he signed on with Hearst's Chicago paper to cover the United Nations' charter conference in San Francisco. With two friends, he bought a small weekly, the *Narragansett Times*, that was circulated in Rhode Island and southeastern Massachusetts. But soon he lost interest and felt at loose ends. "There never was a moment of truth for me when I saw my whole political career unfold," he recalled in an autobiographical note he recorded privately in 1960. "Suddenly, the time, the occasion, and I all met. . . . I began to run. I have been running ever since."

HE BEGAN by running alone, clambering up the stairs of a three-decker to knock on the door of a longshoreman or mill worker. He did not relish making the pitch. Sometimes people slammed the door in his face, or muttered something in a foreign language, or thought he was a salesman. He had to say quickly, "I'm Jack Kennedy and I'm running for Congress." Gaunt and spindly, his back in a brace, he still showed the effects of wartime malaria. But he had a winning smile, and once he got his foot in the door he captivated voters.

It was 1946—the first election since the war—and the 28-year-old upstart was running for Congress in the Eleventh Massachusetts District for the seat of that indestructible Irish pol, James Michael Curley, who had served in various city, state, and federal offices since 1899. He had also served a term in jail for fraud. In Congress since 1942, Curley was induced by Joe to give up his seat for another run for mayor of Boston. Joe would finance Curley's campaign—and pay off his heavy personal debts.

Joe Kennedy not only cleared the way for Jack's run, he paved it. It was Joe who set strategy, lined up key supporters, handled press publicity, hired an advertising agency, and controlled who would—and would not—serve as campaign managers in the wards. Every major decision had to be cleared with Joe. He could do all this because of paternal authority—and because he controlled campaign spending, as much as several hundreds of thousands of dollars, almost all of it his money.

Massive help seemed necessary because at the start there appeared to be a total misfit between candidate and constituency. Jack was different from the pols Bostonians were accustomed to. Hard and aggressive men like Curley— loud-talking, florid, paunchy—had long been fixtures in the city's politics. Boyish Jack Kennedy even seemed shy when you first met him. People knew little of him, other than his name. And he knew little of the voters, of their needs and attitudes and their local leaders. Many of those leaders resented him for running for Congress, for not starting his political career at the usual low level—in the state legislature or city council—and waiting his turn. Those who wanted the seat themselves were especially bitter. City councilman Joseph Russo, who lost a race for the seat in 1942, had put together "a very nice organization" for 1946 and thought he had "a good shot at it" this time.

He had waited his turn, but "here is a young man and he runs into my district. And there I am."

Jack Kennedy did not even live in the district, adversaries complained; he simply resided in the Hotel Bellevue, near the state capitol on Beacon Hill. But Kennedy had two powerful personal connections with Boston politics that his sternest critics could not disparage. One was 83-year-old John Francis Fitzgerald, Rose's father. "Honey Fitz" seemed such a sentimental old windbag by 1946 that many people had forgotten he had served three terms in the U.S. House of Representatives and three as mayor of Boston. The "darling of the North End," Fitzgerald had been a member of the "Board of Strategy," an inner circle of Democratic bosses that had dominated politics and patronage city-wide at the turn of the twentieth century. So had Jack's other grandfather, P. J. Kennedy, who had ruled East Boston for decades and served in both the lower and upper chambers of the state legislature.

Even with this heritage and Joe's resources, the Eleventh District itself was formidable. Its wards and precincts sprawled across not only the family's old domains of the North End and East Boston, but also the West End, Cambridge, low-income Brighton, and more middle-class Somerville. Culturally, it embraced not only the Irish, but also hosts of Italians and at least thirty ethnic clusters, including Chinese, Syrian, and Yankee communities. Each section had its own ward politicos and tribal chieftains—and its own candidate in the congressional primary. Indeed, Italians found they had a choice of not one but two Joe Russos on the ballot. Of Kennedy's foes, the most formidable by far was the popular mayor of Cambridge, Mike Neville. No one expected Jack to carry that city—his Harvard links would make little difference—or, for that matter, any other ward. The Kennedy strategy was to run second everywhere and thus win the biggest overall district vote.

Such a plan demanded face-to-face campaigning across the whole district, and Kennedy was coming to find handshaking easier, even a bit enjoyable. "Irish Patsy" Mulkern, a self-appointed authority on street campaigning, had to credit the rich kid. "Kennedy covered every street in da district," Patsy would rave years later. "Every street, for chrissakes. . . .

Shook hands wit more people than I ever knowed in a campaign. People wouldn't go for him at first. Then he caught on. . . . He kept goin'. Never ate much. Great frappe drinker. Frappes, frappes, frappes. . . ."

KENNEDY RECRUITED helpers as he campaigned, mobilizing a bevy of young enthusiasts who soon developed into a close-knit political clan—a "band of brothers." Most were veterans who felt a strong personal bond with the candidate. "There was a tremendous ferment after the war" among young vets, recalled one of them, Mark Dalton, who became Jack's campaign manager in 1946. "The whole feeling of taking over—that it's a new era." John Galvin, a Navy vet who handled the campaign's publicity, remembered that they "really and truly had a great desire to bring about some changes in American political life." This infused the campaign, he said, with "the kind of enthusiasm you can't buy," giving it the energy of a crusade. Few of these young followers had political backgrounds or connections to other politicians. They were devoted less to party or platform than to Jack Kennedy, who seemed to represent that new era and hope for change.

From the start, personality, not politics, was the campaign's centerpiece. Jack's campaign talks played up his war experience rather than an agenda for change. He made the most of the sinking of his PT boat, telling it as a dramatic story of disaster and survival. But modesty was part of his appeal; he directed attention to the heroism of his crewmates. In memory of his older brother, the family had established the Joseph P. Kennedy Jr. Post of the Veterans of Foreign Wars, of which Jack was post commander. Jack created a powerful bond with Gold Star mothers, whose sons had been killed in the war, when he told a group of them, "I think I know how all you mothers feel because my mother is a gold star mother, too."

Later, with the help of Harvard advisers, the candidate dwelt more on issues closer to the needs of the district's voters—jobs, a minimum wage, union rights, tougher rent controls, and, for veterans, the GI Bill and low-cost housing. In choosing to sound more like FDR than Joe Kennedy, Jack was responding to his constituency. On his campaign rounds, he encountered the dark and shabby world of the abjectly poor for the first time, and gained a truer understanding of people's real needs.

Still, Kennedy was no firebrand for Democratic causes. He told a reporter from the Harvard *Crimson*, "I'm not doctrinaire. I'll vote them the way I see them." Jack invited him, the reporter wrote, to "look at his record in two years and see what he stands for." Likewise, Kennedy's speech to the Junior League late in the campaign, titled "Why I Am a Democrat," was hardly a profession of faith and passion. Kennedy saw "the two party system strained as never before" as the "traditional parties" were becoming indistinguishable and ineffective amalgams of conservative and liberal elements while being challenged by "the large growth of those who call themselves political independents who owe allegiance to neither party—but only to the individual." Jack made clear that for himself political loyalty was a matter not of a fighting faith in political doctrines but of a detached and rational scrutiny of the comparative merits of the two parties. He indicated that he would reserve his own independent judgment, pointing out that, "All the things the Democratic Party has done I cannot approve." That led him to an unresounding peroration: He was a Democrat because on balance "most things done by the Democratic Party have made us stronger at home and abroad."

In any case, it wasn't the candidate's ideas that made the deepest impression on the district's voters. It was his house parties. They were nothing new in Boston politics, but the Kennedys raised them to new heights of elegance and efficiency. The parties were so successful that they had pride of place in every succeeding campaign. The family's women—especially sisters Eunice and Pat, but Rose too—were enlisted to provide coffee and cookies, flowers and silver, to housewives eager to open their homes for the handsome young bachelor's cause. Campaign headquarters followed up with letters to all who had assembled. The street man, Patsy Mulkern, remembered decades later how wowed he had been by the whole Kennedy operation. "He had the biggest rallies ever held in the North End; rallies, house parties, dances, every girl there was gonna be Mrs. Kennedy, for crissakes."

On primary day, June 18, 1946, Jack Kennedy won the Democratic nomination for the Eleventh Massachusetts Congressional District with 40 percent of the vote against nine opponents. He took twice the number of votes of his nearest competitor, Mike Neville, and even ran a close second to Neville in the mayor's own Cambridge. Honey Fitz sang his famous "Sweet Adeline" at the victory party.

Flush with victory, few in the Kennedy corner bothered to note that, with turnout low, Jack had seized the nomination with the votes of only 12 percent of the district's eligible Democrats. It didn't matter. Nor did the bruised feelings of the old pols—the party regulars—he had licked on their own turf.

In the Eleventh District, Democratic nomination was tantamount to election. No Republican had held the seat in decades. That fall, with his family and growing political clan behind him, Kennedy ran like an incumbent—but full speed ahead, like a man in a hurry.

∽

WINNING HIS OWN race by a margin of better than two to one, Kennedy had expected to join a large Democratic majority in the House of Representatives. But the 1946 midterm election was a shocker. In the first election after Franklin Roosevelt's death, the Democrats lost the control of Congress they had held since his 1932 sweep. Nineteen forty-six was a low year for the Democracy. The approval ratings of FDR's successor, Harry Truman, had fallen dramatically, and the great political coalition that had formed under the New Deal banner seemed in danger of breaking up. After the election, a noted Democratic senator, J. William Fulbright, observing the leadership vacuum at a moment when the Soviet Union was aggressively challenging the United States, proposed that Truman appoint a Republican senator to serve as secretary of state and then promptly resign so that the Republican could take over in the White House and, with Congress, provide unified government. "Halfbright," Truman called him.

To these conditions of flux and risk for Democrats, Kennedy brought from home the reputation of a man loyal to nothing but his own ambitions. He had developed little connection with the Massachusetts delegation in the House. Despite the weak Republican opposition he faced in the fall of 1946, he had offered almost no help to his party's candidates fighting tougher races. He arrived in Washington with no great respect for the Democratic leadership in Congress or the administration and had few close friends in either place. The national publicity he had already received—big plays in *Time* magazine and the *New York Times* for his primary win—had marked him as a comer, but now he found himself as but one of hundreds of members of Congress, a mere freshman in the minority party, with little scope for action.

Boyish-looking, not yet thirty years old, often dressed in the casual uniform of an undergraduate, Kennedy had small regard for the ancient folkways of Congress. Go along to get along—that age-old advice given to newcomers for rising very, very slowly through the House ranks to real power—held little appeal for Jack. No wonder that Sam Rayburn, the Texas Democrat who had held the Speakership before the 1946 losses and who better than anyone embodied the values of the House, quickly took a disliking to this young congressman who didn't do his homework, wasn't dependable, who clearly was no regular party man.

Nor did Kennedy share with regular Democrats like Rayburn veneration for the memory of FDR, whose long leadership still shadowed Washington; his irreverence reflected in part his father's enduring bitterness toward his late boss. Young Kennedy even voted for the twenty-second amendment to the Constitution, which barred presidents from serving more than two terms, thus joining Republicans in their crusade to defeat the four-term FDR retrospectively.

But Jack insisted on his political independence, even from his own father. When Joe said that the fledgling congressman was making a "terrible mistake" with a certain vote, his son turned on him: "Now, look here Dad, you have your political views and I have mine. . . . when it comes to voting, I'm voting my way."

FOREIGN POLICY was the area in which Kennedy felt most confident, where he was most assertive in displaying his independence—independence from the president, from the congressional leadership, from the Democratic party and its liberal wing. At a time when American anxieties about the Soviet threat were at fever pitch and Truman and the Democratic party were under furious Republican assault for "softness" in meeting it, Kennedy embraced a militant anti-communism. He echoed Republican charges that Poland had been "betrayed" at the Yalta conference in 1945—the *Boston Herald* headline: KENNEDY SAYS ROOSEVELT SOLD POLAND TO REDS. He laid blame for the "tragic" fall of China to communists in 1949 "squarely with the White House and the Department of State" and lamented that "what our young men had saved" in World War II "our diplomats and our President have frittered away." He followed that up by charging that the administration had no plans to protect American civilians against nuclear attack. So unrelenting were Jack's criticisms of Truman's foreign policies that the *Haverhill Gazette* back home suggested that "the political point" of one Kennedy speech in 1950 seemed to be "that the Republicans should try to sign him up for a job with their speaking bureau." To the indignation of liberal Democrats, Jack was reported to have committed the ultimate heresy in 1950 by saying that Joe McCarthy—the Republican anti-communist demagogue who charged that the Roosevelt and Truman administrations were rife with subversives—"may have something." That same year, he indicated that he was pleased by Richard Nixon's brutal victory over liberal icon Helen Gahagan Douglas in a California Senate race.

On domestic issues, Kennedy did tend to take orthodox liberal positions. He strongly supported public housing, social security, unemployment insurance, and federal aid to education. He did so, he later admitted to journalists, less from conviction than because "naturally the interests of my constituents led me to take the liberal line; all the pressures conveyed toward that end."

But even here Jack was not afraid to run away from his party. He had arrived on Capitol Hill as a fiscal conservative—doubtless due in part to his father's dinner-table lamentations over government spending and taxation. In 1950, he opposed a Democratic proposal to expand social programs because it might lead to "dangerous" budget deficits. Instead he recommended a 10 percent reduction in spending across the board. He did not hesitate to offend even the labor unions that had become the bulwark of the Democratic party under FDR. In 1947, he described them as "selfish," clinging to "special privileges and unfair advantages" over management.

Kennedy appeared undaunted by controversy—indeed, he often provoked it. A champion of federally financed housing for millions of World War II veterans who were still living in basements, attics, and garages, Jack was outraged when the powerful leaders of the American Legion joined realtors' groups and other conservative interests in opposition to the program.

He called the nation's foremost veterans' organization a "legislative drummer boy for the real estate lobby" and escalated the dispute by remarking on the floor of the House that "the leadership of the American Legion has not had a constructive thought for the benefit of this country since 1918." When he got back to his office, Kennedy joked, "I guess we're gone. That finishes us down here."

Why this brashness, this independence?, I asked Kennedy in 1959. "I came back from the Service," he said, "not as a Democratic wheel horse who came up through the ranks but I came in sort of side-ways so that I didn't have this drilled into me that I'm responsible to some political boss back under the Democratic Party in the Eleventh Congressional District." But I pressed him. The issue, I said, was not just "some political boss," but his connection with the Democratic party as a whole. Would he not need the help of President Truman some day? "I never had the feeling that I needed Truman." What about his fellow members of Congress? He got along well enough with the rank-and-file but had little connection with the leadership. What about the members of the House Foreign Affairs Committee, given his interest in international issues? "To be honest with you, I could not name the members. . . . "

This brash Kennedy seemed remote from the somewhat shy or aloof young man of Harvard or Hyannisport. What was he up to? In fact, he was less confident than he appeared. He wasn't equipped for the job, he acknowledged to a reporter in 1959. "I didn't plan to get into it, and when I started out as a congressman, there were lots of things I didn't know, a lot of mistakes I made, maybe some votes that should have been different." Still, it was during these early years that he forged the political style that would define him throughout his career. From the moment he arrived in Washington, he was sure that the House was not his destiny. Occasional acts of political audacity and courage reflected his restlessness, to be sure, his impatience with conformity. But in breaking with party orthodoxies he could also distinguish himself from the horde, from his fellow "worms," and he suspected that outspoken independence might appeal to voters. Certainly it appealed to voters in the Eleventh District. In 1948, when he ran for reelection, no Democrat or Republican dared challenge him. Two years later, he trounced his Republican opponent by nearly five to one.

He was running hard. He had never really stopped. Running for what? He wasn't sure yet. But almost every weekend he flew back to Massachusetts, politicking across the state. "No town was too small or too Republican," Dave Powers, his friend and "booking agent," recalled. "He was willing to go anywhere." The key to political success, Kennedy himself would say, was the "long, long, long labor" of running, the fierce drive to "move on."

Chapter 2

PUSHING AND
SHOVING

K ENNEDY TAKES ON LODGE, the banner headlines proclaimed
when Jack Kennedy announced his candidacy for the Senate early
in 1952. The Massachusetts political community was mesmerized. Senator Henry Cabot Lodge Jr. was heir to the most formidable name in the
state's politics. Grandfather Henry Cabot Lodge was the Republican senator credited with single-handedly defeating Woodrow Wilson's Versailles
Treaty and League of Nations. He had beat back Honey Fitz's challenge
in the election of 1916 and died in harness after serving in the upper
chamber for more than three decades. Now his grandson seemed to have
an equally tight grip on the Senate seat he had first won in 1936, and
Lodge was gaining new prestige in 1952 for his leading role in the campaign to draft General Dwight Eisenhower as a Republican candidate for
the presidency.

Even people in Kennedy's entourage spoke of Lodge's charm and polish,
and some were appalled by Jack's audacity in challenging him. But Joe urged
his son on: "When you've beaten him, you've beaten the best. Why try for
something less?" The press was excited by this battle between two Brahmins,
one Protestant and one Catholic, a fight to the death between what I later
described as a "blueblood" and a "greenblood" (the latter did not catch on).

Still, the contest between the youthful opponents was a small patch in a broader and more complex political quilt. In 1952, the fundamental political conflict in Massachusetts, as in much of the nation, lay not only between the two major parties but *within* each of them, making for a "four-party" combat. The GOP was riven between a moderate wing coalescing behind Eisenhower and conservative militants backing Robert Taft. In contrast to his grandfather, Lodge was a leader of the moderates. He spent weeks working for Eisenhower's nomination at the expense of his own Senate campaign. The Taft forces, headed in Massachusetts by Basil Brewer, the powerful publisher of the *New Bedford Standard-Times*, attacked the Eisenhower forces with a ferocity that presaged the conservatism of Barry Goldwater and George W. Bush of the years ahead.

The Democrats were also divided nationally, between Northern liberals and Southern conservatives, as well as over the extent of communism's threat at home and abroad. But the defining conflicts among Democrats in Massachusetts were less ideological than personal. Massachusetts was a "personality state," one practitioner said, the Democratic party there being "a federation of the followers of individual officeholders or candidates." Prominent among those factions was the "party of one" of John F. Kennedy, or of two, including his father, with their expanding base of loyalists that dated back to the first campaign in 1946.

Even after his six years in Congress, it was hard to place Jack Kennedy ideologically. His domestic record in Washington on the whole reflected the prevailing Democratic liberalism, but on international questions he appeared to lean more to Taft's anti-communist nationalism than to the internationalism of Truman and Eisenhower. He candidly agreed with a reporter's suggestion after the 1952 election that he might be a "popularist," willing to give people what they wanted on a particular issue. He would, he said, be very happy to tell his liberal critics, "I am not a liberal at all." More than anything, Kennedy's ideology was political independence, from his party and from true believers. He maintained cordial relationships with most of his fellow politicians, however, and especially with his father's old friend Paul Dever, the popular governor, who chose to seek reelection rather than challenge Lodge and thus helped clear the way for Jack.

KENNEDY'S RUN for the Senate in 1952 was essentially an enlargement of his first congressional race—with a campaign organization that was separate from the Democratic party, total mobilization of an ever-broadening political clan, endless tea parties, and the rest. And with its remarkably diverse constituency, Massachusetts was a magnification of Boston's Eleventh District. Extending west of the Hub 150 miles to the Berkshires, the battleground embraced several large industrial cities that had seen better days, a host of smaller one-company towns, and rural areas that typically voted Republican by ten to one. Democratic candidates feasted across the state on political polyglots of Irish, Italian, French-Canadian, Portuguese, and dozens of other ethnic communities, most of them Catholic. Age-old conflicts ran deep. Irish hopefuls had run against entrenched Protestant power, then Italians against the Irish and French-Canadians against the Italians, with African Americans and other minorities often feeling excluded by most of the ethnic leaders and by both parties.

Once again, Kennedy would mobilize his own personal organization, creating a network of 286 "secretaries"—local campaign managers—in cities and towns across the state, even in places where, as a close aide said, "Democrat was a dirty word" and "nobody had ever tried to start an organization of any kind." Jack had laid the groundwork for his organization over the preceding years. This was a "ready-made group," Kennedy lieutenant John Droney said. "I think he spoke for six years at every parish and every church and every Holy Name group in the Commonwealth, so he had this group ready to take over and ready to start working for him." Secretaries were instructed to work only for the congressman, not for the party or its other candidates. Not that most needed to be told. Few secretaries had political experience or loyalties to other politicians, and some were even Republicans. But all would become Kennedy people.

As before, Joe took a dominating role. He financed the campaign, probably to the tune of several million dollars—astronomical in those days—but no one will ever know for sure because few records were made, or kept. When the campaign's manager seemed to flounder, Joe pushed him out and demanded that son Robert quit his job in the Justice Department and report for duty. Bobby did so, though reluctantly. A novice in politics, he was afraid he would "screw it up," but insiders begged him to come handle the domineering patriarch. There was little chance of that, but Robert, the son Joe thought most resembled him, drove himself relentlessly. Politics, he concluded, was mainly organization and effort, the art of getting "large numbers of people to work, doing lots of different kinds of jobs. And that was the philosophy of the campaign." Fiercely purposeful, he trampled the sensitivities of those he considered political hacks. At a meeting of local worthies, Robert nearly provoked a fistfight when he accused a candidate for some minor office of trying to cling to Jack's coattails, shouting, "I don't want my brother to get mixed up with politicians!"

Far tougher to shake off was Governor Paul Dever. While Jack was still scrambling to put together his network of political secretaries, he had agreed to run a joint campaign with Dever in Suffolk County, which included Boston. This was the governor's stronghold, and Kennedy hoped to exploit Dever's popularity with rank-and-file Democrats. In return, Dever would get Kennedy money and organizational support.

The relationship broke down, though, after Dever made a disastrous appearance at the Democratic national convention in July. The governor lost his voice at the rostrum while delivering a keynote address and continued to orate in a hoarse whisper, sweating miserably before the pitiless TV lenses. His standing dropped like a stone. Desperate, he reached out to Kennedy for a handhold, pleading for a joint statewide campaign. Dever regulars appeared at local Kennedy offices across the state, asking to be let in. In Fall River, a truck bearing a sign with the governor's smiling face "as big as City Hall" was sent to Kennedy HQ. Could the Dever campaign put the sign up on the building? But the governor was now a liability and in September Jack decided to cut him loose. He dispatched Robert to give Dever the news, "but don't get me involved in it," he said. "Treat it as an organizational problem." Robert, however, was no diplomat, and the meeting was stormy, with only Joe's ministrations preventing a complete break. "It was rather a big debacle," Robert later reflected, apart from its outcome: "We ran our own campaign, which is all that I wanted."

WHILE KENNEDY distanced himself from the Massachusetts Democratic establishment, he actively courted the state's Republicans, exploiting a conflict far bitterer than his own against Lodge: the battle within the GOP between Lodge's moderates and the conservative Taft faction led by publisher Basil Brewer. The Taftites had glumly swallowed Eisenhower's defeat of "Mr. Republican" at the 1952 national convention and supported the general's campaign against Democrat Adlai Stevenson. But they would never forgive Lodge the apostate.

Seizing a big opening for Jack, his father persuaded a Boston banker to set up an "Independents for Kennedy" committee that would offer an easy road for Taft people to switch their loyalty to his son. In late September, Basil Brewer called a press conference to announce his newspaper's endorsement of Kennedy. "If a real Republican was running in this state," the publisher said, "I'd support that Republican against Kennedy." It was Jack's militant anti-communism that gave Brewer political cover for his vendetta against Lodge. A *Boston Globe* headline caught his message: SEES CONGRESSMAN MORE AKIN TO TAFT.

Joe was suspected of offering a financial incentive to the publisher, but probably there was no need to—Brewer's almost fanatical opposition to Lodge was motive enough. Day after day, his editorial page extolled Kennedy's independence, his willingness to attack the Truman administration. "Not blinded by party ties," the congressman showed a real understanding of the "nation's struggle for survival."

Money—in the form of a $500,000 loan from Joe—probably did play a role, however, in the sudden switch of John Fox's conservative *Boston Post* to the Kennedy side. Coming less than two weeks before the election, the endorsement was thought to be worth tens of thousands of votes. Certainly Lodge was convinced that Joe had bought Fox's backing, "though I imagine he handled it pretty subtly, with all sorts of veiled promises and hints rather than an outright deal." Jack Kennedy was less circumspect, blurting out to a journalist in 1960, "You know we had to buy that fucking paper."

Throughout the campaign, the father and son wove their way through the state's complex politics, building alliances across party and ideological lines while casting off dispensables. They exploited the basic strength of the Democratic party but ultimately campaigned independently of it.

Running alone worked. On election day, Kennedy gained a slender plurality of 70,000 votes over Lodge. Stevenson lost. Dever lost. The Democrats lost control of Congress. Kennedy won.

❧

JOHN KENNEDY entered the Senate with one overriding purpose: to use it as a stepping-stone to the presidency of the United States. He would have the ardent support of his father and siblings, of the whole political clan of loyalists and operatives. But he could not expect much backing from his new political home, the Senate, composed of rival Democrats and hostile Republicans. Indeed, he had no greater respect for most of his fellow senators than he'd had for his colleagues in the House. He saw them as mainly transactional politicians, wheeling and dealing brokers, cautious and self-protective, certainly not profiles in courage. He did not exempt himself. He considered himself one of the "worms."

How then was he to set himself apart? Kennedy faced the dilemma of every ambitious senator: to be a national leader but at the same time a spokesman for his state. Here he showed a measure of courage steeled by ambition. Knowing that he probably would have to run for reelection to the Senate before seeking the presidency, Kennedy would protect his state's special needs—especially its economic base in textiles, fishing, shipbuilding—with the help of a large and talented staff, paid in part by his father. After all, he had campaigned in 1952 on the promise to do "more for Massachusetts."

On major national issues, though, he would assume a national posture. It was easy enough to position himself as a serious and independent commentator on national security with frequent speeches on defense policy and international affairs. A harder test came in 1954 with the proposed St. Lawrence Seaway, which would allow shippers to bypass Atlantic ports in trade with the Great Lakes region. The seaway promised an economic boon to the Midwest at the expense of Northeastern seaports. Originally conceived in the 1930s, the project had been defeated in Congress six times in twenty years. Not one Massachusetts congressman or senator had ever supported it. Kennedy himself had spoken against it in his Senate campaign.

When Jack switched to support of the seaway in January 1954, the decision outraged his constituents, as he knew it would, especially the Boston longshoremen who had been among his most loyal backers. He was warned to stay away from that spring's St. Patrick's Day parade in Boston. Newspapers condemned him for "ruining New England."

But Kennedy's reversal was in fact a carefully weighed turning point in his political career. He had decided, a journalist recalled, "that if he was ever going to be bigger than Massachusetts, then he'd better go against public opinion in his state." The young senator won national attention for his courage in sticking to his guns with a notable address to the Senate that asked New Englanders to recognize "the legitimate needs and aspirations of other sections" of the country. He concluded with a reference to Daniel Webster, the great Massachusetts nationalist: "Our aim should not be 'States dissevered, discordant [or] belligerent'; but 'one country, one constitution, one destiny.'"

ONE DAY between campaigns, I found Jack Kennedy in an untypically reflective mood. Instead of raising day-by-day issues, I asked whether he had any long-run plan or strategy, or even a philosophy. Not really. "You just keep pushing everybody," he said. "I think there are an awful lot of accidents in this business—some help you and some hurt you." I asked him what he meant by "pushing."

"It's like when we're sunk in the navy," he said. "There really is no point in going from island to island but, I mean, when you keep moving then you—that's how you really ever get any breaks through. . . . If you just keep shoving ahead then you're in motion and something—then there may be luck attached to it."

Pushing and shoving—nothing better summarized the political arts of the Kennedys. Jack was pushing himself forward, of course, but he was also ready to shove people aside. That was the fate in 1956 of William "Onions" Burke, chairman of the Massachusetts Democratic Committee and collector of the Port of Boston. From the start of his career, Kennedy had paid as little attention as possible to the state party. Suddenly, in 1956, the senator could not ignore it, because it became an obstacle to his own ambitions.

The state committee was controlled by a powerful rival, the majority leader of the U. S. House of Representatives, John McCormack, through his henchman, Burke. Kennedy had long had a wary relationship to McCormack. Tip O'Neill, who succeeded Kennedy in Congress as representative from the Eleventh District, would describe it as "natural resentment" between "the old and the new, between the established and the maverick." A few years before, Joe Kennedy had intervened to end a burst of hostilities over a report that the majority leader's staff had made disparaging comments about Jack, reassuring McCormack that "there is nothing in Jack's hopes for the future that would ever conflict with your wishes." After that, the two got along mainly by avoiding each other.

For his part, "Onions" Burke stood in for those Democrats who, in the words of John's nephew Edward McCormack, resented Kennedy "for not involving himself more in party politics," those who had felt the sharp Kennedy elbows and learned that "you're either with the Kennedys in every effort, on every issue, or you're drummed out of the regiment." Kennedy in turn detested the rotund politico who epitomized the patronage-mongering Irishman above whom the Kennedys had risen.

Personal feeling alone would not have drawn Kennedy into a power struggle that promised to become an ugly brawl. But Burke's state committee controlled the selection of delegates to the 1956 Democratic national convention. Kennedy early on had decided to back Adlai Stevenson for the presidential nomination. Stevenson was the front-runner, and there was talk, which Kennedy did not discourage, that he might pick him as his running mate. To claim consideration for the nod, though, Jack needed to control the Massachusetts delegation and swing it Stevenson's way at the convention in Chicago. McCormack and Burke were as determined to block Kennedy—and block me too, a Stevensonian whose hopes for a place in the delegation McCormack had tried to veto. For the senator, it was also a matter of prestige. Either he could demonstrate that he was, in an aide's words, "a political figure of some strength in his own state" or he would play second fiddle to John McCormack.

Once engaged in a battle he could ill afford to lose, Kennedy mounted a full-force effort. He mobilized his whole power base, from his Senate office to the statewide network of political secretaries created for the Lodge campaign to friendly reporters. The senator came up from Washington to campaign personally against Burke. He lobbied all the uncommitted members of the state committee, even dropping in on them at home to explain his hopes for a "constructive, vital and enlightened state party." Reformers, surprised and pleased by Jack's new commitment, signed on. Editorialists applauded Kennedy's "firm stand in favor of the best possible type of leadership for the party."

Behind the scenes, both sides played dirty. Kennedy circulated a list of charges against the chairman—"It should not, of course, be attributable to me"—but after Burke misrepresented a conversation between them, the senator sent an angry telegram to newspapers statewide, accusing Burke of lying. The only issue, Kennedy wrote, was Burke's "own unfitness for the position he now holds."

The climactic vote for chairman was set for May 19, 1956, in a Boston hotel. The Kennedy team had prepared a six-page "scenario" to guide them through each step of the meeting. "But, you see," one of Jack's closest advisers, Dick Donahue, would say years later, "if you get eighty Democrats from Massachusetts in a room, parliamentary procedure is not always their first concern." No sooner did the committee convene than pandemonium broke out, straight from the pages of Edwin O'Connor's *The Last Hurrah*. Burke himself got into a shoving match with an off-duty policeman hired by the Kennedy forces. In a room rapidly filling with smoke, sweat, and high temper, it took an hour to elect a temporary chairman to preside over the vote.

But with the senator in an upstairs room of the hotel keeping a safe, watchful distance from the tumult, the meeting ended as he had hoped: with Burke deposed and a Kennedy man, Pat Lynch, in as head of the state party. Though I had played no real part in the Burke drama, I won too, becoming a Massachusetts delegate to the convention.

The relieved senator issued a statement that heralded "the beginning of a new era of the Democratic party in Massachusetts." But it was nothing of the kind. Those of us who hoped Kennedy now would *lead* the party he had seized with such abrupt efficiency were to be disappointed. Jack had acted against his own inclination and against his father's urgent advice: "Don't get into the gutter with those bums up there in Boston." Whatever his "honest intention of doing something," as Donahue put it, to reform the fragmented, corrupt, ineffective state party, "there were other things with higher priorities from '56 on." With Burke pushed aside, his rear secured, Kennedy was shoving ahead on his own.

THE 1956 vice-presidential nomination was John Kennedy's immediate target. As the leader of a state delegation committed to Stevenson, with a starring role in a convention film extolling the Democratic party called *The Pursuit of Happiness* and a strong nominating speech for Adlai, the senator pushed his way onto the shortlist for the vice-presidential nod. Whom would Stevenson choose? No one, it turned out. On the evening of his own nomination, he threw the vice-presidential nomination open for the convention to decide. Now everything was changed. Kennedy had to gain the votes overnight of six hundred or more delegates. With characteristic alacrity in seizing a chance, the senator, backed by Robert and a claque of loyalists, ran an intense, frenetic twelve-hour campaign, rushing from delegation to delegation. But his efforts were in vain. Senator Estes Kefauver of Tennessee beat him on the second ballot by a hundred votes.

Kennedy was bitterly disappointed—he hated to lose—but soon he realized what he had won by losing. Stevenson's race against the popular President Eisenhower was doomed; Robert Kennedy traveled with the candidate, making extensive notes for a primer on how *not* to run a presidential campaign. He was shocked by Adlai's disdain for politics and politicking, appalled by his disorganization and indecision. Stevenson was "just not a man of action at all," and his campaign, Robert concluded, was "the most disastrous operation you ever saw." It was good luck that John Kennedy had no part of that. Instead, the public was left with the image of him at the convention: a bold warrior, fierce in battle, gallant in defeat. Even Stevenson acknowledged that Kennedy had been "the real hero of the hour," adding "we shall hear a great deal more from this promising young man."

That might have been some consolation to Joe Kennedy. He had objected violently to his son's push for the nomination from the beginning. During the convention, Joe called Robert from the French Riviera, where he was vacationing. "Blue language flashed all over the room," an aide recalled, as Joe denounced Jack "as an idiot who was ruining his political career." The father foresaw Stevenson's defeat and feared Jack's Catholicism would be blamed, damaging his future presidential prospects. There was no sense risking that for what was, after all, second place on the ticket. The real goal was Number One. On this, father and son agreed. Meeting a few weeks after the November 1956 elections, Jack said to Joe, "Well, Dad, I guess there's only one question left. When do we start?"

∽

KENNEDY'S ELECTION to the presidency in 1960 was greeted at the time as an astonishing win for so young a candidate. Time has not dimmed this view; indeed, a half century later the victory appears almost miraculous in the light of what we did not know about Kennedy but have learned since. Most Americans were unaware of medical problems so dire that survival for four or eight years was not certain. The family drew a tight veil of secrecy around questions of his health. I ran head on into this in writing my 1960 biography. There were indications that he had developed Addison's disease, but this was a dread term bound to frighten voters. I was denied access to his medical records, and the best I could bargain out of the senator and his doctors was the statement that, "While Kennedy's adrenal insufficiency might well be diagnosed by some doctors as a mild case of Addison's disease, it was not diagnosed as the classic type of Addison's disease." They insisted that the symptoms could be fully controlled by medication.

Nor did Americans know of Kennedy's sexual adventurism, which might at any time have exploded into headlines, with an assist from the opposition. His marriage to Jacqueline Bouvier in 1953 had for a while diminished reports of his obsessive womanizing, but the rumors surfaced again as the couple drew apart. Jack was often away politicking, and Jackie became despondent that he sometimes ignored her even when he was in town. Staffers feared that Kennedy's lapses could jeopardize the campaign.

Less concealed was another threat to Jack's aspirations: anti-Catholicism. The savage defeat of the 1928 Democratic presidential nominee, Al Smith, weighed heavily on the Kennedys. The New York governor, the first Catholic major-party presidential candidate, was beaten by Herbert Hoover in an election that was more church war than political campaign.

Thirty years on, prejudice had scarcely disappeared. Polls in the late 1950s showed that many Americans would not vote for a Catholic presidential candidate. It was not only the rank bigotry of rural nativists that Kennedy had to overcome. Liberal Protestants, a strong force in the Democratic party, clung to the notion that the Catholic church was pursuing political power to impose its conservative dogmas on the country through its authoritarian command over a dedicated army of tens of millions of believers. Catholic politicians, supposed to be under church discipline and beholden to the votes of their co-religionists, could not be trusted to put American interests ahead of those of the Vatican.

But Kennedy's faith was only the beginning of his troubles with his party's liberal wing, which was made up of the activist and ideologically committed Democrats who had twice secured Adlai Stevenson's nomination. Though Jack had a respectable voting record on Democratic bread-and-butter issues, he had made no secret of his distaste for liberal true-believers. "I'm not comfortable with those people," he had told a reporter shortly after becoming senator. Their fervor and doctrinal certainties irritated him. An "idealist without illusions," as he was now casting himself, Jack resented pressures—which intensified as 1960 approached—to prove whether he would stand with them or against them.

For many liberals, Kennedy had already chosen to stand against them on what they believed was the defining issue of the 1950s, the anti-communist crusade of Senator Joe McCarthy. In 1954, Kennedy had failed to vote for Senate condemnation of the Wisconsin bully. To liberals, the McCarthy issue was black and white: McCarthy represented a grave threat to civil liberties that the Senate had properly—if belatedly—put down. For Jack, the controversy was characteristically a blur of personal and political grays. He had had to face the awkward fact that his father liked and supported McCarthy and that in 1953 Robert Kennedy briefly worked for McCarthy's Senate committee. Moreover, Jack could not overlook McCarthy's popularity in Massachusetts, especially among Catholics. And while he considered McCarthy's methods reprehensible and counterproductive, he could not, he said, "get as worked up as other liberals did." To him, the vote was less a supreme moral issue than a technical one of whether McCarthy had violated Senate rules. Jack was hospitalized at the time of the vote, which provided an excuse, but he could have been paired with a pro-McCarthy senator. He was the only Democrat who failed to vote.

Liberals would not let him forget it, least of all the grande dame of the New Deal, Eleanor Roosevelt. She harbored old grievances against Joe Kennedy and saw the son as merely the puppet of his reactionary father.

Opposing Jack's presidential hopes, she struck publicly at his sensitive points. A suggestion on national TV in 1958 that Joe was out to buy Jack the presidency—"spending oodles of money all over the country"—sparked an acrimonious exchange of letters between the senator and the former first lady. Roosevelt played to anti-Catholic prejudices that same year by doubting that Kennedy, if elected president, would be able to separate church from state. Most woundingly, in a 1958 magazine article she revived her earlier charge that Kennedy had "dodged the McCarthy issue in 1954."

Given all the political problems and obstacles in the way of Kennedy's candidacy, why was he running at all? Not for ideological reasons—Jack did not think ideologically. He was not pursuing an overriding cause or even an arresting new program—that was not his way. His motivating force was mainly his love of campaigning, of beating the odds, of besting the other guy and, above all, of reaching for the highest stakes. It was the ultimate game.

JACK EXPECTED that the Democratic nomination lay open, since few thought that the twice-defeated Stevenson would try again. But he faced redoubtable foes from the Senate with much more experience than he had: Lyndon Johnson, the majority leader from Texas; Stuart Symington of Missouri; and Minnesota's folksy, warm-hearted Hubert Humphrey, who was running as the favorite of the party's liberals—that is, so long as Stevenson stayed out. If the expected candidates found themselves in a stalemate at the convention, Adlai might yet be tempted to return, seducing nostalgic delegates with one of his inspiring addresses.

To overcome the doubts about his electability, Kennedy adopted an arduous but straightforward strategy: to be first in the field and to run faster and harder than the opposition—which meant Humphrey, since Symington and Johnson had decided to avoid the primaries. The Kennedy team identified a handful of key battlegrounds: New Hampshire, where Jack, as a neighbor, could expect to get off to a strong start; Wisconsin, in Humphrey country; and West Virginia, with its depths of poverty and large, devout Protestant population.

Kennedy's push through the primaries was to be the campaign of 1952 replayed as a nationwide effort. Local influentials were recruited to manage city and county campaigns, supported—and sometimes overrun—by political roughnecks shipped in from Massachusetts. Kennedy-for-President clubs were set up wherever an organizer could be found—in small towns, farm communities, suburbs. They worked to build Jack's grassroots appeal—canvassing, passing out literature, staging rallies, and getting crowds to meetings. National strategy was set at headquarters in Washington, with Robert Kennedy, as campaign manager, the fearsome enforcer. The candidate himself campaigned ceaselessly, coping both with his throbbing back pain and with the fans who crowded around him all too closely on the hustings.

The campaign's dazzling success in the primaries became part of America's political saga. After the expected easy win in New Hampshire, it was on to Wisconsin, where Jack had been campaigning since 1958. Here, Humphrey, on his own turf, swung onto the attack. After statements of his own impassioned liberal faith, he would ask if there was anything more to Jack Kennedy than organization and efficiency. "Every now and then," Humphrey said, "I read in the paper how disorderly Hubert Humphrey's campaign is and I say, 'THANK GOD.'" Humphrey's campaign was not only disorderly, it was understaffed and short of funds. It proved no match for the massive Kennedy operation. Jack got a clear win, but not yet a knockout blow.

West Virginia, with its rural Protestant vote, became Kennedy's harshest test and Humphrey's last stand. When Robert Kennedy arrived in the state to launch the month-long push, he asked a group of campaign workers, "Well, what are our problems?" After an uneasy silence, one stood up and shouted, "There's only one problem. He's a Catholic. That's our Goddamned problem!" West Virginia gave the Kennedy politicos, Dick Donahue recalled, "the coldest bath of our lives."

Jack decided he had to confront the religious issue quickly and directly. On his first day in the state, he told an outdoor rally in Morgantown that an America that disqualified Catholics from its highest office "wasn't the country that my brother died for in Europe, and nobody asked my brother if he was a Catholic or a Protestant before he climbed into an American bomber plane to fly his last mission." The appeal to tolerance and fair play made an impression on Jack's audience, but, despite a vast outpouring of Kennedy money, muscle, and organization, few in the campaign were confident that the religious divide could be bridged. They were amazed when their man won easily, with 60 percent of the vote. Donahue called the turn-around "the wildest, craziest, dizziest thing that we've ever done." It shocked Democratic leaders everywhere. No one could now doubt John Kennedy's vote-gathering skills, even under the worst conditions. Humphrey dropped out. By the time Kennedy won a string of five more primary elections, his nomination was a near certainty.

WINNING THE nomination on the first ballot at the convention in Los Angeles filled the Kennedys with a new confidence going forward into the fall campaign. But first a decision had to be made about a running mate, and Kennedy was not well prepared for this. The obvious choice was Lyndon Johnson, who could be expected to help carry much of the South, where Eisenhower had twice broken the traditionally strong Democratic grip. Kennedy had had the same wary relationship with the majority leader as he had with other Senate bosses. But Johnson had also challenged Kennedy for the nomination—not openly, in the primaries, but through a backstage campaign of insult and innuendo that had persisted into the convention.

The main objection to Johnson, though, was not personal but political. The party's liberals loathed the Texan for using his power in the Senate to stifle coordinated Democratic opposition to Eisenhower's agenda. Kennedy had managed to grab the nomination with little backing from liberals, but the mobilization of activists—"kinetic people," as Harvard historian Arthur Schlesinger Jr., an activist himself, called them—was considered vital to give the campaign "crusading urgency" in the fall.

The night after his own nomination, a curious impasse divided Kennedy and his advisers as objections to Johnson flooded in from unionists, African American leaders, and others on the left. "If you do this," a labor boss told Robert Kennedy, "you're going to fuck everything up." One of Jack's closest campaign aides told him, "This is the worst mistake you ever made." Some liberals threatened to put up their own nominee and embarrass Jack with a floor fight. "It was the most indecisive time we ever had," Robert Kennedy recalled. "We changed our minds eight times during the course of it."

After long hours of hesitation and confusion, Kennedy turned his back on the liberals and made the final decision for Johnson. It would prove to be the most important act of the campaign. The Kennedy team shoved the nomination through the convention by a voice vote of delegates. The "ayes" and "nays" sounded about evenly divided, but the convention chairman declared LBJ the nominee by acclamation.

In his acceptance speech the next night, John Kennedy rose far above party wrangles—and far beyond partisanship—to kindle a sense of shared purpose in Americans as they confronted the future. "The old era is ending," he proclaimed. "The old ways will not do." It was time, he proclaimed, "for a new generation of leadership—new men to cope with new problems and new opportunities. . . . We stand today on the edge of a new frontier—the frontier of the 1960's—a frontier of unknown opportunities and perils—a frontier of unfulfilled hopes and threats." The nation must make a choice between the public interest and private comfort, between national greatness and national decline. "A whole world looks to see what we will do. We cannot fail their trust."

As he plunged into the national campaign, Kennedy lost no time in planning grand strategy. It became clear that the "new generation of leadership" would offer few new ideas to address all those new problems and opportunities. Jack had said in his acceptance speech that the "New Frontier" was "not a set of promises—it is a set of challenges." Yet the party platform approved at the convention had been filled with promises. The committee that drafted it was dominated by liberals, above all by Paul Butler, the party chairman until Kennedy exercised the prerogative of presidential nominees and replaced him after the convention. For his half-dozen years as party head, Butler had been pushing Democrats to define, as James Sundquist, an ally on the platform committee, put it, "a concrete program that presented the voters with a true choice." The 1960 platform was the climax of Butler's efforts. With its bold planks on civil rights, Medicare, federal aid to education, and economic policies aimed at benefiting working-class Americans, it was, in Sundquist's words, "the most outspokenly liberal platform the party, or any party, had turned out in our time."

Such a platform would have thrilled Stevenson or Humphrey, had they won the nomination. For John Kennedy, however, even though he had backed some of these measures in the Senate, the platform complicated his strategy to run an essentially nonideological campaign pitched strongly to centrist voters. And it was the platform's sweeping civil rights plank that had given special urgency to JFK's decision to appease whites in the South by bringing their fellow Southerner Lyndon Johnson onto the ticket. So Kennedy became neither the first nor the last presidential nominee to vow loyalty to the party platform and to invoke it where it suited his immediate purposes, but otherwise to steer his own course, untethered by its promises. Soon Arthur Schlesinger was warning the candidate of an "intellectual and emotional vacuum" in the campaign. He quoted one liberal as saying that the issue wasn't religion—"It isn't what Kennedy believes that worries me. It's whether he believes anything."

Schlesinger objected to the dominance of the "organization politicians," but that term fit Kennedy himself perfectly. He believed passionately in organization—not the party's, but his own—with money and people deployed strategically and with maximum force. The money was, as ever, mobilized by Joe, and Jack himself told the story that his father had said that he would pay for a victory, but he was damned if he would buy a landslide. Kennedy's political clan of loyalists, now so large and dispersed as to form a base across the nation, was set into highest gear. A large headquarters staff attended to the grubby practicalities. For Bobby and the rest, the angel, not the devil, was in the details.

∽

IN THE FALL of 1960, the Kennedy organization launched the biggest and toughest selling job in America. A presidential race resembles a military campaign, with its officers, troops, and strategists. But a nationwide campaign is intertwined with a maze of smaller battles among contenders for Senate, House, and state offices. They would all be running together under the Democratic banner but also, to lesser or greater degrees, alone, as they sought to exploit or evade their party identity.

The Kennedy organization could hardly serve as generalissimo of the whole campaign because its single and complete focus was the election of John Kennedy. Robert Kennedy made this fact brutally plain to a distinguished gathering of New York liberal Democrats: "I don't give a damn if the state and county organizations survive after November, and I don't give a damn if *you* survive." Neither Bobby nor his brother understood the risk they were taking. If other Democratic candidates—especially for the House and Senate—were cast adrift, forced to run alone, the entire ticket, bottom to top, would be weakened. It would lose strength in depth. Without help from the Kennedys or from the Democratic National Committee John Kennedy now controlled, the shunned candidates would turn to other sources for support and incur other loyalties and obligations. And if congressional candidates had to run alone, they would be more likely to legislate alone—or at least not together with a president who had spurned them in the clutch.

Yet the Kennedy people also realized that if they were to elect Jack, they had to make overtures to vital constituencies. The most important were the Democrats of the South, for whom desegregation had become the defining issue. Kennedy himself made only a few forays to the South during the campaign and never spoke of civil rights to Southern audiences. It was left to Johnson, riding the rails on his campaign train, the *LBJ Victory Special*, to distance the ticket from the liberal civil rights plank in the party platform and from the "radicals" in Congress. For an old New Dealer like LBJ, who was convinced that segregation was holding his native region back, herding racists into line behind the ticket was often hard going. Presenting himself as the grandson of a Confederate soldier, Johnson reassured Southerners that a Kennedy administration would not attempt to turn the civil rights plank into law. He promised to serve as a moderating influence both in the new administration and with Congress.

As LBJ was disassociating the ticket from civil rights down South, Kennedy, campaigning up North, managed with a good deal of care and finesse to associate himself with the cause of black Americans while evading substantive discussions or commitments, except to aim fire at the Eisenhower administration's failings. The running mates were attempting, as *Time* noted, to "project double images without being accused of being two-faced."

It was this sort of political hypocrisy that enraged committed liberals. Egged on by Schlesinger, who warned that liberal apathy was the Republicans' "great secret weapon," Jack embarked on pilgrimages to three prominent antagonists after his nomination. First was Adlai Stevenson, whom Jack appeased by letting him lead a foreign policy task force. Traveling to Independence, Missouri, Kennedy sought to woo Harry Truman, who had angrily opposed his candidacy and remained barely reconciled to his nomination. It turned out that Jack's opponent was even more offensive to the former president, who said, "That no-good son-of-a-bitch Dick Nixon called me a Communist and I'll do anything to beat him." And what about Kennedy's old critic, Eleanor Roosevelt? It was as a humble suppliant that JFK visited Hyde Park, leaving the former first lady with a new feeling, as she wrote a friend, that "here was a man who could learn," with "a mind that is open to new ideas" and a genuine interest "in helping the people of his own country and mankind in general."

For all Jack's success in making peace—or at least a truce—with these icons, liberal doubts about Kennedy were far from assuaged. Late in August, the nation's leading liberal group, Americans for Democratic Action, offered Kennedy its endorsement. But Schlesinger reported to Jack that it was made "with the utmost tepidity." He quoted someone at the meeting as saying, "We don't trust Kennedy and we don't like Johnson; but Nixon is so terrible that we have to endorse the Democrats."

JACK KENNEDY was lucky in his opponent. Eight years as Eisenhower's loyal vice president had not altogether erased the reputation Richard Nixon had earned as a viciously opportunistic, Red-baiting congressman and senator, a man ready to destroy other people's reputations to advance his own fortunes. Not only liberal Democrats but also many in his own party mistrusted him.

Nixon had beaten New York's liberal governor Nelson Rockefeller for the GOP's presidential nomination, and to reconcile party liberals and moderates to his candidacy, he enlisted Jack's old foe Henry Cabot Lodge as his running mate. He had agreed to a "compact" with Rockefeller on the party platform, with especially progressive planks on civil rights and federal aid to education. It was not only to appease Rockefeller that Nixon compromised. He knew that these planks would appeal to a broader range of Americans in the general election than his party's traditionally conservative positions. Predictably, the Republican right erupted. Conservatives were as much enraged by the secrecy of the Nixon-Rockefeller negotiations—an end run around the convention's rightist platform committee—as by their substance.

But that was Nixon's way. He rarely sought advice from others. He made his own decisions—to the most minor details—and kept his own counsel, mainly because he distrusted even his close associates—distrusted their judgment, motives, and good faith. He could not be dissuaded from making a showy but empty pledge to the GOP convention that he would "carry this campaign into every one of the 50 states of this Nation." The mad dash to fulfill that rash promise—he covered twenty-five states in the campaign's first two weeks—left him exhausted. He vented his rages on aides and almost sacked a key staffer. Always surrounded by supporters, party officials, advisers, speechwriters, advance men, secretaries, Richard Nixon was in 1960, biographer Stephen Ambrose wrote, "one of the loneliest men in the United States."

But Nixon welcomed almost any direct confrontation with his adversaries and had high expectations as he approached his four televised debates with Kennedy. He was so confident that he ignored pleas to prepare for the encounters. "He hadn't done anything except to tell me that he knew how to debate," his frustrated campaign manager recalled. "After all, he was the master debater. Who were any of us to presume to insist?"

The debates evoked huge excitement; later, they were hailed by a communications professor as "the most significant, groundbreaking American political campaign events of the twentieth century." If hardly that, they did enable 70 million Americans to see the candidates alone, without advisers or speechwriters. After the first debate in late September, each side felt that its man had won, and each was right. Television viewers admired the relaxed and engaging Kennedy compared to Nixon, whose image came across as gaunt and shadowy. The much smaller radio audience gave Nixon the edge.

It was fitting that judgments of the debates turned so much more on images and personalities than on substance. Far more effectively than Nixon, Kennedy exploited burgeoning media fascination with candidates' personalities and lifestyles. Rich, youthful, handsome, and married to a beautiful and stylish wife, Jack was an irresistible magnet for the editors of mass-circulation magazines, who covered him as they would a movie star. His growing celebrity showed in the enthusiasm of the vast crowds on the campaign trail, most notably spawning the phenomenon of the Kennedy "jumpers." At first, these were teenaged girls who bounced up and down as his motorcade passed. But late in the fall, a reporter noted, the girls were joined by middle-aged ladies in bathrobes, pregnant mothers, and even nuns jiggling beneath their black robes. Kennedy's novel fusion of politics and sex appeal moved a Southern senator to remark that Jack combined "the best qualities of Elvis Presley and Franklin D. Roosevelt."

For all the heat generated in the 1960 campaign, there was remarkably little distinction between Kennedy and Nixon on the issues. Both stood deliberately away from the most activist wings of their parties—for Kennedy, the liberals; for Nixon, the hard right—and both tended toward the wide center of political opportunity. Nixon's most marked shift left was on domestic policy, where his party had been weakest since the days of Herbert Hoover, while JFK played to the right on international affairs, where the toughness of Democrats in meeting the Soviet threat was perennially in question. Debate over foreign policy was especially shrill but shallow. Both sides denounced communist expansionism without offering realistic strategies for dealing with it. The old and fatuous convention of bipartisan foreign policies—that politics stops at the water's edge—blocked any chance that the two parties would offer meaningful alternatives to the voters.

Even on the most potentially inflammatory issue—Kennedy's Catholicism—there was no difference between the campaigns. Both agreed it should be no issue. Fearing a backlash, Nixon resisted private urgings from Protestant leaders such as Norman Vincent Peale and Billy Graham to promote a Protestant bloc vote against Kennedy. In the South, LBJ evoked the story of Joe Kennedy Jr. and his copilot from Fort Worth, Texas—presumably a Protestant—together on their last mission: "When those boys went out to die so that you could live, nobody asked them what church they went to." As he had done in the primaries, Kennedy decided to meet the issue directly and before an unfriendly audience—this time, at a September gathering of Protestant ministers in Houston. "I am not the Catholic candidate for President," he told the group. "I am the Democratic Party's candidate for President, who happens also to be a Catholic." He did not speak for the church nor the church for him. "If this election is decided on the basis that 40,000,000 Americans lost their chance of being President on the day they were baptized, then it is the whole nation that will be the loser." At the end, the ministers stood and applauded. All that Nixon could say was that his rival's statement "should be accepted without questioning."

THE ABSENCE of real conflict between the campaigns was reflected in the election results. The popular vote ended in close to a dead heat, with Jack ahead by little more than a hundred thousand out of nearly 70 million votes cast, the smallest margin since 1888. Kennedy's electoral college lead was wider, 303 to 219, due largely to Lyndon Johnson's work in securing seven Southern states, including his native Texas.

The election had an extraordinary outcome: Not only the losers, but also the winners were disappointed. After the debates, Kennedy's campaign seemed to be coming to such a huge climax that the staff, along with outside analysts, expected that he would win a comfortable majority, especially given the sizeable Democratic edge in voter registration. The persistence of anti-Catholicism contributed to the narrowness of JFK's victory, costing him millions of Democratic votes. Never before had a president been elected with a minority of Protestant voters.

Joe Kennedy, after all, had not bought a landslide. The implications were portentous. In a campaign so much driven by the candidates' appearances and personalities, Jack's youthful vigor and charisma drew a healthy celebrity vote and only just edged out Nixon's gravitas and experience.

For a man who frequently spoke of the 1960s as a potentially revolutionary decade, what kind of mandate was this for transforming leadership?

Chapter 3

THE POWER BROKER

John Kennedy had been pondering the presidency ever since he was a teenager. At Harvard in the 1930s, he had studied political science with Arthur N. Holcombe, who had also taught Jack's older brother, Joe, and their father. In graduate school at Harvard some years later, I studied with Holcombe too, so I know not only what he taught but what he did *not* teach. For one thing, he would have discouraged any speculation by Kennedy about altering the constitutional system. When in my own class with him I delivered myself of some fanciful plan for reform, Holcombe—a master of the Harvard put-down—dismissed it. "A dubious idea," he said, unsmiling, "at best."

Only when I returned to Holcombe's ideas to prepare for this work did I realize the intellectual modernity of the man we called Uncle Arthur. Primarily interested in political institutions, especially the presidency and the parties, Holcombe was a conservative who nevertheless was determined to bring politics up to date. He sought to apply a rational, scientific approach not only to the study of politics, but also to its practice, an emphasis on objective analysis that must have had strong appeal to Jack. Still, Holcombe understood the "intrinsic power" and "independent force" of transcending ideas as a "vital factor in the course of events." Holcombe's theme of the interplay of great ideas, political action, and key institutions, of leadership able "to organize the thought, the will, and the happiness of a nation," had special impact on his students during the intellectual ferment and political turbulence of the New Deal years.

How much did Holcombe and Harvard's other political science teachers shape young Kennedy's understanding of the American political system? Certainly Jack would not have missed their emphasis on the system's intractability, with powers separated among the president, Congress, and the courts, and divided between the state and national governments. But the leadership of Franklin Roosevelt, pushing through the sweeping New Deal program shoulder to shoulder with the Democratic party, empowered by the great 1932 election mandate, was for Holcombe an object lesson in how leaders could overcome the political system's brakes on change—by "generating political power from the energy which emanates from the will of the people," uniting them through a political party behind "a common national policy."

As he began his campaign for the presidency a quarter century later, Kennedy too saw such possibilities for dynamic, Rooseveltian leadership. In "the challenging, revolutionary Sixties," the senator told the National Press Club in January 1960, the country would need in the presidency not a passive broker, not a bookkeeper-in-chief or "casual bystander" to congressional action, but instead "a Chief Executive who is the vital center of action in our whole scheme of government." This was, Kennedy claimed, "what the Constitution envisioned." Only the president, he asserted, "represents the national interest. And upon him alone converge all the needs and aspirations of all parts of the country, all departments of the government, all nations of the world." Only the president could provide the leadership—political, legislative, moral—to "summon his national constituency to its finest hour."

Kennedy's was a heroic image of the presidency, and hardly what the Founders, with their fears of unchecked monarchical rule, had envisioned. In part, Kennedy's comments were meant as a scathing reflection on the Republican incumbent, the war hero turned complacent and detached executive, Dwight Eisenhower. But Kennedy's "vital" president, though "in the very thick of the fight," was nevertheless a strikingly isolated one. Repeatedly in the campaign he pictured the president "alone—at the top—in the loneliest job in the world," a solitary figure at the pinnacle unable to share his power and responsibility.

That image of isolation to a degree anticipated the realities Kennedy would face after his election. Unlike Holcombe's ideal leader, JFK had a relatively weak basis for governing. His old professor would remember that while young Jack rejected ideologies, he understood, "more clearly I think than most people ever do, that ideas are among the most important realities there are." Yet for all his oratorical brilliance in the campaign, what ideas had Kennedy articulated that might serve as "vital factors" shaping events? Political parties, Holcombe had said, empower leaders, but Kennedy was weakly linked to the most energetic force in the Democracy, the liberals. And "the will of the people"? During his presidency, Kennedy would sometimes carry a slip of paper in his pocket with a number jotted on it—118,574. It was his margin over Nixon in 1960, and it served to remind the president that half the American people had sought leadership from someone else.

SO WHAT WOULD the "awesome power" of the presidency amount to for JFK? To the National Press Club, he had said that the next president must be ready "to exercise the fullest powers of his office—all that are specified and some that are not." To help him prepare for his role, Kennedy sought advice weeks before the election from Richard Neustadt, a young professor of government at Columbia who had recently published a widely admired work, *Presidential Power*. In the book, Neustadt had emphasized not the formal or institutional powers of the president but his informal or personal powers. This was not in itself a novel approach. For decades, scholars and journalists had been stressing political as well as constitutional power in their studies of the president's relation to Congress, the courts, parties, interest groups, and other elements of the fragmented system. But Neustadt's angle was different. In a series of memos, he counseled Kennedy not on how to deal with Congress or other external forces but rather on how to master power *within* the executive branch.

Neustadt much admired Franklin Roosevelt's genius in presiding over a dozen sprawling and often quarreling White House offices while always keeping on top of his staff, deftly inspiring, managing, and exploiting aides. Neustadt advised JFK to assert his personal leadership by setting his own agenda, serving as his own chief of staff, safeguarding his own reputation, and protecting his own freedom of action. And how to do all this? By using his authority not to dictate to subordinates but to influence them to go along because it would be in *their* interest to do so. Kennedy could maintain that authority by shifting assignments, keeping staff and associates guessing, putting people of sharply differing views in charge of projects so that they would rely on him in case of conflicts. Hence, he would protect his interests against theirs where these might diverge. In essence, Neustadt advised JFK to run the executive branch alone.

Neustadt's highly personalized presidency suited Kennedy. It placed the president squarely at the "vital center," at least of the executive branch, and put a premium on the mastery of persons rather than institutions. Jack had never administered anything larger than his Senate office, but he was no novice in interpersonal clout. As a campaigner, he had effectively mobilized and controlled a large phalanx of loyalists who worked with fierce devotion for his ambitions. He had been an amused spectator of the petty machinations of Boston pols even before he ran for Congress; he had experienced the endless give-and-take of House and Senate politics. His father had taught him about the lethal rivalries of highly charged politics in London and Washington, including lessons from his experiences of dealing with that master of the art, Franklin Roosevelt.

But Neustadt's advice poses two key questions for Kennedy's leadership. If he had to struggle and scheme so hard to keep control over the branch of which, after all, he was chief executive, how could he influence separate and autonomous branches, notably Congress? This question poses a second. If even in his own bailiwick he had to act as power broker, maneuvering and manipulating his assistants and department heads, would he become merely a more "vital" Eisenhower, no more than bargainer-in-chief—a transactional rather than a transforming leader?

BEFORE HE COULD exert clout over his subordinates, the president-elect first had to hire them. For most office-winners, handing out jobs—rewarding the faithful, punishing the straddlers—was the most delicious of tasks. But Kennedy approached it with little enthusiasm. He grumbled to his father, "Jesus Christ, this one wants that, that one wants this. Goddamn it, you can't satisfy any of these people."

During the transition, Jack confessed to aides that he was little prepared to make key appointments. "I spent so much time getting to know people who could help me get elected President," he acknowledged, "that I didn't have any time to get to know people who could help me, after I was elected, to be a good President." And of those he did know, some he didn't want around him. Adlai Stevenson, for instance, was widely expected to be given the top job at State. But Kennedy didn't like him and resented his involvement in a futile "stop Kennedy" effort at the convention. Besides, Adlai might "forget who's the President and who's the Secretary of State." Foreign relations had been a consuming interest for Jack since the 1930s and he intended to keep policymaking under his direct control. "It is the President alone," he had said during the campaign, "who must make the major decisions of our foreign policy." So, dismissing Stevenson—"fuck him," Jack said—he turned finally to a man he barely knew, Dean Rusk, head of the Rockefeller Foundation. Rusk was experienced and competent—and, most importantly, willing to let Kennedy run foreign policy.

Because JFK had so much run alone for the presidency, he felt fewer obligations to party leaders and factions than his predecessors had. And because his victory margin was so thin, he was eager to appoint "a few smart Republicans" to reassure the country of his nonpartisanship. In piecing together his administration, Kennedy cast a wide net. He put a brother-in-law, Sargent Shriver, in charge of a nationwide talent hunt.

Among JFK's early choices was Robert McNamara to lead the Defense Department. McNamara was president of Ford Motor Company and a liberal Republican. Jack had never met him before offering him the job. In searching for a Treasury secretary, Kennedy, who had little experience of finance, said his priority was to find someone "who can call a few of those people on Wall Street by their first names." The first choice was Robert Lovett, a worldly Republican banker, and when he declined the post, Kennedy named another Republican financier, C. Douglas Dillon, Eisenhower's under secretary of State. The nomination triggered complaints from liberals. Arthur Schlesinger reminded Jack that if Nixon had won the election, he might have given Dillon the same job. "Oh, I don't care about those things," Kennedy replied. "All I want to know is: is he able? and will he go along with the program?" But could Dillon really be trusted to go along? It was Robert Kennedy who raised the question of loyalty, first with his brother and then, bluntly, with Dillon himself, who assured him that if he felt obliged to resign, he would go quietly. Dillon proved to be one of JFK's best appointments.

Kennedy filled out the rest of his Cabinet mainly with skilled and experienced liberals who had backed him strongly in 1960, including Stewart Udall for Interior, Arthur Goldberg for Labor, and Abraham Ribicoff for Health, Education, and Welfare. One exception—exceptional in every sense—was his choice for attorney general, who was not only inexperienced but also happened to be the president-elect's brother. "I decided I wasn't going to do it," Robert Kennedy would recall in 1964. This meant withstanding intense pressure from Joe Kennedy, who "wouldn't hear of anything else." But over breakfast one morning, Jack pleaded with his brother. In a government of "people he didn't know particularly well," he needed someone whose "motivation really could never be questioned," someone he might trust, well, like a brother. So Robert agreed, not so much to be attorney general, but to serve as his brother's confidant and protector—the quintessential insider.

Kennedy created another layer of trust and protection by filling the White House staff with men who had campaigned with him, some since 1946. In the Roosevelt style, JFK accepted—even encouraged—disagreement among his staff. "When you people stop arguing," he told an aide, "I'll start worrying." Since he had made personal loyalty the basis for most of his staff appointments, he was confident that once he made a decision everyone would fall into line. Though each staffer was given an area of responsibility, all ranged through wide realms of policy and politics. This reflected Kennedy's disdain for the rigid, hierarchical staff structure of Eisenhower's White House. With such freedom and their closeness to the president, Kennedy's staff became unusually powerful, often preempting the strangers in the Cabinet and projecting presidential authority through the departments and agencies.

"I want to be in the thick of things," Kennedy said of serving as his own chief of staff, as the hub of a wheel whose spokes were members of his staff. But by narrowing his base of advisers and surrounding himself with men whose "loyalty to Kennedy transcended everything," as one of them put it, he cut himself off from the broader range of people and ideas that might be needed as new problems and crises arose.

∽

IN THE COLD WAR of the 1960s, the acid test of Kennedy's leadership would be his ability to confront hostile nations and peoples. That in turn depended heavily on his ability to manage his own administration and extract and evaluate the knowledge he needed to make wise decisions. Less than three months into his presidency, tiny Cuba would afford the first and most humbling of a crescendo of learning experiences, a test of his mettle that would expose weaknesses of his Neustadtian style of leadership.

From the Eisenhower administration, Kennedy inherited a CIA plan to send a brigade of Cuban exiles to invade Fidel Castro's island nation. Although Kennedy had made Castro's overthrow a central theme in the 1960 campaign, the scheme seemed risky, resting on a host of dubious assumptions: that the invaders would have the advantage of surprise, that the invasion would trigger an armed uprising against Castro, and that the American role could be concealed. The CIA, for its part, assumed that once the invasion was launched, JFK could not allow it to fail, even if that meant direct American intervention.

By Kennedy's own design, the decisionmaking process centered squarely on him. He had abolished checks and balances within the White House that might have produced a more searching evaluation of the plan—that might, for instance, have brought to light doubts within the military about its soundness. Instead, the new president was exposed to the unfiltered enthusiasm of the CIA's experts, who played to JFK's bias for action and eagerness to project strength. The White House had no process for registering dissent, or for bringing in independent voices from the outside. Arthur Schlesinger, one of the few on JFK's staff to challenge the experts, fired off a series of private memos to Kennedy expressing opposition to the invasion. But in group meetings, intimidated, he later acknowledged, by "a curious atmosphere of assumed consensus," he sat silent. Still, for all JFK's readiness to act, the president was apprehensive, and he framed a compromise. The United States, he decided, would aid an attack by the exiles, but under no circumstances would American forces participate directly. It was the worst possible decision.

Code-named "Bumpy Road," the operation ended as one of those rare events—"a perfect failure," as the historian Theodore Draper called it soon afterward. By the time the brigade sailed into the Bay of Pigs, Castro had mobilized his army and air force and moved to arrest tens of thousands of Cubans suspected of oppositional activities. There was no surprise, no uprising—and no denying an American role. But when the CIA and the Joint Chiefs of Staff appealed to him for air support, JFK stood firm. "They couldn't believe that a new President like me wouldn't panic and try to save his own face," Kennedy told an aide. "Well, they had me figured all wrong."

Publicly, the president took full responsibility for the debacle. Privately, he was distraught and bitterly self-reproaching for following the CIA and the top military brass despite his own reservations. Arthur Schlesinger wrote that JFK had "become a prisoner of events." Even more, though, he was a prisoner of his style of personal leadership.

"EVERY DAY there was a new problem," Robert Kennedy recalled of 1961. Soon after he took office, the president faced a communist insurgency in Laos with a seeming choice between "appeasement" and military intervention. In June, Kennedy was browbeaten by Nikita Khrushchev, the aggressive Soviet leader, at a showdown summit in Vienna. Emboldened, Khrushchev then stepped up pressure on the American presence in divided Berlin. The confrontation threatened to escalate into nuclear war.

Crisis followed crisis, with the administration merely reacting, improvising. The main fault lay in Kennedy's fluid, informal management style, which placed enormous burdens of coordination and follow-through on the president himself. As the hub of the wheel, he controlled the paper flow, gave assignments to staff, sifted through options from the ground up. He insisted that everything be brought before him. He was governing almost alone and he was overwhelmed by it. There was little chance for reflection, planning, anticipation.

The strains of 1961 forced Kennedy to adapt his leadership. He defined areas of responsibility more sharply and curtailed freelancing. He set up committees and task forces to study problems before they exploded into crises.

Crucial was JFK's growing trust in his national security adviser, McGeorge Bundy, a Harvard dean and a lifelong Republican. Bundy became Kennedy's filter, the one man to whom others on the staff and in the departments reported and who in turn reported directly to the president. Yet JFK balanced these concessions to more formal organization with an increased dependence on Robert Kennedy. Much as he had done as manager of his brother's campaigns, Robert served as the president's personal troubleshooter, his eyes and ears throughout the government, ensuring that Jack knew what he needed to know, protecting his interests and enforcing his decisions.

The crises of 1961—and what the president learned from them—prepared him for a far greater challenge that lay ahead. Again it involved Cuba. In the summer of 1962, U.S. intelligence picked up signs that Moscow was increasing military shipments to Cuba. In October, two U-2 surveillance planes brought back photographic proof that the Soviets were secretly constructing launch sites for offensive nuclear missiles that could reach two thousand miles into the United States. Khrushchev was planning to present the Americans with a fait accompli when the missiles became operational in November. In the most serious of many miscalculations, the Soviet leader expected a president he considered weak and indecisive to swallow it.

Kennedy quickly convened a small group of advisers from the State and Defense Departments and the White House staff—ExComm, it came to be called. Crucially, he included his brother Robert to offer antidotes to conventional institutional wisdom. In contrast to the Bay of Pigs, there was no rush to action this time, no overreliance on the advocacy and assumptions of experts. Kennedy invited outsiders into the deliberations, most notably former ambassador to the Soviet Union Llewellyn Thompson, who brought to the table shrewd evaluations of Russian intentions. Over days of wideranging discussion that often featured sharp disagreement, ExComm developed a remarkable cohesion under extraordinary tensions. Guided by the president—and by pointed interjections from Robert Kennedy, who reflected JFK's thinking—the group gradually worked toward a consensus for an alternative to the immediate use of force. This time, the president had the needed leverage to reject pressure from the military for an invasion or at least direct strikes on the launch sites. In a dramatic televised speech on October 22, he revealed the Soviet buildup and announced a quarantine of

Cuba. That was also risky: The Soviets might challenge the blockade or even launch a preemptive strike of their own. But it gave Khrushchev—and Kennedy—room to maneuver. A flurry of communications, through private as well as public channels, followed, and slowly Khrushchev, realizing his mistake, began to back down. In a breathtaking climax, Moscow ordered ships headed for Cuba to turn back just before the quarantine line. A few days later, the Soviets announced that the missiles would be withdrawn.

In the aftermath, the resolution of the Cuban Missile Crisis was portrayed as a triumph of collective deliberation. And so it was. But there was no mistaking its orchestrator. In 1961, Bundy had noticed, JFK seemed determined to hold all the threads closely in his hands, as though he could assure his clout and authority only by governing alone. Yet this often had the opposite effect, reducing his power and limiting his choices. Now, by widening his circle of advice, pushing against pressures for a premature consensus, encouraging orderly but free discussion, the president had protected his options and maintained control. It was his greatest triumph as a power broker.

But Kennedy could not always bring that operating style to bear. In the Third World, Kennedy faced what he called a "battle for minds and souls" as colonial empires collapsed and new nations struggled to be born, often amid conditions of direst poverty and political chaos. "The great battleground for the defense and expansion of freedom today," the president told Congress in 1961, "is the whole southern half of the globe—Asia, Latin America, Africa and the Middle East—the lands of the rising peoples." In one of those lands—Vietnam—JFK inherited the most intractable of conflicts. Despite American support, South Vietnam's Ngo Dinh Diem regime was faltering in its struggle with the communist North.

In late 1961, with the situation approaching a critical point, Kennedy was under heavy pressure from leading advisers—Bundy, McNamara, Rusk, as well as the military brass—to send combat troops to Vietnam. The president resisted, asking skeptical questions about domestic and international reaction and the wisdom of making a full, open-ended commitment to South Vietnamese independence. "Troops," he told them, "are a last resort." But the president was also determined to preserve a noncommunist bastion in Southeast Asia and rejected suggestions from another faction of advisers that he pursue negotiations that could lead to Vietnam's neutralization and American disengagement.

Playing one faction against the other, Kennedy brokered a middle way. He decided to increase the number of American "advisers" supporting the South's army from the 1,200 he had inherited from Eisenhower. These men—eventually there would be 16,000—were supposed to stay out of combat, but inevitably they got involved in firefights and sometimes major battles with the Viet Cong. Their presence helped stabilize South Vietnam's defenses, and for over a year Vietnam receded from the president's view.

But by 1963, the crisis was escalating again, as the military situation deteriorated and violent protests erupted against Diem's poor leadership. Contradictory intelligence left the president uncertain as to his choices. While JFK had been paying little attention to Vietnam, his advisers had divided more bitterly than ever, between those calling for more intervention and those who feared a quagmire, between those who advocated the ouster of Diem and those who warned that a coup would hasten South Vietnam's collapse. Constantly seeking more information, Kennedy sent a general and a State Department official together to Vietnam; they returned with such conflicting reports that the president asked, with his typically biting humor, "You two did visit the same country, didn't you?" The internal debate over Vietnam became so divisive that in a moment of sheer aggravation—and exaggeration—the president exploded to a friend, "My God! My government's coming apart!"

What had happened to the power broker? Years earlier, Senator Kennedy had proclaimed Vietnam "the cornerstone of the Free World in Southeast Asia, the keystone to the arch, the finger in the dike." In his inaugural address as president, JFK had vowed that Americans "shall pay any price, bear any burden, meet any hardship, support any friend, oppose any foe to assure the survival and the success of liberty." Even as he came to doubt their wisdom, such sweeping rhetorical commitments severely constrained Kennedy's range of options. If he withdrew from Vietnam, he told an aide, he would be "damned everywhere as a Communist appeaser."

And so the president faced a dilemma: He had to avoid a "betrayal" of Vietnam, which would damage the American cause in the Cold War and his own political standing, yet do so without the cost of greater American intervention. The president's vacillations as he tried to square this circle only widened the polarization among his advisers. Unable to resolve their conflicts, yet never doubting that there was an American solution to the problem of Vietnam and that American security depended on finding it, he was left almost alone in pursuit of nearly irreconcilable goals. In the missile crisis, the president had orchestrated a process that enabled him to come to a clear decision on the course of action. With Vietnam, every discussion, every decision, every action seemed to lead him into deeper uncertainty. No wonder that decades after his death, Kennedy's intentions in Vietnam remained a matter of furious debate.

But there was an even more potent constraint on the president's leverage: the nature of the enemy. Few Americans, despite the tenacity displayed by their own revolutionary forebears, recognized the passion of the Viet Cong. They would have to learn that military power was not enough to cope with revolutionary ideas zealously embraced. Foes with powerful motivations would triumph over men with machines. The old shibboleth was in fact the truth: The crucial struggle lay in the war to win men's minds and souls.

ᖃ

To win people's minds, John Kennedy, on January 20, 1961, had delivered one of the most riveting inaugural addresses in American history, a vow to wage "a long twilight struggle" against "the common enemies of man: tyranny, poverty, disease and war itself." The words of Kennedy's speech were militant, but they also represented a Jeffersonian evocation of the values of liberty and equality and an assertion of their interdependence: that the success of freedom could not be assured so long as men lived in bondage to "mass misery." If that was true in Southeast Asia, Africa, or Latin America, it was also true, Kennedy knew, in the dockyard areas of Boston and the hollows of Appalachia.

Addressing misery and inequality at home, however, would call for comprehensive policies and big programs. Most of the ambitious ideas for change JFK adopted were not new. Many—such as federal aid to education, Medicare, urban renewal, and regional development for depressed rural areas—had appeared in the 1960 Democratic platform that Kennedy had alternately run on and away from. They had been introduced even earlier, in the Eisenhower years or before, but never enacted into law. It was that inertia that Kennedy had campaigned against, with his promise to get the country moving again. Could he deliver?

To do so, the power broker in the White House would have to confront the barons in Congress whose formal power, under the Constitution, was equal to his own and whose informal power could, if they chose, be nearly tyrannical. After fourteen years in Congress, Kennedy knew these men, but did he know how to bend them to his purposes? Unlike Lyndon Johnson, JFK had never been a member of their inner circles, but rather a young man in a hurry who looked down on them and their folkways. And for all his appreciation of clout, Kennedy lacked Johnson's raw appetite and skill for horse trading, arm twisting, and knocking heads together.

Nor could he claim a mandate in domestic policy from the 1960 election. He had no coattails from that election. His party had lost ground—twenty seats in the House, two in the Senate—and most Democrats had outpolled him in their constituencies. He could expect little sympathy for an ambitious domestic program from conservative Democrats, especially the Southerners who had often effectively countered FDR and Harry Truman and were still entrenched in key committees. They were masters in the arts of delay and obstruction.

The citadel of their power was the House Rules Committee under Chairman Howard W. Smith of Virginia, who had the mien and manner of a plantation overseer. For years, his committee, which controlled the sending of bills to the House floor, had bottled up liberal measures. How to attack the citadel? By weakening Smith's grip through the addition of new committee members, including liberals. After intense pressure from White House politicos, Northern Democrats and a few Republicans eked out a deal a week and a half after the inauguration that expanded the twelve-member committee by three, including two liberals. However gratifying at the time, this was a puny victory. The congressional balance of power remained tilted in favor of inaction.

KENNEDY HAD made education a major issue during his campaign, pointing to the crisis of overcrowded schools, underpaid teachers, and decaying facilities. It was, his longtime aide Ted Sorensen wrote, "the one domestic subject that mattered most" to Kennedy. Yet the question of federal aid to education was among the harshest political battlefields in the postwar Congress. The white South had always vehemently opposed federal aid as a threat to its system of racially segregated schools. To conservatives, it represented big-government interference in state and local affairs. Bitterest of all was the religious conflict: whether federal aid should be extended to Catholic schools. Kennedy had experienced the intractability of the issue firsthand as a young congressman when in 1950 he tried to broker a compromise between Catholics and Protestants on a bill that would give limited aid to parochial schools. He had been stymied within his own committee.

A month after his inauguration, the president sent Congress a comprehensive package of aid for elementary, secondary, and higher education, with emphasis on "areas of special educational need," including "depressed areas" and "slum neighborhoods." Kennedy hoped to neutralize Southern Democrats by assuring them that segregated schools would not be denied aid. In an attempt to defuse the religious issue, he ruled out any funding for parochial schools, despite his earlier support for such aid, citing the constitutional separation of church and state.

The Senate swiftly passed the package almost intact. But in the "reformed" Rules Committee of the House, a full-tilt religious battle erupted. Catholic leaders mobilized against the exclusion of church schools, and when Kennedy indicated a willingness to compromise on the point, Protestants became enraged as well. As the fight grew fast and furious, JFK seemed unprepared for the intensity of the opposition. The new president had put his prestige behind the bill—he had named education his "No. 1 priority" during the transition—and had taken confidence from polls showing that three-quarters of Americans favored federal action. So he had planned no public campaign for his proposal and, behind the scenes, left the heavy lifting to his congressional liaison staff. With Southern Democrats watching "with hawk-like vigilance," as a journalist noted, "for the first sign that the Administration is dominated by the Catholic hierarchy," Kennedy was hesitant to parley with church leaders. Neither was he willing to bring the hammer down on a key Catholic Democrat in the House Rules Committee who opposed the bill, giving the impression of a president who could be defied without consequences. And both sides defied him, as Catholics rejected compromises that failed to grant them equal treatment, while Protestants refused to give Catholics anything at all. Kennedy's measure never reached the House floor. It was a total defeat.

In 1962, the president renewed his proposals, insisting to Congress that he saw "no reason to weaken or withdraw that bill," declaring it the minimum "required by our needs." This time, the outcome was even worse. With no stomach for another religious war, Congress virtually dismissed Kennedy's ambitious program.

Furious, Kennedy returned to the fray in 1963, but now he focused on the limited and less contentious area of higher education, where a "long-predicted crisis," Kennedy declaimed, was "now at hand." Even his more modest hopes dwindled by summer, though. "We will probably get our jocks knocked off," he told Sorensen. But with less at stake and some deft management by supporters in Congress, conflict was defused and in the fall Congress passed a measure providing grants and loans for higher-education facilities. It was a far cry from the president's original aspirations for fundamental change.

COULD KENNEDY do better in another area of urgent human need, health care? Doubtless, his own medical problems and extensive hospitalizations deepened his conviction that something must be done for the millions of poor and elderly people who could not afford decent care. Health insurance for seniors—Medicare—appeared less intractable politically than education because it would not face the religious and racial obstacles that had doomed the school bills. Still, since its first introduction in 1952, Medicare had repeatedly been defeated in Congress, with the prospect of federal health benefits inevitably spurring conservative denunciations of creeping "socialism" and warnings that the nation would go broke.

Blocked by the House in 1961, Kennedy insisted that he would make Medicare "the highest priority" the next year. But now, as the bill was again bogged down in House and Senate committees, the administration split bitterly over strategy. Some frustrated advisers proposed "going to the people" to spark a grassroots pressure campaign, while others feared this would merely stiffen congressional resistance and favored quiet negotiations with key legislators. Kennedy could not bring the factions together to frame a coordinated strategy. The administration tried both approaches, but they often worked at cross purposes. The public campaign was undermined by talk of dealmaking in Congress, while the nationwide rallies organized in the spring of 1962 by the AFL-CIO with White House support irritated lawmakers weighing the political pros and cons of the bill.

Most disappointing of all was the president's appearance at Madison Square Garden in May for a nationally televised address. His fighting stump speech for Medicare roused the thousands of senior citizens in the Garden crowd but did little to persuade his more important audience—the tens of millions of skeptical viewers at home. Editorialists condemned the president for bringing "hippodrome tactics" to the grave topic of health care. In fact, JFK was easily outdueled by Dr. Edward Annis, a Miami surgeon who delivered the American Medical Association's rebuttal on TV the next night. Annis made a strong, reasoned appeal urging viewers to trust their doctors—not the government—when it came to their health and well-being.

"The President's performance just let the steam out of the whole effort," a Medicare supporter lamented. It weakened the administration's hand with Congress. Any hope of action in the House now faded. The bill was still in play in the Senate, where Kennedy took the, for him, rare step— "unprecedented," Sorensen called it—of organizing a pressure campaign to win the support of a single key senator, Democrat Jennings Randolph of West Virginia. But Randolph defied the president and cast the vote that sank Medicare.

By spring 1963, Kennedy appeared to weary of the struggle, but wanted credit for another good try. He suggested to his Health, Education, and Welfare secretary that they go through the motions—"The failure then will not be ours" —and hope for better political weather in 1964. Neustadt's advice on the limits of presidential power hardly steeled his resolve, for it had confirmed Kennedy's own deep instincts: If the object was to win, there was nothing to be gained by battling for lost causes.

The president's fatalism hardly squared with the promise of heroic, transforming leadership he had pledged in his inaugural address, or his campaign vow to bring "a real fighting mood" to conflicts with Congress and make the presidency "the vital center of action" in the government. How could Congress be made to follow a "vital" president's lead? As the cases of education and Medicare showed, Kennedy relied above all on the soundness of his proposals—that they responded to recognized and important national needs. He shared a widely held but mistaken belief that, as Neustadt wrote, "a reasonable President would need no power other than the logic of his argument." But Congress—an aggregation of shifting and fragmented interests that nevertheless saw itself, not the White House, as the center of action—was rarely a reasonable beast, and Kennedy had little faith that he could truly tame it.

The distance he had felt from his colleagues on the Hill grew when he reached the White House. Now the gap was not merely personal, but also institutional, and his lack of feel for the mood and dynamics of Congress, as the miscalculations in the education and Medicare fights demonstrated, had serious consequences. His congressional liaison office—headed by Larry O'Brien, master strategist of Kennedy campaigns since 1952—was tireless and efficient, but the president did not see himself as working shoulder to shoulder with congressional Democrats to shove his agenda through. He had never been aligned with either of the party's two main factions, the Northern liberals and Southern conservatives, nor did a strong, solid "Kennedy bloc" form under his leadership. Always keenly protective of the limited political capital he had earned in 1960, the president typically approached Congress not in a fighting mood but deferentially. "Kennedy was not as aggressive as he could have been," remembered Senator Allen Ellender, one of the South's barons. "He was a little shy; he wasn't forward." In the 1962 Medicare battle, JFK had badly needed the support of Wilbur Mills, chairman of the powerful House Ways and Means Committee, where the bill was stalled. But he feared that if he pushed Mills too hard, the chairman would turn against other pieces of Kennedy's agenda. Medicare never found its way out of Mills's committee.

The president's legislative leadership—marked by appeals to the national interest and nonpartisanship—was more statesmanlike than political. So too was his reluctance—surprising for a president with exceptional rhetorical skills—to transcend the mire of congressional politics by taking the fight to the people. His ill-calculated address on Medicare was a rarity, and it probably reinforced his reluctance to speak out boldly. That reluctance was rooted in part in JFK's bias for consensus over conflict and his distrust of emotion in politics. But, as Lewis Paper, a student of Kennedy's leadership, noted, the president also believed that "he should wait until some specific event or crisis penetrated the public's apathy and made them receptive to his explanations and exhortations." But this rendered him incapable of moral leadership without a major crisis and made him "even more the servant rather than the master of events." What would he do—how would he assert his leadership—when events overtook him?

ᢏᢏ

THE MOST ENDURING political and moral crisis in the history of the United States has been the struggle for the rights of African Americans, a crisis that would reach a climax during John Kennedy's presidency. Racial inequality was not an issue Kennedy had felt deeply about as a young man. Robert Kennedy would recall that while his brother was "shocked" by all manner of injustice, the Kennedy boys were not "extra concerned about" the condition of African Americans as they were growing up.

During his congressional career, Kennedy saw African Americans through the prism of vote harvesting. It was a matter of cultivating their leaders, who, in Kennedy's view, were interested not in black empowerment, but, like white politicians, in their own personal power and advancement. These leaders, Robert recalled, would "deliver the Negro vote, and you never had to say you were going to do anything on civil rights." In 1957, the senator, already eyeing the presidential prize and hoping to avoid alienating either blacks or white Southerners, supported a proposed civil rights bill while also backing an amendment that weakened it significantly. Though that bill did little to advance black freedom, it was the first civil rights law enacted since Reconstruction and a signal of the gathering force of the civil rights movement. In the 1960 campaign, Kennedy used the same political calculus as in 1957. While he paid lip service to civil rights, he sent Lyndon Johnson to the South to dampen fears about JFK's intentions.

But Kennedy had not been able to avoid the issue altogether. Besides vague promises to use the "immense moral authority" of the presidency to offer "leadership and inspiration," he made an implicit commitment to action when he belabored Eisenhower for failing to abolish racial discrimination in federal housing programs "by a stroke of the presidential pen"—the president's prerogative to issue executive orders that required no congressional approval.

This unilateral power was what Kennedy needed in 1961 to appease civil rights advocates while avoiding fights with Southern Democrats in Congress—fights he was sure he couldn't win. In March, he told reporters he would propose legislation only when he felt that "there is a necessity for a congressional action, with a chance of getting that congressional action." The first-year strategy, he said to Harris Wofford, his special assistant for civil rights, was "minimal civil rights legislation, maximum executive action." So he made safe gestures. Noticing the absence of any black representative of the Coast Guard in the inaugural parade, he ordered the agency to recruit African Americans. He appointed the first African American ambassador to a non–Third World country.

But month after month passed with no action to ban discrimination in housing. Activists sent thousands of pens to the White House marked, "One stroke of the pen." Still the president delayed, into the second year of his presidency. When I talked with him in 1962, I was struck by the depth of his concern with "this Southern problem"—not racial discrimination but rather the power of the Southern bloc in Congress that had, to his mind, a stranglehold on his agenda and therefore on his presidency. To JFK and his brother, the attorney general, African American activists and liberals impatient for presidential leadership on civil rights had no appreciation of the complex challenges the administration faced. A reason for postponing the executive order to bar housing discrimination, for instance, was that it would jeopardize a pending bill to create a Department of Urban Affairs, which would have responsibility for fair housing practices. (The proposal failed anyway.) And then, as the 1962 elections neared, there was the fear of white backlash at the polls, and not only in the South.

When Kennedy finally announced the order, after the midterm elections, almost two years after he took office, it was sandwiched between other major announcements on the day before Thanksgiving. "He underplayed it all the way," Ted Sorensen acknowledged. Nor was the order as sweeping as his campaign words had implied it would be. It banned discrimination only in new housing owned or financed by the federal government, not in existing housing or loans by banks or savings-and-loans institutions. Rather than an example of presidential authority, Kennedy's "stroke of the pen" became a confession of political weakness.

BY THEN, events were far outrunning the president's leadership. Some events were appalling. In May 1961, a group of civil rights activists embarked on two buses for a "Freedom Ride" from Washington through Southern states to test compliance with a recent Supreme Court decision that outlawed segregated bus terminals. In Anniston, Alabama, a bus carrying activists was attacked by a white mob and set ablaze. In Birmingham, another mob assaulted the riders with baseball bats and lead pipes, igniting an international uproar.

Kennedy was furious—at the Freedom Riders. "Tell them to call it off!" he snapped at Wofford. Robert Kennedy sent marshals to protect the activists but asked for a "cooling-off period," noting that the president was about to leave to meet Khrushchev in Vienna. James Farmer, organizer of the Freedom Rides, replied sharply: "We have been cooling off for 100 years. If we cool off any more, we will be in a deep freeze."

As the president struggled to react to crises and searched for ways to dampen activism, new leaders were emerging from within the movement itself and gaining national stature. Foremost among them was Martin Luther King Jr. In October 1961, King became the first African American to dine with a president in the private quarters of the White House. Showing him around, Kennedy led King into the Lincoln bedroom, where a replica of the Emancipation Proclamation hung above the fireplace. "Mr. President," King said earnestly, "I'd like to see you stand in this room and sign a Second Emancipation Proclamation outlawing segregation, one hundred years after Lincoln's." Kennedy showed interest in the idea and asked King to prepare a draft, but when King did, the president never responded.

Would JFK's personal touch with King work? Words and gestures meant little if the president remained unwilling to follow them up with action—congressional action, actual laws. King understood the realities of congressional power—he had witnessed at close hand the infighting and maneuvers that had neutralized the 1957 civil rights bill—but he could not accept the president's subordination of moral imperatives to narrow political consider-ations, his repeated dismissal of deeply felt claims to freedom and equality as "unhelpful" and "untimely" embarrassments to the rest of Kennedy's agenda. "I have almost reached the regrettable conclusion," King wrote, "that the Negro's great stumbling block in the stride toward freedom is not the White Citizens Council or the Ku Klux Klanner, but the white moder-ate who is more devoted to 'order' than to justice," who "paternalistically feels that he can set the timetable for another man's freedom."

IT WAS THE ESCALATION of events—white violence, black protest—that jarred Kennedy into assuming leadership. Under mounting pressure from African American leaders—and from liberal Republicans who moved to fill the legislative void—Kennedy sent Congress a limited set of propos-als in February 1963 that would chip away at discrimination in voting and education. He accompanied the bill with his strongest language yet in sup-port of civil rights, pointing out that "the harmful, wasteful and wrongful results of racial discrimination and segregation still appear in virtually every aspect of national life." A little earlier, he had declared that "the distance still to be traveled one hundred years after the signing of the Emancipation Proclamation is at once a reproach and a challenge."

Events in Birmingham soon showed that the president had not yet met the challenge. In April, King launched a campaign of nonviolent protest in this citadel of segregation. After a month of demonstrations and arrests—King himself spent a bleak week in a Birmingham "dungeon"—conflict in-tensified when King mobilized the city's black children to join the marches. His aim, King wrote in his "Letter from the Birmingham Jail," was "to cre-ate a situation so crisis-packed that it will inevitably open the door to nego-tiation." Police chief Bull Connor reacted with fury, attacking the protesters with clubs, dogs, and water cannon. Images of the violence shocked the world, and Kennedy declared himself sickened. "I am not asking for pa-tience," he said. "I can well understand why the Negroes of Birmingham are tired of being asked to be patient."

The president intervened to prod Birmingham's business leaders to "meet the justifiable needs of the Negro community." They agreed to desegregate public facilities such as stores and restaurants and to offer job opportunities to African Americans. But the truce lasted only a day before three bombs targeting King and his brother triggered a new round of violence.

At the same time, JFK faced a separate confrontation with Alabama's governor, George Wallace, over Wallace's defiance of a federal court order to integrate the state university. Before he was sworn in earlier that year, Wallace had vowed, "I'm gonna make race the basis of politics in this state, and I'm gonna make it the basis of politics in this country." Then, at his inauguration, he had shouted, "Segregation now! Segregation tomorrow! Segregation forever!" Disgusted by Wallace's posturings as the last defender of white rights, Kennedy commented bitterly that such Southerners were "hopeless, they'll never reform."

The president was meeting regularly now with a compact group of advisers to discuss the ongoing crises and administration strategies. The group resembled the ExComm team that had served JFK so well during the Cuban Missile Crisis. Members included the attorney general and his deputy for civil rights, Burke Marshall, as well as speechwriter Ted Sorensen and legislative strategist Larry O'Brien. In bringing information from diverse sources and offering multiple perspectives on developments, the group helped the president to shape and refine his options.

One such meeting, on May 20 in the Oval Office, reflected the evolution in JFK's understanding of the civil rights struggle. Already battered by months of confrontation and violence, Kennedy was shaken by estimates that the upheaval would only worsen and spread. "There's going to be an awful lot of trouble," Marshall told him. O'Brien reported that moderate African American leaders were growing increasingly militant. "You're going to have an eruption," Robert Kennedy warned.

At long last the president was coming to realize, as Marshall remembered it, that the racial problem wouldn't go away. It was a moral and political crisis "that he had not only to face up to himself, but somehow to bring the country to face up to and resolve." JFK was reaching the conclusion, as he said on May 20, that the only answer was "real progress." This meant bold legislation that would establish a "remedy in law"—rather than in the streets—for black grievances.

By June 11, Kennedy had maneuvered George Wallace into permitting the peaceful integration of the University of Alabama. Seizing on that rare unalloyed success, the president went on television that night with a moving call to action, declaring that "now the time has come for this Nation to fulfill its promise." Americans, he said, were "confronted primarily with a moral issue" that was "as old as the scriptures" and as clear as the Constitution. With "fires of frustration and discord" burning in every city, "a great change is at hand, and our task, our obligation, is to make that revolution, that change, peaceful and constructive for all."

The next week, to fulfill his vow to act, Kennedy sent Congress a package of civil rights measures that in its breadth went far beyond what any president had proposed since Reconstruction, striking fundamentally at racial discrimination in public accommodations, voting, education, and federally funded programs. Kennedy understood that he was in for the fight of his life—he thought it might be his "political swan song." He was unsure of his chances but knew he had to push very hard. "You've got to get it done," he told Senate Majority Leader Mike Mansfield. "It's the heart of the matter." He repeatedly sought advice on strategy from Mansfield's predecessor, Lyndon Johnson, and consulted and exhorted key Republicans, including Dwight Eisenhower, realizing that he would need substantial support from the opposition party to offset defections among Southerners in his own. For the first time in his presidency, JFK was starting to fashion a wide collective leadership to meet a supreme domestic challenge.

Most crucial in mobilizing this collective leadership—and as a measure both of Kennedy's new commitment to civil rights and of his deep worry about the political risks it entailed—was his effort to establish a working alliance with African American leaders whom he had kept at a distance, whose expectations he had so often frustrated. Eleven days after his speech, he met a group of them at the White House, including Farmer, King, and A. Philip Randolph, who had been in the forefront of the campaign for federal action since the days of Franklin Roosevelt. "This is a very serious fight," Kennedy told them. They would doubtless have disagreements. They faced different pressures—Kennedy from Congress, the African American leadership from within their movement. But, he emphasized, they were all in it together now. "What is important is that we preserve confidence in the good faith of each other."

Taking leadership of the fight for civil rights at last, the president was reaching out to a black constituency he had failed to connect with and to the liberal community that still viewed him with much reserve. His shift was more than an abandonment of his failed political strategy of brushing aside black calls for action to avoid confrontation with Southern Democrats. It marked a moral commitment, both of himself and of the nation, to the renewal and achievement of basic American values of freedom, equality, and justice, a commitment so strong it could not be shirked, and one that would have a dramatic long-term impact on the lives of African Americans, on his political party, and on his country.

ᔓᕽ

ONE EVENING late in October 1963, President Kennedy invited a handful of trusted members of Congress to the White House for drinks, snacks, and political talk. As Tip O'Neill, who had taken over Kennedy's House seat in 1952, remembered it, the president was concerned about the status of his bills—Medicare, a tax cut, a salary increase for federal workers—and especially about the timing. JFK didn't need to explain to them that 1964 was an election year. "What's going on in the House?" he asked. "Why can't we get our program through?"

After an hour's discussion, Kennedy waved O'Neill into an office. "Come on in. I want to talk about old times." The president began to reminisce about his first campaigns and some of the men who had been with him then, those "who had more or less drifted away" as JFK had surged ahead. He remembered the names—Dalton, Kelly, Cloherty, Sutton, Mulkern, Healey—and asked O'Neill about their health and wealth, how they were getting along. The president "still had a feeling in his heart for those old friends that started with him."

It was hardly a coincidence that Kennedy was recalling those early races even as he was starting to plan his next, and last, campaign—and even as he worried about the progress of his legislation in Congress and the record of achievement he might have to offer voters in 1964.

A FORTNIGHT after this evening, the first grand strategy council of the reelection campaign—a three-hour marathon—was convened in the Cabinet room at the White House. It was presided over by the president and attended by all the veteran chiefs of his political clan, including the attorney general. Robert Kennedy had no intention of managing another campaign, but the top job would stay in the family: It would be handed to the husband of sister Jean, Stephen Smith.

"As usual," the president announced, "the campaign will be run right from here," and, as usual, he wanted to be clued in on everything. Topics ranged from the "loyalty oaths" required of convention delegates—"Should stricter and more comprehensive tests of loyalty [than in 1960] be applied?"—to the allocation of delegates among the states, to voter-registration programs—in which "reelection of the President," not general party-building, would be the primary goal. The group examined the latest polls, which showed "solid gains for JFK" over 1960 among African Americans and young men, "soft gains" among women and Catholics, and no gains among older men. Kennedy's careful handling of the religious issue had put to rest Protestant fears of a Catholic conspiracy. The Irish, though, were down surprisingly as "shaky for JFK." Reports had been prepared on the president's prospects in the states—"The situation in Virginia is not entirely hopeless"—and local allies and contacts were identified.

The meeting's focus was organizational, but the president laid out what he hoped would be the campaign's main theme: peace and prosperity. In keeping with that, JFK wanted to project strength and confidence, but he was concerned that his connection with voters was superficial, based less on his leadership and convictions than on the glamour of his image. As Robert Kennedy recalled, JFK worried that "he had not gotten himself across as a person with much compassion" and that people "didn't feel personally involved with him."

These were old political craftsmen in their workshop, overlooking nothing, taking nothing for granted. But they were optimistic. Earlier that year, in January, Kennedy was anticipating "another tough campaign" in 1964. By the fall, though, prospects had so much improved that even a hard-bitten vet like Dick Donahue, who had a seat at the strategy conclave, thought it might be "an easy one for a change."

Most encouraging, Barry Goldwater was gaining ground in the fight for the Republican nomination. The ultraconservative senator from Arizona led a faction of Republicans—and a small but burgeoning radical-right move-ment outside the party—that rejected the compromises with New Deal lib-eralism represented by moderates like Eisenhower and Lodge and by his leading opponent for the 1964 GOP nomination, Governor Nelson Rock-efeller of New York. Goldwater's militant stand against civil rights would cost Kennedy votes in the South, but the president expected that with LBJ on the ticket again he could hold moderate Southerners for whom prosper-ity, not race, was the leading issue. And Goldwater's extremism would bring offsetting gains elsewhere.

Best of all, the lines of conflict would be drawn brightly, the choice clear. Liberals were buoyed by Kennedy's commitment on civil rights and by his efforts to de-escalate the Cold War in the aftermath of the missile crisis. In June 1963—a day before his address on civil rights—the president had made a "peace speech" that called for serious engagement with the Soviets in a spirit of "mutual tolerance." Two months later, he reached agreement with Khrushchev on a limited nuclear-test ban. With Goldwater as the alterna-tive, liberals were sure to be mobilized. They, along with JFK, looked for-ward to the chance for a real mandate in 1964 that would allow the seeds of change Kennedy had planted in his first term—civil rights, education, Medicare, urban renewal, action against poverty, and the rest—to come to fruition. On that clearly defined battlefield, the president would run as he always had—long and hard—but he would perhaps this time not run alone.

THERE HAD been such hopes before. John Kennedy had entered the White House with great expectations of transforming leadership. Many of us who heard his inaugural address—that stirring call to action—shared those expectations. After the torpor of the Eisenhower years, there really seemed to be an appetite, even an *imperative*, for change. If the 1960s were to be, as JFK had so often said during the presidential campaign, a revolu-tionary decade, then leadership of the kind he promised—vital, creative leadership like FDR's—would surely be needed. So hopes had been high on January 20, 1961.

How naive we were. Kennedy's running alone, which seemed so captivat-ing and even courageous at the time, ended up as a poor, even impossible, strategy for a leader hoping to weld government together to create some kind of transformation. Strong leadership required that a president mobilize and unify followers numerous and committed enough to overcome the many forces resisting change—not only our fragmented constitutional system but also opposing leaders and *their* followers.

To mobilize followers, President Kennedy had two potential bases—his nationwide personal organization and the Democratic party that had nominated him. For his 1960 campaign, Kennedy had relied on the former. Working outward from his core of Massachusetts loyalists, he created a network of activists that reached down to the grass roots of cities and counties. These activists cheered on election night—but then what? They were not organized to carry on; they could not readily be transformed into a base for governing. Built specifically for elections, Kennedy's personal organization evaporated—until the next campaign.

With his other base—the Democratic party faithful—Kennedy had long had a mutually frustrating relationship. He set the tone with his very first campaign in 1946. Running for Congress as an outsider, he had created a personal organization in order to win the Democratic primary against a host of party regulars. JFK had strengthened and broadened this personal organization for later campaigns, leaving Massachusetts Democratic leaders—and, in 1960, the party's national leadership—feeling ignored and bypassed. Kennedy's attitude was that he owed the party nothing. At the 1960 Democratic convention in Los Angeles, a powerful city boss, hoping to influence the vice-presidential pick, reminded Kennedy of the help his organization had given him. "Not you nor anybody else nominated us," JFK replied sharply. "We did it ourselves."

After he won the presidency, Democratic leaders continued to complain that Kennedy neglected the party. White House politicos in turn found the Democracy inadequate when most needed, while they did nothing to strengthen it. Party leaders and functionaries still had a role in day-to-day transactions in Washington and state capitals, but they were denied a part in the transforming leadership Kennedy hoped to provide. As the ultimate test, the party could not marshal the following Kennedy needed for his big bills on issues such as education, Medicare, and civil rights.

This was nothing new in presidential history. FDR had known similar frustration—to the point that he tried to drive reactionary Southern Democrats out of office in 1938. Yet Roosevelt took this risk because he believed that a Democratic party of committed followers, united around common principles, "willing to stand up and fight night and day" for the cause, was the best and strongest base for his progressive leadership. Like Kennedy, FDR was sometimes accused of running alone, ignoring the party when it suited him. Unlike Kennedy, Roosevelt fought to transform that mutually frustrating relationship into one of collective leadership. Ultimately, the fault for the party's inability to provide effective support for JFK's program fell on Kennedy himself. His was a failure of presidential leadership whose roots were laid at the very beginnings of his political career.

All of the presidents who followed Kennedy into the White House took lessons from his highly personalistic leadership and personalized presidency. Each subsequent president in his own way depended heavily on his personal organization, ran to some degree apart from his party, and found himself to some extent governing alone. Too often, this led to failed presidencies, even national crises. Some presidents, empowered by their convictions and determined to forge a collective leadership, were able to transcend their isolation and leave a lasting mark on their party and on the country. But every presidency after his was stamped with Kennedy's special brand of leadership.

JFK AND LBJ:
GOVERNING TOGETHER

Americans have long been familiar with the "balanced tickets" that produced presidents and vice presidents of sharply different backgrounds and philosophies. But American politics has rarely thrown together men less alike than John Kennedy and Lyndon Johnson. Johnson's background—the lonely and impoverished childhood in the arid, remote Texas Hill Country; the hard work in menial jobs such as road building and trash collection; the degree from Southwest Texas State Teachers College—could hardly have been more different from Kennedy's. Even more contrasting were their personalities. Kennedy shrank from physical contact except with intimates, hated long-windedness, and rarely expressed emotion publicly. Johnson used hugs and pats as a form of persuasion and even intimidation, pontificated endlessly and often boringly, and erupted over trifles into torrents of rage and denunciation.

One thing they had in common was a childhood fascination with politics—Johnson's adored father served several terms in the Texas House as an ardent populist, until illness and poverty drove him out—but Johnson's ambition burned earlier and brighter. A childhood friend remembered him saying, "I want to wind up just like my Daddy, gettin' pensions for old people." Desperate to escape the grindstone of life in the Hill Country, Johnson found in politics a way out and up.

Kennedy had to overcome his personal distaste for the Texan when he chose him as his running mate. Once in the White House, he sidelined LBJ almost completely. Johnson, in turn, judged Kennedy and his leadership style harshly. In the end, though, their greatest achievements were linked inextricably. It was LBJ's presence on the ticket in 1960 that secured Kennedy's election. And it was JFK's program and, even more, the aura of idealism and sacrifice surrounding the murdered president that helped to power the greatest burst of presidential leadership since Franklin Roosevelt.

THE KENNEDY-JOHNSON presidency had its roots in the Eisenhower years. Ike's decisive win in 1952 over Adlai Stevenson carried Republican majorities into both houses of Congress. Among the Democrats to fall was the Senate majority leader, Ernest McFarland of Arizona, and Democrats turned to his young, go-getting deputy, Lyndon Johnson, to lead their caucus. It was a remarkable rise for a first-term senator in a body that valued seniority above all things.

Managing Democrats in the Senate was no easy task, given their wordy fractiousness, their jealous possessiveness of their own prerogatives, and the historic differences in the party between Northerners and Southerners. As minority leader, Johnson made it his business to study his colleagues closely—"the beliefs and values common to all of them as politicians," as he later put it, and "the emotion most controlling that particular Senator when he thinks about this particular issue." He learned their views, biases, work habits, their strengths and, especially, their weaknesses. Thus he possessed the most crucial information for a leader: the intimate motives and vulnerabilities of his potential followers. And he knew how to use it.

As a Southerner, Johnson's greatest leadership challenge was to work with Northern—mainly liberal—Democrats. He himself was no rock-ribbed conservative. He retained his populist roots, the faith that the fundamental purpose of government was to help the needy and the weak, and in his early career—as Texas director of the New Deal's National Youth Administration and then, after 1937, as a member of the House—he distinguished himself by his devotion to FDR. But as he moved forward, his close ties to Texas business interests, his reputation as a wheeler-dealer, and his raw ambition cast him in liberal eyes—even those of old New Deal allies—as a power-hungry opportunist.

Adlai Stevenson's elevating campaign for the presidency in 1952 had brought to Capitol Hill new liberal cadres who were intensely policy-minded. They wanted the Democratic party to take a more substantive and committed posture. After his defeat, Stevenson proposed a "system of consultation" through which he and other titular party leaders might "be advised of party policy" and even "shape that policy." And Senator Estes Kefauver urged Johnson to call a party caucus to build a stronger platform.

Johnson would have none of it. Not only would these initiatives have enflamed his other Senate constituency, the South's conservatives, but they also threatened his own power. He wanted to keep control of the party's agenda in his own hands and preserve his freedom of action in bargaining with the Republican White House. This left no organized Democratic opposition to Eisenhower's centrist leadership.

When Democrats regained control of both houses in the 1954 elections, conflict within the party intensified. Newly elected activists joined the liberal bloc even as Johnson became majority leader, the most powerful elected Democrat in the United States, and established himself as bargainer-in-chief with the Republican president. Liberals rallied against Johnson's domination. With a presidential election two years ahead, they argued that Democrats should use their control of Congress to confront the Republicans in the White House on major issues and, win or lose, build a clear partisan record to take to the voters in 1956.

But for Johnson, the consummate transactional leader, compromise was the coin of his realm. His aim was to turn bills into laws, not lost causes. "What do you want," he would demand, "housing or a housing issue?" And no one in the Senate knew the difference better than Johnson. "Because he spurned the hopeless fight," political scientist Ralph Huitt wrote, Johnson "was able to fashion a myth of invincibility which was itself mightily persuasive: when he moved, it was taken for granted that 'Lyndon's got the votes.'"

After Stevenson's 1956 defeat, liberals began to build party machinery of their own. In 1957, backed by the party's chairman, Paul Butler, they established the Democratic Advisory Council as an arm of the Democratic National Committee. The DAC was charged with the task of formulating party policy and aggressively attacking Eisenhower's presidency. Its membership included such luminaries as Stevenson and Harry Truman as well as hosts of governors and mayors. Eleanor Roosevelt chaired a panel on civil rights.

Senators were invited to join the DAC, but Johnson declined, as did John Kennedy. In fact, only two senators dared to become members—Kefauver and Hubert Humphrey—after Johnson announced to the press that he considered the group an unwarranted intrusion into the rights and responsibilities of elected officials. He spoke for his constituency, the Senate Democracy. Many of the rank-and-file followers—and not only Southerners—agreed.

The DAC's research and advocacy groups have hardly come down in history as exciting campaign lore, but their much-publicized findings, based on extensive research and analysis, had a lasting impact on the future policies and politics of the Democratic party—even, eventually, those of President Johnson. Most notably, the DAC took an uncompromising position on freedom and equality for African Americans and scorned the majority leader's proudest achievement: the 1957 civil rights law. Without Johnson's tireless bargaining to forestall a Southern filibuster, no bill would have been passed. But what remained after all the wheeling and dealing was more symbolic than substantial—Eleanor Roosevelt called it an attempt to "fool the people."

EVEN SO, Johnson's role in the fight—a Southerner taking leadership for civil rights—raised his national profile. He now appeared a serious contender for the 1960 presidential nomination. Yet he was as much worried as gratified. His Senate leadership was both an asset and a liability. He had a national rostrum, often appearing side by side with Eisenhower, but the job also shackled him. Not only did the press of business—and his determination to keep control—limit his campaigning, but his image merged with that of an institution many Democrats held in low esteem. The slate of achievements he hoped would impress voters, built on compromises with Republicans and conservative Democrats, inevitably tilted right, putting him out of step with the national Democracy. He could only envy independents like Kennedy who floated far above the Senate and seized targets of opportunity across the nation.

Yet for LBJ the Senate was also a safe harbor. As majority leader—and not a declared candidate—he was insulated from attack by other aspirants. If he really got into the presidential campaign, he worried, "they'll gang up on me and chop me up as leader so that I'll be disqualified for the nomination." LBJ's strategy, then, was to stay out of the primaries, where he expected that the other contenders would chop each other up and no clear victor would emerge. As a moderate Southerner with old New Deal ties and a record of Senate leadership, Johnson thought he would be the inevitable choice of a divided convention.

Even as Kennedy intensified his campaign and began to ring up primary victories, Johnson refused to declare his candidacy. He gave help to Humphrey, fueling talk that the Minnesota senator was a stalking horse for Johnson, and ran down Kennedy's prospects. "He's just a flash in the pan," Johnson insisted, "and he's got no record of substance to run on." And indeed the majority leader, who was putting all his political chips on his own record of substance, persistently underestimated Jack's raw political appeal and organizational power. But "the boy"—as Johnson was now calling Kennedy—kept winning.

After JFK's victory in West Virginia, Johnson realized he had to get going if Kennedy was to be stopped—but still made no formal announcement that he was in the race. Instead, he waged an aggressive behind-the-scenes campaign to win over uncommitted delegates, while publicly raising questions about Kennedy's youth and inexperience, his religion, his health. To one reporter, he dismissed Jack as "a little scrawny fellow with rickets." He also charged that Kennedy was under his father's thumb. "Old Joe," he said, would run the country if "Sonny Boy" became president.

Johnson's insults and insinuations embittered Kennedy's political clan. Many, especially Robert Kennedy, would never forgive him. But John Kennedy understood that politics could be the roughest of games—his own campaign was spreading rumors about Johnson's financial dealings and heart condition. He was more concerned that Johnson had gone so far out on a limb that he could not accept second place on Kennedy's ticket without a humiliating reversal.

Second place, it proved, was the best Johnson could hope for. His strategy to leverage his power and prestige as majority leader directly into the

nomination, without openly competing for it, failed utterly. When he finally announced his candidacy, five days before the convention opened, his
fate was sealed.

KENNEDY'S CHOICE of Johnson as his running mate was not the amaz-
ing rapprochement of bitter rivals that some at the time believed. To
Kennedy, the choice was almost inevitable. "He's the natural," Kennedy
said. Their partnership would greatly improve JFK's chances in November,
and Johnson's congressional experience would help them to move the administration's legislative agenda.

Johnson's own decision was inevitably more complex, the outcome of
conflicting emotions and motivations. Arthur Schlesinger—no friend of
Johnson's—believed that he was moved to agree to join the ticket in part by
a "deep sense of responsibility" to the South, a real desire to help lead his native region forward from its futile defense of the past and "back into the Democratic party and the national consensus."

In courting Johnson, JFK made the usual assurances of wide-ranging and
meaningful vice-presidential responsibilities. LBJ, who had turned every job
he had held into a powerhouse, wanted to believe that. And not only Johnson thought the two men might creatively govern together. Kennedy's national appeal combined with Johnson's Southern standing might mobilize a
broad voting base behind an energetic leadership that would seek to meet
the human needs neglected during eight years of a Republican presidency.

Yet the ticket's razor-thin margin of victory in November banished bold
hopes of collective leadership. Johnson's plight in the vice presidency was
worsened by his own rash attempts to secure power. Even before the inauguration, he was swiftly and embarrassingly rebuffed by his Senate colleagues when he proposed to continue to run the Senate from the executive
branch by presiding over the Democratic caucus. He fared little better in attempting to extend his reach within the administration. Just after the inauguration, Johnson's aides drafted an executive order for the president's signature that would give LBJ "general supervision" over a number of agencies.
Johnson would receive copies of every important document sent to the president. Kennedy, astounded by this grab for power, politely ignored the draft
order. The two men never mentioned the subject again.

Still, the president brought his vice president into White House councils more than most of his predecessors had done. He gave LBJ some key assignments—economic opportunity for black Americans, the space program—and sent him abroad on goodwill trips. But there was no chance of their governing together. The two had a mutual respect, but little rapport. In a White House where power was rooted in clan ties and exclusive loyalties, Johnson could not have been more the outsider. And once that realization sank in, LBJ became, in Schlesinger's words, "almost a spectral presence" in the White House. He sat silent through meetings, muttering a few words when the president asked him directly for his views. In Kennedy's greatest test, the missile crisis, the vice president was but a background figure. Few men knew better than LBJ the difference between real power and its trappings. "The Vice-Presidency," he would later say, "is filled with trips around the world, chauffeurs, men saluting, people clapping, chairmanships of councils, but in the end, it is nothing. I detested every minute of it."

The president understood LBJ's despondency. He couldn't cure it, but he was generous with gestures. He made a special point of recognizing the vice president at public ceremonies. When Johnson held back, the president would call out, "Where's Lyndon? Where's Lyndon?"

∽

SOONER AND MORE SADLY than anyone could have imagined, Johnson was there, in front. With Kennedy's murder, Johnson abruptly recovered from the sullen dormancy of his vice presidency to regain the energy and skill that had made him master of the Senate. The new president did not need Richard Neustadt's book to gain control of the executive branch. He had a technique of his own—direct, overbearing pressure bordering on intimidation and abuse. He threatened, ridiculed, humiliated. "How can you be so god-damn stupid!" he shouted at one staffer. "Why can't I get men with the brains of the Kennedy bunch?" At other times, he could be charming and even contrite as he handed out small gifts. While demanding loyalty, LBJ also offered it.

From his first days in the presidency, Johnson knew what he had to do. "My job," he told historian Doris Kearns Goodwin, was "to take the dead man's program and turn it into a martyr's cause." In a dramatic noon address to Congress two days after JFK was buried, Johnson declared that "the ideas and the ideals which he so nobly represented must and will be translated into effective action." Embracing his slain predecessor's domestic agenda—"above all, the dream of equal rights for all Americans"—Johnson asked that the country "highly resolve that John Fitzgerald Kennedy did not live—or die—in vain."

To build this legislative monument to the dead president, Johnson drew on his experience as majority leader. He knew that the sort of presidential bullying he visited on his staff would not get him very far with prickly legislators. But they had to be pressed hard. Kennedy, Johnson believed, had not been forceful enough. There was but one way for a president to deal with the Congress, he told Kearns Goodwin, "and that is continuously, incessantly, and without interruption. If it's really going to work, the relationship between the President and the Congress has got to be almost incestuous." Johnson's ever-ready channel to lawmakers was the telephone, but he also sent little notes and worked them face to face. Nothing better represented the difference between LBJ and his predecessor in their approaches to persuasion than what came to be known as "the treatment." Johnson would lean his bulk in on a doubtful legislator, his face inches away, supplicating, cajoling, accusing, complaining, sometimes with a tear or the hint of threat. It was, as two reporters wrote, "an almost hypnotic experience and rendered the target stunned and helpless."

JOHNSON'S LEADERSHIP of Congress achieved historic results in his first year in office, none more remarkable than the passage, virtually intact, of the civil rights measure President Kennedy had proposed in June 1963. African American leaders, recalling Johnson's role, as majority leader, in gutting the 1957 civil rights bill, had feared for Kennedy's proposals when Johnson succeeded him. But the compromising boss of the Senate now went all-out in his fight for the Civil Rights Act, enlarging Kennedy's proposals, rejecting every weakening amendment, giving to the struggle, he later wrote, "everything I had in prestige, power, and commitment," both as a fitting tribute to his slain predecessor and as a simple and necessary act of justice.

Johnson had been highly critical of JFK's handling of civil rights. In the summer of 1963, during initial discussions of Kennedy's program, LBJ made a rare attempt to thrust his expertise on the White House. He told Ted Sorensen flatly that the administration hadn't done its homework for the bill. Kennedy needed to rally the country around civil rights as a moral issue. He had to prepare the way with congressional leaders, including Republicans, while organizing outside interests—not only civil rights activists, but also labor leaders, educators, the business community—to pressure lawmakers. Without such an effort, LBJ predicted, Kennedy's bill would suffer a disastrous defeat.

JFK had followed much of that advice, and now Johnson built on those foundations. He mobilized the strength of public opinion and of citizens' groups behind the moral cause of civil rights. He teamed with the attorney general, Robert Kennedy, and Senators Mansfield and Humphrey, and forged an alliance with key Republicans, to inflict a stinging defeat on Howard Smith in the House, liberating the bill from his Rules Committee, and then to beat a Senate filibuster by Southerners. The passage of the bill represented the triumph of a kind of collective leadership that Kennedy had rarely mobilized during his thousand days in office.

In 1964, the president made a second momentous commitment—this time, to an "unconditional war on poverty in America." It would not, he acknowledged, be "a short or easy struggle," but "we cannot afford to lose it." As a first salvo, Johnson pushed through an Economic Opportunity Act that fleshed out and enacted ideas developed under his predecessor. From it flowed job-training programs for disadvantaged youths, provisions for adult education, community health and family-planning centers, Volunteers In Service To America (VISTA) and Head Start, as well as development loans to small businesses and innovative community-action programs designed for "maximum feasible participation" by the poor themselves to create change where they lived.

Yet Johnson's leadership of Congress had its limitations. Many of his early successes were hard-won. They often turned on cooperation from Republicans to overcome resistance from the Democratic party's conservative wing. Even more, Johnson had exploited the fresh pain of John Kennedy's murder, the aura that clung to the dead president's causes. To achieve his grand ambition of a "Great Society"—and to emerge from Kennedy's shadow—Johnson knew he needed a mandate from the 1964 election and coattails long enough to fill Congress with like-minded legislators. There was much work to be done.

THOSE OF US attending the 1964 Democratic National Convention in Atlantic City were amused by a huge billboard for Barry Goldwater that loomed across from the convention hall. IN YOUR HEART YOU KNOW HE'S RIGHT, it proclaimed. We admired the chutzpah but brushed off the challenge as a joke. It would take us another decade or so to acknowledge that the Arizona senator was far more than a billboard.

The convention itself was the typical orchestrated tribute to a party's sitting president. But matters did not proceed altogether smoothly for LBJ. African American activists from Mississippi demanded that their Freedom Democratic Party be seated in place of the state's "official" slate of lily-white segregationists. Disturbed that the party's deepening rift over civil rights should receive such a high-profile airing—and outraged that his coronation might be tainted—Johnson ordered Hubert Humphrey and labor leader Walter Reuther to work out a compromise. Outraged in turn when they were offered two token seats and the promise of nondis-crimination at the *next* convention, embattled activists wanted to quit the conclave, but Martin Luther King Jr. and others urged them to stay. In the end, the activist band had its big moment. When the whites learned of the two-seat compromise, *they* walked out. Black Mississippians happily grabbed the vacated chairs under the glare of television lights.

Though this skirmish was heavy with portent for the party, in 1964 it was mainly an infuriating deviation in Johnson's march to victory. With Goldwater's rigid conservatism as the perfect foil, the incumbent reaped vic-tories from the broad fields of support he had won through his wide-rang-ing legislative program. In the fall, he took forty-four states, with a share of the popular vote—61 percent—that rivaled FDR's landslide of 1936.

Unlike JFK in 1960, Johnson had not run alone. In fact, he had run to-gether with his predecessor. Even as he began gingerly to distance himself from Kennedy, Johnson frequently invoked the late president in his speeches, offering himself as JFK's rightful heir. And despite their mutual contempt, LBJ and Robert Kennedy campaigned together in New York, where Kennedy was running for the Senate. Johnson urged New Yorkers to elect JFK's brother to guarantee that "we win President Kennedy's program and my program."

More significantly, Johnson used that program—the Great Society, with its values of social progress, racial justice, and economic opportunity for all—as the unifying theme of his campaign. He stumped aggressively for a true policy mandate—a national consensus—for himself and his party. He worked hard for Democratic candidates while also inviting moderate Republicans frightened by Goldwater into his fold. The reward was a Democratic sweep down to the grass roots, with a gain of more than five hundred seats in state legislatures as well as a dozen governorships. Above all, the president carried a huge Democratic majority into Congress on his coattails, with a better than two-to-one margin in each house.

SAVORING THEIR sweeping majorities, Johnson Democrats derided the Goldwaterites who had been convinced that they could mobilize a "hidden majority" of "forgotten" Americans. That majority sure remained hidden, they scoffed.

But the Democrats underestimated the long-run significance of the Goldwater crusade. For the first time, the right wing of the GOP had won control of the party and its apparatus. Old Midwestern conservatives like Robert Taft with their simple, small-government beliefs had never overcome moderates like Eisenhower and Governor Tom Dewey of New York. Now a new, insurgent Republican right had not only captured the party but had done so without compromising their hard-line set of doctrines. They were far more antigovernment than Taft, who had accepted some federal responsibility in economic areas. And whereas Taft Republicans had their roots in "America First" isolationism, the Goldwaterites were aggressively interventionist in the fight against communist tyranny around the world.

Even more, the Goldwaterites were taking aim at the Democrats' ancient white Southern bastion. Goldwater portrayed his vote against the Civil Rights Act in 1964 as a defense of states' rights—that code for racism with roots in America's founding period. His campaign linked civil rights protests to "the growing menace to personal safety" and African American activists to street criminals. Bigotry worked. Of the six states the Republicans carried, five were in the Deep South. The other was Goldwater's native Arizona.

Goldwater had set out to transform American politics. He shocked Eisenhower and even Nixon with his extremism. In the New Hampshire primary campaign alone, Goldwater suggested that Social Security be made voluntary, that another Bay of Pigs–style invasion of Cuba be mounted, and that diplomatic relations with the Soviet Union be broken. Political writer Theodore White quoted a reporter as exclaiming, "My God, he's going to run as Barry Goldwater."

Transforming leaders like FDR and LBJ knew they had to be transactional too, as brokers, negotiators, compromisers. Goldwater declined to compromise. Rather than balance his ticket, he tipped it even more sharply by picking a fierce right-winger, Congressman William Miller from upstate New York, as his running mate. His ideological campaign team erupted in quarrels and made serious errors of judgment. But Goldwater was in his glory as a militant ideologue, pledging to "chart a new course of peace, freedom, morality, and constitutional order."

Accepting the Republican nomination, he uttered remarks that signaled political catastrophe: "I would remind you that extremism in the defense of liberty is no vice! And let me remind you also that moderation in the pursuit of justice is no virtue!" To the Goldwater slogan—IN YOUR HEART YOU KNOW HE'S RIGHT—Democrats replied, IN YOUR GUTS YOU KNOW HE'S NUTS.

In the end, Goldwater appeared to be virtually running alone, on his narrow and virulent conservative base. The "hidden majority" would wait for a better day.

⁓

HOW WOULD Lyndon Johnson exploit his landslide? First, he would move quickly. Ten days after his unremarkable inaugural address in January 1965, the president summoned his legislative aides not for a pep talk but to get them going. He exhorted them:

"I want you to get all my legislative proposals during this session, now!" And he meant *now*—in weeks. He warned them that every day he was in office, "I lose part of my power. Every day that I use that power, I have less power left. . . . I want you to get this legislation through now—while I still have that power."

That year, with the mandate he had won and the new support in Congress, Johnson pushed through measures that had frustrated Kennedy again and again—above all, aid to elementary and secondary schools and Medicare—as well as the Voting Rights Act, which expanded on JFK's proposals of 1963 and secured to African Americans "the most basic right of all," as Johnson said, the "right to choose your own leaders." An omnibus housing act to promote urban renewal was followed by the creation of the Department of Housing and Urban Development, three years after Kennedy's proposed new urban affairs department was blocked in Congress. Johnson's choice as the first head of HUD was the man Kennedy had envisaged in that role, Robert C. Weaver, who became the first African American Cabinet secretary. And because LBJ, like his predecessor, saw the arts and scholarship as essential to a great society, he drew on a report commissioned by JFK to establish the National Foundation on the Arts and the Humanities. Johnson also secured passage of landmark environmental laws to stem air and water pollution. All these bills—the greatest outpouring of major legislation since the New Deal—passed in a seven-month explosion of activity.

Yet even as he continued to invoke his predecessor's memory and draw on his plans, Johnson was coming to feel trapped by a legacy he had done so much to shape. Even his 1964 landslide was inevitably seen as, in part, a memorial vote for JFK. While LBJ's policies won enthusiastic backing from those New Deal liberals he had antagonized as majority leader—and one of them, Hubert Humphrey, had become his loyal vice president—it was Kennedy who posthumously won their hearts. Often frustrated by JFK's vacillations and ineffectiveness before his murder, liberals credited Kennedy's vision and words for Johnson's successes. LBJ was the workhorse—still the opportunist and wheeler-dealer, but now serving the martyr's cause.

Johnson grew impatient—even defensive—with this portrayal, stung by having to share credit for achievements he believed JFK could never have realized. Even more, LBJ resented the suggestion that had it not been for the aura of John Kennedy, *he* could never have achieved what he had. To him, the truth was in the numbers. As he had when he was in the Senate, Johnson measured leadership—his and others'—by tallies of legislation, and now he was pushing historic laws through at a pace that equaled that of his hero and model, Franklin Roosevelt. That many of those measures had their origins in the Kennedy administration was beside the point. "They say Jack Kennedy had style," LBJ told a group of senators in 1966, after he had proudly read out statistics that showed enormous spending increases for domestic programs since the Kennedy years, "but I'm the one who's got the bills passed."

JOHNSON'S STRATEGY with Congress was simple: Jump in ahead of the opposition, propose measures shaped for maximum impact, and prepare the ground thoroughly with every kind of presidential persuasion—telephone calls, public appeals, face-to-face pressure, and much else that was off the record. And he urged his aides to try everything too—"to bowl with those Congressmen," to "sleep with those Congressmen if you have to." The aim always was to connect with the followers in Congress, to take care of them, to understand *their* needs, remembering, as he told his staff, that "these men have to go back home and get reelected every two years."

LBJ's leadership in pushing through the federal aid-to-education bill—closer even than civil rights to the heart of this one-time teacher of impoverished Mexican-American children in South Texas—typified his approach. As Kennedy had learned, education reform faced the perils of conflict over the "three Rs"—race, religion, and Reds—with its alleged implications for school segregation, parochial schools, and "socialist" government. To overcome these obstacles, the president was purposeful, unrelenting, and resourceful. He set a task force to planning the bill many months before he sent it up to the Hill in January 1965, conferred endlessly with members of Congress, and told his Cabinet to give their full support. He refused to submit it to Congress without first getting the agreement of two key lobbying groups—representing public schools and parochial schools—whose irreconcilable conflict had badly hurt Kennedy's bills. His shrewdest stroke was to present the bill as a program to provide funding not for schools, but for poor *children* whether they attended public or parochial schools, thus minimizing the religious issue. Hardly revised by Congress, the measure easily passed the

House and won a remarkable Senate majority of 73-18. An exuberant president signed it into law in April 1965 at his boyhood one-room schoolhouse in the Hill Country. The bill had been enacted in less than three months.

Not all of Johnson's big bills passed so smoothly, but pass they did as the White House plotted and pressured. Pundits expected that 1965 would be Johnson's main and final legislative year, but he put through another set of major laws in 1966: a highway-safety act, an increase in the minimum wage, the Model Cities program, and the establishment of the Department of Transportation.

But in 1967, even though LBJ still had a large agenda and continued to pass legislation at an impressive rate, the number of significant bills declined sharply. Johnson's momentum stalled. The reasons were not far to seek. Not only did Democrats lose seats to Republicans in the 1966 elections—forty-seven in the House, three in the Senate—but the liberal coalition that had provided the muscle behind the president's domestic agenda began to splinter as LBJ turned to court conservatives whose support he desperately needed for another venture. Without formal declaration, by gradual steps but inexorably, Lyndon Johnson by 1967 had become a war president.

IT CAME to be called "Lyndon Johnson's war," but the president could reflect bitterly that Vietnam was an inheritance from at least four predecessors. Franklin Roosevelt had condemned French colonialism in Indochina without daring to veto French repossession of the area. Since then, American involvement there had deepened, with the United States taking over the French role of opposing a communist insurgency, as Vietnam came to be seen as a vital front in the Cold War. From Kennedy, Johnson had inherited not only a team of hawkish advisers but what Defense Secretary Robert McNamara called "a hell of a mess" in South Vietnam—an unstable client state whose army, despite American arms and 16,000 American "advisers," was barely able to fend off, much less defeat, the growing might of North Vietnam.

Johnson was no militarist. Mainly, he was a standard-issue Cold Warrior who saw his country as the bulwark of freedom against communist expansionism. Over his years in Congress and then as vice president, he had had wide exposure to international issues. But at heart his interests were domestic, where he felt far more capable and controlling, and where, he said, "I've got some bigger things to do." The president, an aide remarked, thought "foreign policy was something you had, like measles, and got over with as quickly as possible."

But LBJ could not get over Vietnam, and by the mid-sixties he was in a terrible bind. He had committed ground troops in the months after the 1964 elections on warnings from McNamara and other advisers that otherwise "Asia goes Red." But again and again the generals had come to him asking for more men, until hundreds of thousands of Americans were fighting over there, accompanied by massive waves of bombing. The escalating costs threatened to drain funds from his Great Society programs, posing a choice between guns and butter. Though a majority of Americans continued to support the war, anxiety was rising, and along with it discontent with Johnson's leadership. Antiwar rallies spread and grew, including a march on the Pentagon by a hundred thousand protesters in October 1967. By then, Johnson had long abandoned any thought of beating the North Vietnamese. The best hope was to force them into peace talks that would allow an American withdrawal that did not amount to surrender.

Under siege, Johnson's leadership imploded. Its great outward, embracing thrust died. LBJ's flexibility and resourcefulness, his huge appetite for new people, new data, new ideas, new causes withered as he turned and turned in search of the solution to the puzzle of Vietnam that had eluded JFK. Johnson's drive for mastery, which had powered his collective leadership, confronted a situation he could not master and collapsed inward. Now he struggled, as JFK had, merely to control the inner circles of his own administration.

He narrowed his team of advisers to hard-core loyalists and spent more time with military men, picking bombing targets and poring over battle reports. In White House conferences, there was rarely deliberation over the broader issues of the war. Cabinet meetings decayed into dull, scripted ceremonies; doubts about Vietnam were not on the agenda. And one by one, those who developed doubts abandoned the administration—finally, in November 1967, the war's main architect, Robert McNamara.

LBJ never engaged real dissent on the war. He convinced himself that the protest movement was nothing more than a mob of ignorant young people, cowardly intellectuals, sensation-seeking journalists, Eastern elitists who had always resented him because he was from Texas, hadn't gone to Harvard, and wasn't John F. Kennedy. He blamed them for the "credibility gap"—the fact that even among Americans who backed the war, the president's constantly optimistic reports of its progress were disbelieved. He blamed them for destroying the aura of his leadership, as his image as a populist passionately committed to building a Great Society gave way to caricatures of an unprincipled, bullying political operator and warmonger. LBJ was stunned by this depth of ingratitude. "Deep down," he would later say, "I knew—I simply knew—that the American people loved me. After all that I'd done for them and given to them, how could they help but love me?"

Now the test was approaching, the 1968 election. Vietnam grew ever more polarizing. The liberals who had been the most stalwart supporters of his Great Society were deserting the president in increasing numbers. Foremost among them was Senator Robert Kennedy of New York. Kennedy was one of many men in power who had once believed that "we will win in Vietnam," but in March 1967, he made a strong speech calling on the administration to stop the bombing of North Vietnam. The president, who had persuaded himself that he was honoring JFK's commitment to defend South Vietnam, attributed the public attack to personal animosity and presidential ambition.

But Robert Kennedy was not the Democrat who raised the first electorial challenge to LBJ. In November 1967, Eugene McCarthy, a little-known senator from Minnesota, announced that he would run against Johnson in the March 12 New Hampshire Democratic primary. Though a strong liberal, McCarthy had been no rebel against Johnson's Senate leadership, and in 1964 LBJ had almost picked him for the vice-presidential nomination before settling on his fellow Minnesotan, Humphrey. But by 1967, McCarthy had concluded that the Vietnam War reflected a wider lack of restraint in American ambitions abroad. Even more, McCarthy maintained, LBJ's own lack of restraint in the crisis of Vietnam had created a dangerously "personalized presidency, somewhat independent of the government and somewhat independent of the political party from which the president has come." Hoping to counter the "growing sense of alienation from politics," of "political helplessness," especially among young Americans, McCarthy decided to step to the fore of the "Dump Johnson" movement.

The president and his political people dismissed McCarthy's threat, and a poll three weeks before the primary showed the senator backed by only 11 percent of New Hampshire Democrats. But even as McCarthy's grassroots effort led by students and housewives, nuns and mill workers slowly gathered force, the Viet Cong's Tet offensive, launched at the end of January and targeted at South Vietnam's cities and provincial capitals, was giving the lie to Johnson's claims of progress in the war. On primary day in New Hampshire, McCarthy came close to beating the president, with 42 percent of the vote to Johnson's 49 percent. Four days later, Robert Kennedy leapt into the race.

EARLY IN 1968, I asked the White House for an interview with the president. It was granted. One dark night, I walked across Lafayette Park to a mansion—was I imagining this?—that seemed shrunken, almost besieged. But once I was ushered to the "family floor," I joined a lively and talkative group. The president entered, detached himself from the other guests, and sat me on a sofa in the corner. I started to ask him about his presidency, about his use of power, about his values. He did not want to talk about the presidency or big ideas—he wanted to talk about himself. I could not squeeze in a question or take a note. He talked all through dinner and long into the evening. What I remembered later were his references to his mother and father. He felt that he had failed them; he wanted them to be proud of him.

Johnson was humiliated, besieged, depressed, and bone-tired. He dreamed of paralysis, of lying in bed listening through a doorway as aides he could no longer command fought to share out his power. Suddenly, at the end of March, after New Hampshire and with another potential embarrassment looming in the Wisconsin primary, he ended a televised speech that proposed a bombing halt in Vietnam with a stunning announcement: "I shall not seek, and I will not accept, the nomination of my party for another term as your President."

This shock did not stop the spiral of events. On April 4, Martin Luther King Jr. was murdered in Memphis, and riots exploded in cities across the country. Two months later, Robert Kennedy was assassinated in California. Hubert Humphrey, rewarded for his loyalty with LBJ's support, was duly nominated in August at a bitterly divided convention in Chicago, whose streets rang with violent clashes between police and antiwar protesters.

Why did Johnson, the transforming leader of the mid-sixties, now appear far more the servant of events than their master? It was partly the intractability of the Vietnam War and the passions surrounding it. Even more, his loss of power reflected a profound shift in the nation's axis of conflict. Johnson had emerged from an era of clear and meaningful conflict between conservative Republican nationalists and liberal Democratic internationalists, a rational frame within which ideological and policy battles could be fought out. Vietnam changed all this. The Democratic party became deeply divided between "hawks" such as Johnson and Humphrey and "doves" like Robert Kennedy and Eugene McCarthy. All of these men were liberals on domestic issues but now found themselves politically at dagger's point. As Johnson and the old Cold War liberals on the national level lost their familiar guidelines, as a younger generation mobilized by the causes of the 1960s pushed a "New Politics" up from the grass roots, the Democratic party seemed set on a course of self-destruction.

IF VIETNAM and its divisions were Johnson's legacy—and they proved to be a long one, for both his party and the country—so was his campaign to build a Great Society. Was he, in the end, a transforming leader? He hardly fit the type, from George Washington and Thomas Jefferson to the two Roosevelts. Almost as tall as Charles de Gaulle, LBJ lacked the Gaullist mien. He was too crude, this man who pulled his beagles up by their ears, who gave reporters a graphic account of the sex life of a bull while careening around his ranch at ninety miles an hour. In Washington, he put people off with his earthy talk and huge encircling arms. As much as LBJ resented the thought, it was the memory and legacy of John Kennedy that supplied a note of grace and an intangible measure of political force essential to Johnson's leadership, especially in its first year. To that extent, the two men can be said to have "governed together" during Johnson's presidency as they never had when Kennedy was alive.

Still, as he insisted, Johnson was the one who passed the bills. His epitaph was not a Gettysburg Address or a declaration of Four Freedoms but legislative achievements too long even to list here. He liked keeping score of the "major" bills he had passed—for 1966–67 alone, the White House inventory claimed eighty such acts. Some of Johnson's accomplishments were indeed major, historic: civil rights, antipoverty programs, housing, health, education. Others appeared minor and turned out to be major, such as public broadcasting. But even laws with dull, innocuous titles—water research, traffic safety, flammable fabrics—could enhance people's lives. Change that originated in Washington would induce change in state legislatures, city councils, and town boards, far down into the grass roots. The test of transforming leadership lay in this—not in presidential pronouncements but in the daily lives and hopes, security and liberty, opportunity and happiness, of 200 million people.

Johnson himself was poignantly aware of the transience of power, of how fragile his 1964 consensus proved to be. By 1968, he felt spurned and abandoned. But for a time, he had demonstrated, better than anyone since Franklin Roosevelt, how a president and his party, empowered by values and by the hopes and demands of people in need, could govern together to accomplish enduring change.

Chapter
5

NIXON-REAGAN:
THE GRAND NEW PARTY

The European press had derided John Kennedy's choice of Lyndon Johnson as his running mate in 1960. How could the aristocratic young Jack tie up with a crude Texas cowboy? They failed to understand that balancing the ticket was one of America's oldest political pastimes. By adding a "different"—even a rival—man as running mate, a candidate could widen the appeal of his ticket immensely. Often the running mate was a congressional leader who might line up support on the Hill. A well-balanced ticket might even reach out to state and local politicians, ideally creating a broad coalition that could run together under the party banner and even govern together.

Ticket balancing had not always worked, of course. Franklin Roosevelt's selection in 1932 of Texan John Nance Garner, the Speaker of the House, gave a traditional North-South balance to the Democracy, but Garner's hostility to the New Deal meant that he was of little help in putting through Roosevelt's program. FDR's choice of Missouri Senator Harry Truman twelve years later, on the other hand, produced both a balanced ticket and an effective postwar leadership.

Sometimes the *only* link between a presidential candidate and his running mate appeared to be their common party membership. But that was just the point—their party loyalty and party obligation had joined an FDR with a Garner or a Truman, an Eisenhower with a Nixon, in the party fold. When Ike accepted Nixon as his running mate in 1952—and eventually, in 1960, as his successor at the head of the GOP—it was not because he agreed with all of Nixon's party stances, or even liked him, but because Nixon was a fellow *Republican*.

But wearing a party label is not the only—or true—test of party identity, of genuine partisanship. In the 1938 off-year elections, Franklin Roosevelt, the leader who had mobilized the Democratic party behind the deep reforms and progressive ideology of the New Deal, confronted conservative Southern senators of his own party who were dedicated to repealing those reforms. He launched one of the most audacious adventures in American political history—a party "purge." He toured the South urging Democrats to throw out their reactionary leaders in favor of young New Dealers Roosevelt had handpicked.

The outcome was a flat failure—all of FDR's targets were renominated— but not before Roosevelt had put before audiences *his* test of party identity. "First, has the record of the candidate shown, while differing perhaps in details, a constant active fighting attitude in favor of the broad objectives of the party and of the Government as they are constituted today; and secondly, does the candidate really, in his heart, deep down in his heart, believe in those objectives?"

Common party membership united Richard Nixon and Ronald Reagan, Jimmy Carter and Bill Clinton, the two George Bushes. As they ran for office and as they governed, what did their party identity amount to?

From Nixon to Reagan to Bush II, with Newt Gingrich providing a brief and unusual episode of leadership from the House of Representatives, America has witnessed the steady rise and transformation of the Republican party. In an era when the demise of party politics was widely foretold, the GOP accomplished a remarkable recovery from its perpetual minority status in the aftermath of the Depression to become a vigorous instrument for the conservative movement, proving Barry Goldwater a prophet. In their different ways, Nixon, Reagan, Gingrich, and Bush II all were Goldwater's heirs. Even Nixon, no ideologue and a party man mainly by convenience, helped put in motion the Republican revolution that his successors helped to complete. Together, these leaders built a party whose candidates would embrace FDR's tenets of partisanship.

But they could not have done so without the fracturing of the Democratic party after the Kennedy-Johnson era. Rather than regroup to meet the Republican surge, Democrats fell further apart. In a vicious circle, the party's divisions encouraged its candidates to forsake Rooseveltian partisanship. That weakened the party further, inducing Democrats like Jimmy Carter and Bill Clinton, the only Democratic presidents elected in this era, to turn away from their party—to run alone.

❧

AS BIOGRAPHERS assessed and reassessed Richard Nixon in the years after his resignation from the presidency, they variously labeled him a right-wing conservative, Republican moderate, secret liberal, warmonger, and peacemaker, but he was always one thing: a supreme opportunist. He was consistent mainly in his inconsistency. He not only seized opportunities as they offered themselves—he created opportunities that he then exploited.

The times indeed favored the opportunist quick to adapt to new situations and openings. The shots that struck down John Kennedy in 1963 ushered in a decade that saw the mobilization of millions of Americans to new causes—not only civil rights for African Americans, but antipoverty, feminist, environmentalist, and other movements—as well as conservative backlashes provoked by rapid and unwelcome change. But the decade also unleashed darker forces of violence and upheaval—more assassinations, racial tumult, and an escalating war in Vietnam that in turn triggered massive protests.

In these volatile times, Nixon seized any opportunity in sight. Still hurting from his knife-edge loss to JFK in 1960, he ran for governor in his native California two years later and suffered a humiliating defeat. Burning with mortification, he told the hated press he blamed for his defeat that they should think what they would be losing: "You won't have Nixon to kick around any more, because, gentlemen, this is my last press conference." Political obituaries were duly written.

But even as he was being buried, Nixon plotted resurrection. And not somewhere down the road. Within months, he began to position himself to exploit an impasse among the leading contenders for the Republican nomination in 1964. To moderates, he offered himself as a sensible alternative to Barry Goldwater; to conservatives, a safer choice than Nelson Rockefeller, the liberal New York governor.

But Nixon watched carefully as the ground continued to shift. When Goldwater appeared unstoppable, Nixon declined to join the "stop Barry" movement, though he was ready to pick up the pieces if it succeeded. While Nixon recognized what he called "the terrible liability of the extremist tag," he saw that Goldwater was on to something that could be useful to him in the future. That fall, he campaigned hard across the country for Goldwater—as a Goldwaterite.

AFTER THE DEBACLE in California, the man who had almost beaten Kennedy deserted his ungrateful home state for New York City, where he established a law practice designed to allow ample time for the campaign trail. Satisfied that he had restored his standing with Republicans by his loyal support for Goldwater, Nixon went to work crafting a strategy for 1968 that would keep him close to the party but carefully separated from other Republican hopefuls. He had a simple but demanding plan: to woo potential delegates to the convention far in advance by campaigning for congressional and state candidates in the 1966 off-year elections. Week after week he traveled out into the hinterland, visiting eighty-two congressional districts in 1966 alone, stumping for liberals and conservatives alike, while seeking pledges from local politicos likely to become convention delegates. Reporters noticed that Nixon was spending a lot of time in the South—campaigning in all eleven states of the old Confederacy—and speculated that he intended to make the region his base in 1968. Nixon brushed aside talk of his intentions, but he didn't mind claiming credit for the GOP's gains that November of forty-seven seats in Congress.

Never was Nixon's opportunism more tested than in the volatile election conditions of 1968. He was the favorite of neither the Republican party's liberals—that would be Nelson Rockefeller—nor its conservatives, who were looking to Governor Ronald Reagan of California as Goldwater's heir. But his Republican opponents appeared irresolute in the face of political and social turmoil. Rockefeller announced for the presidency, pulled out, entered again; Michigan Governor George Romney, a moderate, quit after his early promise fizzled; and Reagan hesitated until it was too late. Only Nixon stayed on course, shifting back and forth in the Republican center as opportunities unfolded. He avoided policy commitments as he talked vaguely about a "new alignment for American unity" coming to the fore in the shape not of "a grouping of power blocs" but of "an alliance of ideas" with "traditionally Republican thinking" as its "wellspring."

Ideas were hardly Nixon's forte, though; the pursuit of power was. His main strength lay in strategy and tactics. Though he borrowed from Goldwater's search for a hidden majority, Nixon cast a wider net. He relied less on doctrinal purity than on carefully balanced appeals in his effort to piece together that new alignment.

Nixon was at his most adroit in quietly opening up a "Southern strategy" that would forecast a transformation of American party combat. He refined the tactics of the 1960 Democratic ticket, when JFK had backed civil rights in the North while Johnson placated Southern segregationists. But while LBJ had sought merely to hold the South for the Democracy, Nixon's goal was to bring Southerners over into his camp. More subtly than Goldwater, he played to the racial prejudices of traditionally Democratic whites in the South, while at the same time taking a moderate civil rights posture in Northern cities. He vowed to carry out Supreme Court school desegregation decisions while "interpreting the old doctrine of states' rights in new ways." He courted civil rights activists with calls for new initiatives that would foster "black capitalism" while deploring urban violence and promising a regime of tough "law and order." By squaring this political circle, Nixon also fended off a strong thrust from George Wallace. The Democratic former governor of Alabama had battled the Kennedys over civil rights and now was pushing to expand beyond his segregationist base in the South with a "Northern strategy" of racial and economic populist appeals to disaffected whites.

Nixon's most striking feat, though, was his success in selling himself to press and public as a fresh face on the political scene, born again as a "new

Nixon." To stage his political rebirth, he borrowed from the repertoire of the man who had defeated him in 1960. Journalist Theodore White heard "echoes of the phrases of John F. Kennedy" in speeches that strained for soaring eloquence. Another reporter commented that by parading a group of "young intellectuals" before the press corps and making a fuss about his "youth movement," Nixon was trying "to create the impression that he was building up his own New Frontier."

This Nixon was not the Red-baiter of the postwar decade—"McCarthy in a white collar," as Adlai Stevenson had called him. Nor was this the political hatchet man of the Eisenhower administration, nor the embittered loser of the early 1960s. This was not "Tricky Dick" but a man of "Experience, Courage, Integrity, Ability, and Action," as the campaign pamphlets had it—a statesman, almost. Even Norman Mailer got the message, discovering a Nixon who was "not without real dignity"—a man "who had risen and fallen and been able to rise again, and so conceivably had learned something about patience and the compassion of others."

Nixon's patience was rewarded and his compassion tested by his politician's luck in 1968, which was catastrophically bad luck for his foes. An anguished Lyndon Johnson, consumed by Vietnam, quit the race and vowed instead to devote all his efforts to the search for peace. Then in California, just after winning the primary there, the Democrats' leading contender, Robert Kennedy, was shot down. Thus was Nixon's way to the presidency cleared. Only Hubert Humphrey remained to carry on the Democratic campaign.

But despite the relentless efficiency of the Nixon operation and Humphrey's burden of the deep rifts within the Democracy over Vietnam, the popular vote was breathtakingly close. Nixon won by only a half million votes out of the 73 million cast. A late Humphrey surge, riding hopes for peace talks, almost made Nixon a loser again. Wallace had run as an independent and drew almost 10 million voters. He cut deeply into Nixon's support, nearly beating him across the old Confederacy and making the Republican a minority president with 43 percent of the national vote. But the two men together took 57 percent of all ballots cast, while Humphrey's share was 20 percent below Lyndon Johnson's in 1964. Worse, Humphrey ran a woeful third in every Southern state except Texas. It was a startling shift and an omen for the future. Even so, although Republicans made small gains in Congress, Nixon was the first president since 1848 to win a first term without his party carrying either house. Only 34 percent of Americans were identifying themselves as Republicans—against 55 percent who called themselves Democrats. In the South, only a quarter of white conservatives were Republicans.

With such a divided, indecisive result, the story of 1968 appeared far less the beginning of a new epoch in American politics—the birth of what a Nixon strategist heralded as "the emergent Republican majority"—than another episode in the rise and fall and rising again of Richard Nixon.

AFTER NIXON'S tacking back and forth during the fall campaign, the American people waited expectantly for his inaugural address and Cabinet-making in hopes of gaining some idea of his plans. They waited in vain. The speech was a call for unity, freedom, and peace, with no guidelines for achieving those noble goals. Nixon's appeal for the end of angry rhetoric fell hollowly on demonstrators who chanted antiwar slogans, burned American flags, and pelted the presidential limousine with stones and bottles during the worst disruption of an inaugural procession in American history.

Nixon's choices for his Cabinet were no more revealing of future plans, except in the omissions. He named not a single Democrat, woman, African American, or Rockefeller Republican. He mainly tapped Nixon loyalists, especially from the business community. Criticized for picking a Cabinet that had no there there, Nixon could hardly have cared less. He did not want a strong or popular Cabinet. He wanted—and he got—an absolutely loyal West Wing staff that could anticipate his needs and quickly act on them. But where John Kennedy's loyal band was made up of hard-bitten political veterans, many of Nixon's people had little experience beyond the 1968 campaign. They were mainly young and callow men, desperate to please and susceptible to maximum discipline.

To crack the whip, Nixon appointed an unlikely troika. H. R. Haldeman, a crew-cut public relations man from southern California who had campaigned with Nixon since 1956, functioned as chief disciplinarian. John Ehrlichman, a Seattle zoning lawyer who had served in Nixon campaigns since 1960, was named White House counsel, but he had broad responsibilities for domestic policy. Henry Kissinger, a German-born Harvard professor of international relations, seemed the odd man out when Nixon chose him as national security adviser. A consultant to the Kennedy and Johnson administrations, he had long served Nelson Rockefeller as a personal foreign policy expert. But Nixon and Kissinger established a quick rapport at their first meeting during a wide-ranging discussion of the president-elect's ambitions and, most importantly, of his determination to cut the State Department out and direct foreign policy from the White House. Haldeman, Ehrlichman, and Kissinger each dominated a small group of devotees. These men composed a tiny power base—the smaller the better, Nixon believed, to insulate the president from the demands of the hated bureaucracy while ensuring that power was centralized in the White House.

Even this tight little staff needed to be controlled. Nixon fashioned an ingenious device to enhance his own personal authority. Where Lyndon Johnson had worked to the blare of news broadcasts from three televisions mounted on the walls of the Oval Office and to the constant clatter of two wire-service teleprinters beside his desk, Nixon preferred to have his news closely sifted and filtered. He arranged for a daily summary of stories from the newspapers and the networks to be compiled overnight in the West Wing by trusted political aides for him to check out when he came to work in the morning. Not only were the summaries tailored to his tastes and political needs, but the president could use them as a launchpad for instructions to his aides that often took the form of angry outbursts against enemies, real or imagined, inside and outside the administration. "FIRE HIM!!!," he would scrawl when learning of some bureaucratic outrage. These written orders minimized his exposure to subordinates outside the powerful threesome. Somehow, amid the intense and even frenzied interaction of scores of West Wingers, the president of the United States remained a loner, seated in an Oval Office as hushed and solemn as a hermitage.

IN HENRY KISSINGER, Nixon had a foreign policy staff of one. That was how both men preferred it. From his first days in the White House, Kissinger exhibited an extraordinary grasp of two qualities alien to many academics: an adroit and even Machiavellian ability to dominate the policy process, fending off powerful rivals in the State Department, the Pentagon, and the West Wing; and a readiness to adapt his own foreign policy ideas to those of Nixon. The two quickly established a partnership in their ambitious and intricate effort to reconfigure the Cold War balance of power.

Kissinger was Nixon's agent in preparing historic summits in Moscow and Beijing, playing those two giant rivals against each other much as he might have two insecure assistants on his staff. He was less successful in persuading them to exert pressure on North Vietnam to end a war that remained intensely and even violently divisive in city streets and on college campuses. Alternating between bellicosity and conciliation, much as LBJ had, to bring North Vietnam to a peace agreement, Nixon and Kissinger together worked out an elaborate disengagement from Vietnam that brought American troops home by putting the military burden on the shoulders of a weakened and disorganized Saigon regime. Somehow they managed to lose South Vietnam while dismissing charges that they were indeed losing Vietnam.

Though Congress enacted a law, over Nixon's veto, which limited a president's authority to wage undeclared war, Nixon otherwise enjoyed the wide latitude that Congress historically had given the president as chief foreign policy maker. This power enabled him to exercise the opportunism he needed and cherished in dealing with the endless flux of world events.

Yet Nixon's refusal to consult with Congress, his rejection of the State Department's resources, his addiction to secret diplomacy, to deception, and to surprises and sudden shifts in course—his intense personalization of foreign policy—ensured that many of his initiatives had little lasting structure. His three major achievements—the agreement with North Vietnam, détente with the Soviet Union and with China—all suffered reverses or collapsed when he left the scene. The collective leadership and shared policymaking that promotes stability and continuity, that provides a base for continuing achievement, meant to Nixon and Kissinger only endless arguments and ultimate paralysis. They would run their own shop with its separate power base. After all, there was a lofty precedent for Nixon's having a brain trust of one. So did John Kennedy with his brother Robert.

ALTHOUGH HE SHARED JFK's fascination with international affairs, where presidents could act virtually alone in matters of the greatest consequence, Nixon knew that if he was going to construct a "new alignment" in American politics, he would have to fight for it on the far more constrained and complex terrain of domestic policy. A prime target of opportunity was a legacy of the FDR and LBJ presidencies—welfare. "From the first days of my administration," Nixon wrote in his memoir, "I wanted to get rid of the costly failures of the Great Society." Providing aid to the blind, elderly, disabled, and families with dependent children, the welfare system was costing $2 billion annually by 1968, and Nixon's political antennae were sensitive to the white backlash against abuses, which was fueled by legends of black men buying Cadillacs with public funds and women shopping for color TVs with taxpayer money meant to feed their children. But Nixon knew that Goldwater's drastic alternative—the complete abolition of the welfare state—would be politically disastrous.

To help resolve the dilemma, Nixon recruited Daniel Patrick Moynihan, an assistant secretary of Labor in the Johnson administration. By the summer of 1969, Moynihan developed the Family Assistance Plan, which would guarantee a minimum annual income to every American family, the working poor as well as the unemployed. By offering direct payments, the program would slash the bloated bureaucracy Nixon loathed as a nest of enemies.

The FAP was Nixon's attempt to thread the needle: drastically overhaul welfare while preserving the principle of government aid to the needy. The plan promised fairness and efficiency and, by including a work requirement, it encouraged self-help. If this seemed a finely balanced compromise, that was also the problem. Conservatives were appalled that a Republican administration wanted to improve on—not eradicate—a Great Society abomination. Liberals considered the income guaranteed too little, and labor unions feared that by pushing the unemployed into the job market, the plan would depress wages.

Three times Nixon sent the FAP to Congress and met deadlock. He blamed "an unholy alliance" of right-wingers and "damn social workers," but the main problem was the president himself. Of course, he was proud of the program and especially pleased by the surprise its unveiling produced. But where Johnson had exhorted his staff to use every means of persuasion on

Congress, Nixon's staff had to beg *him* to do more than go through the motions of lobbying. Even as he persisted in submitting it to Congress, aides decided he didn't care whether the FAP passed. Nixon himself was deadlocked between his desire to appear as a bold reformer and the opposition not only of fellow Republicans but also of a powerful constituency he was eagerly courting, Southern Democrats. On the third go-around, another congressional deadlock looming, Nixon abruptly gave up. "Flush it," he ordered.

CIVIL RIGHTS tested Nixon's determination to thread the needle even more than had welfare reform, with far higher political stakes. His essential position, with roots back in the Eisenhower years, was to cleave to the center by opposing school segregation while resisting "forced integration" by busing and other means. When Northern liberals called this formula a hypocritical copout, Nixon complained to Ehrlichman that they sent *their* children to private schools. Attorney General John Mitchell, Nixon's friend and campaign manager, proposed letting courts take the lead—and the heat—for ordering school districts to desegregate. The president warned aides to "quit bragging" about desegregation. "We do what the law requires—nothing more. This is politics, and I'm the judge of the politics of schools."

Having sought the center, Nixon became trapped in it. As the 1970 congressional elections neared, he was increasingly squeezed politically between angry white Southerners and militant African Americans. In March 1970, he released a statement that condemned segregation and indicated his intent to support the law. But he vowed to cooperate with local authorities in the South to obtain voluntary compliance rather than impose federal power. Civil rights lawyers in the administration complained that this approach would slow or even halt desegregation. Spotting this item in his news summary, the president scratched a furious note to Haldeman: "H—Get their names! Have their resignations on my desk by Monday."

The president resented charges that he was a racist or indifferent to the plight of African Americans. In the 1950s, he would point out, he had had as good a record on civil rights as any national politician. At the same time, he was eager to build on his political gains in the South. Nixon insisted that he was playing the role of unifier on civil rights, earnestly seeking a middle course between extremes, denouncing segregation as a moral wrong while encouraging the South to find its own remedy without federal coercion. In fact, he was attempting a balancing act, a form of transactional leadership, weighing political gains and costs, in the face of the transcending moral issue of the time. But it was more than opportunism. By displaying "sensitivity" to white Southern opposition to desegregation, Nixon was taking a strategic role in the most potent political change of the late twentieth century—the Republican shift to an expanding base in the South.

RICHARD NIXON was perhaps the most misanthropic president in American history, with an astonishing range of targets for his hatred. As listed by biographer Stephen Ambrose, they included liberal editors and reporters, television newscasters such as Walter Cronkite and Dan Rather, African Americans and social workers, bureaucrats and big businessmen. All Democrats from outside the South. All Republicans from east of the Ohio River and north of the Potomac. The entire "American leader class." And most members of his Cabinet. "It was an astonishingly long list," Ambrose wrote. "Nixon hated them all." For Nixon, hate was a lifelong trait, beginning with his early opponents in California, about whom he blatantly lied. Achievement did nothing to dim his hatreds. On the eve of his greatest triumph in 1972, he was telling intimates that after the election he wanted resignations from everyone in the administration. He relished the prospect of saying, "you're out, you're out, you're finished, you're done, done, finished."

But his unwavering hatred did not translate into ideological or political consistency, where his hallmark was raw opportunism, even at the cost of gaping contradictions. He embraced the Republican party but later exploited and degraded it. He resorted to big government even while publicly denouncing it. He cynically shifted alliances among moderate Eisenhower Republicans and Rockefeller liberals, Taft and, later, Goldwater conservatives, as well as Southern Democrats. Early moralistic condemnation of communism gave way to an ardent pursuit of détente with China and the Soviet Union.

These vast inconsistencies, along with the hatreds that spilled out in venomous attacks on anyone who appeared to cross him, reflected perplexities of motivation and character and presented problems of psychological as well as political analysis. Ultimately, Nixon emerged as so divided a person and dysfunctional a leader that only his opportunism remained constant amid the shifts from role to role that ambition and expediency demanded.

What role would Nixon have most cherished for himself? Probably that of political strategist, plotting election victories. He was a brilliant vote analyst, with an elephantine memory for even the pettiest details of city elections. Like earlier presidents, he was a close student of opinion polls, but he went far beyond them to create his own public opinion operation under Haldeman's tight control. Bright young staffers were trained in public opinion analysis and given special access to the sophisticated polls the White House commissioned. Nixon not only harvested but also hoarded the findings by refusing to share them with the Republican National Committee, with his vice president, Spiro Agnew, or even with his own White House politicos. The data were his personal campaign weapon.

Fuller knowledge that has emerged in recent years of this private polling explains a crucial question about his presidency: why this Republican signed into law—and even proposed—a host of laws that matched initiatives of Johnson's Great Society. Even as he contended that most Americans were "simply fed up with government," he announced a "new American revolution" that extended federal power into fresh domains. It was not only the FAP that made right-wingers in his party squeal. In his first term, Nixon signed into law the National Environmental Policy Act, which made the quality of the environment a national priority, the far-reaching Clean Air Act and other measures to counter pollution, and the creation of the Environmental Protection Agency; the Occupational Safety and Health Act, which established federal regulations to protect workers from recognized hazards on the job; and—even as the FAP was failing for the last time—a Supplementary Security Income program that provided a guaranteed annual income for the aged, the disabled, and the blind.

Why such aggressive support for the types of programs that Republicans had spent oceans of ink denouncing? Nixon's motive was pure political self-interest: Polls proved that voters liked them. Year after year, Congresses that had passed such legislation were reelected. And, sure enough, Nixon's policies, even as they cut against the Republican grain, paid off handsomely in his reelection victory of 1972. He beat liberal Democrat George McGovern 60.8 percent to 37.5 percent in the popular vote, which the electoral college converted into a sweep of forty-nine states for the president, leaving one—Massachusetts—for McGovern. Once more, though, Nixon's was a personal rather than a party victory. Despite his landslide, the Republicans lost two Senate seats and gained only thirteen in the House.

NIXON'S YEARNING for power and influence was scarcely assuaged by his reelection. Even before a ballot was cast, he was calculating how he could convert his anticipated majority into a powerhouse that would back him during his second term and, even more, that might ultimately dominate the coming decades as liberal Democrats had since the New Deal.

But Nixon had scarcely sorted out ends and means in this grand strategy. At its core, he wanted to build on the Goldwater effort to draw Southern conservatives, both in Congress and at the grass roots, into the Grand Old Party. The dominance within the Democratic party of the new generation of activists that had ousted LBJ—McGovern was their candidate in 1972—made that possibility all the more enticing. Nixon reveled in the contrast between the sober middle-Americanism of the "silent majority" he aspired to lead and McGovern's following of—as a Nixon campaign aide described them—"the gay libs, the welfare rights, the black militants, the women's libs, the pot-smokers, the long-haired college kids." Nixon saw nothing but political opportunity in stoking social and cultural polarization.

Yet his ambitions for a great political realignment fell victim to his relentless opportunism. The liberal strands in his own programs and his determination to play both sides on fundamental issues undermined his strategy. Nixon was no Goldwater, willing to risk all for purity of doctrine. Nor would he embrace a consistent set of values that could transform that "silent majority" into a real majority of new followers that would empower Republican presidents and Congresses.

For all his relish of the "big play"—the sudden, unexpected turn—Nixon lacked true boldness and the commitment to long-term strategy that would allow him to achieve deep, lasting change. He wanted desperately to be thought of as a philosophical president, a sage able to understand and master the currents of history. In fact, he was impulsive, easily distracted, unable to resist the passing chance to score a point or two.

Nixon's opportunism had served to alienate him from the Republican party. For a former member of both houses of Congress, he was remarkably distant from most lawmakers. Like Kennedy and other presidents before him, Nixon had put his own election ahead of the fate of his party in Congress in 1968. But in 1972, when he had such huge advantages—incumbency, the biggest war chest in political history, a divided opposition—his unwillingness to come to the aid of fellow Republicans—indeed, he seemed to be running away from them—bred resentment. Nixon in turn complained to Ehrlichman that his party had raised the "worst crop of candidates in history." Within the executive branch, Nixon was almost as distant from his own Cabinet. He utterly lacked any wish to work with his party in Congress or with his department heads as a team. "I must build a wall around me," Nixon had told Haldeman on the very first evening of his presidency—an extraordinary statement for a leader who wanted to create a fresh and enduring following.

He had that big White House staff, of course, but this was hardly a team, and it became less of one as years passed. It was unusual for workers in the farther reaches of the White House to glimpse the president. Even the most relevant members of his staff rarely saw him to discuss policy. He mainly communicated with them through Haldeman and Ehrlichman. His organizational base—and his intellectual base to some degree—eventually narrowed down to those two men and a few others.

One of the most poignant moments of Nixon's final departure from the White House was when he apologized to his staff for not having been in better touch with them. "I just haven't had the time," he said.

WATERGATE—THE OUTCOME of Nixon's isolation and enmities, his contempt for the institutions of government over which he presided—brought the collapse of his presidency with his abdication. But it did not put an end to his influence on the White House or on the Republican party.

Before "the Watergate bullshit came along," Nixon said twenty years later, "I was going to build a new Republican Party and a new majority. . . . Yes, a new majority," his voice trailed off. In the scandal's aftermath, Republicans suffered massive setbacks in the 1974 midterm elections. Now only 19 percent of Americans dared to call themselves Republicans. One

GOP pollster feared that "in 20–30 years the party will be extinct." The only hopeful sign for Nixon's new majority came as he was being consumed by the scandal. Even as Republicans abandoned him in droves, standing by him in the last ditch were many of the Southern Democrats he had so aggressively wooed.

Another last-ditch defender was a Westerner, a presidential aspirant himself, Ronald Reagan. Few had observed Nixon's final crisis with more mixed feelings than Reagan. He disliked Nixon as a person, did not admire his style, and opposed such policies as the FAP and the rapprochement with communist China. But Reagan respected him for "getting off the floor when he was down," and he especially respected Nixon's political acuteness, believing that he knew more than anyone about national politics. Reagan would pay Nixon the ultimate tribute by resurrecting his new majority strategy from the ruins of Watergate and bringing it to a fulfillment Nixon himself could never have reached.

༝

RONALD REAGAN long mystified philosophers and pundits alike. How could a youthful New Dealer, Hollywood liberal, and activist union leader transform himself in only a few years into an apostle of conservative Republicanism, a Goldwater promoter, and ultimately America's most right-wing president before the advent of George W. Bush? I see little mystery. Throughout his life, Reagan slavishly submitted to the dominant ideology of his changing environments.

He grew up in a working-class home in Dixon, Illinois, not "from the wrong side of the railroad tracks," but close enough that "we could hear the whistle real loud." As a young man, he was intoxicated by FDR, by his speeches and style, his buoyancy, his enduring liberalism. After moving to California in 1937, Reagan starred in a series of B-plus movies. He not only joined the liberal Americans for Democratic Action but also served as an actors-union president and hard negotiator with the studios.

Then Reagan found himself in a new set of circumstances and underwent a startling alteration. With his movie career flagging by the mid-1950s, he became in effect a very well paid propagandist for General Electric, delivering a pro-business, antigovernment message to hundreds of thousands of employees at more than one hundred plants. In a short time, Reagan turned radically conservative, and by 1964 he was a committed Republican partisan. His stirring endorsement of Barry Goldwater on a special national TV broadcast a week before the presidential election transformed a long-faded film star into a fresh and dynamic figure in national politics.

Mystery remains, though, about the sheer intensity of his new ideology. Why did this seemingly benign, even artless "typical American" become such a powerful, values-grounded ideologue? Why did he push so hard? What fueled the burning ambition that led him in 1966 to run for the top position in the biggest state, and then repeatedly for the supreme national post? Opaque behind a relentless geniality, Reagan revealed little. But the answer must lie in part in the ideology itself. To embrace fervent causes often sharpens the ambition to act for them.

It took the force of this fusion of ideology and ambition to propel the amiable "Citizen Reagan" into the raucous politics of California in the mid-'60s. Political hopefuls in America usually start locally, running for city council or the state legislature. Ronald Reagan would begin near the top, challenging the ebullient incumbent governor, Pat Brown, the man who had won fame by beating Nixon in 1962. But Reagan knew his own strengths. His name recognition was high with movie-loving Californians. He could count on heavy funding from his millionaire friends. He had become the darling of the state's right-wing Republicans for his ardent support of Goldwater when so many others in the party had abandoned Barry. And while he forged an enduring political base in his adopted homeland, southern California, with its conservative political culture, already he was displaying the trademark of his later achievements: a remarkable ability to draw votes from far afield.

After he brushed aside a Rockefeller Republican in the primary, Reagan bested Brown by almost a million votes in November. He won strong support among traditional Democrats in rural central California and even in the more liberal north, proving that, at least electorally, he was something more than a Goldwater clone.

And so now to govern. But Reagan, having vaulted past the apprentice stage, had a monumental ignorance of the realities of California government. His arrival in Sacramento must have resembled a scene from *The*

Candidate, a film in which a newly elected senator blurts out to his campaign manager, "Marvin, what do we do now?" Unlike the film's senator, Reagan had his conservative convictions, but they were a blunt instrument in the hands of the governor and his equally inexperienced team of ideologues in the face of California's huge and complex society. Reagan made an initial stab at fiscal orthodoxy, but taxes and spending grew apace during his two terms. The governor oversaw steady increases in outlays for higher education even as he attacked elitist faculty and vowed to defend university campuses against antiwar protests "at the point of a bayonet if necessary." Reagan won a welfare-reform package with tough "workfare" requirements that put few people to work. After eight years, the antigovernment zealot left California's government—"them," as the governor continued to refer to it—much bigger than he had found it.

BUT EVEN the governorship of California was for Reagan mainly a stepping-stone to the presidency. He made a brief, belated run in 1968 after only two years in Sacramento, but Nixon had the nomination locked up, and in 1972 the incumbent was too well entrenched to challenge. But four years later, another sitting president of Reagan's own party, Nixon's appointed successor, Gerald Ford, was vulnerable to a thrust from the right.

Ford was badly burdened by his predecessor's legacy of scandal and by his own pardoning of Nixon, which abruptly ended his "honeymoon" with the American people only a month after he took office. The economy was staggering under the twin weights of inflation and recession, the price of a decade of guns *and* butter. Ford also faced an aggressive Congress bent on rolling back presidential powers in the wake of Vietnam and Watergate—a "usurpation," his chief of staff, Dick Cheney, termed it, that risked "a permanently weakened presidency."

Ford had never run for office outside of his congressional district in western Michigan. He was a conservative in the mold of fellow Midwesterner Robert Taft, not a Goldwater radical, and as president he had moved toward the center, not only, like LBJ, by embracing many of his predecessor's policies—including détente with the Soviet Union and China—but also to heal the bitter divisions formed by Vietnam and Watergate. He had gone so far as to pass Ronald Reagan over for the vice presidency in favor of—horrors!—Nelson Rockefeller.

Reagan had adopted what in California politics was called the Eleventh Commandment—"Thou shalt not speak ill of any fellow Republican"—but he would make an exception of Gerald Ford; the chance was too good to pass up. He promised that his challenge would not be divisive, but, as Ford wondered, "How can you challenge an incumbent President of your own party and *not* be divisive?" The ex-governor painted the president as a big-government tax-and-spender whose softness on communism would bring the country to its knees. Ford's campaign, meanwhile, tarred Reagan as a war-mongering extremist in the Goldwater mold. That Reagan got as far as he did—winning key primaries after a faltering start and taking the fight to the convention—testified to the insurgent power of right-wing Republicanism. But in the end, he could not overcome Ford's advantages of incumbency and his backing by the Republican establishment. Reagan fell on the convention's first ballot.

It was a fine trial run for 1980, Reagan's last chance. He was approaching seventy with his presidential ambition undimmed. This time, he could go all-out, first against a strong but fragmented field of Republicans in the primaries. Again there was an early defeat—to George Bush in the Iowa caucuses—but Reagan made a stunning recovery a month later in New Hampshire, beating Bush by two to one and eliminating the other contenders. So strong was Reagan's showing that Republican moderates who harbored doubts about the right-wing candidate were discouraged from rallying to Bush's side. Reagan ultimately won twenty-nine of thirty-three primaries and gained 60 percent of the votes cast. Overall Republican turnout for the primaries rose sharply above that of 1976—a good omen for the GOP.

In the fall campaign, Reagan confronted an incumbent president, Jimmy Carter, who was desperately on the ropes. Carter's apparent helplessness in the face of an economic crisis graver even than the one Ford had faced, including an economic plunge early in 1980 that left millions without jobs while inflation soared to almost 18 percent, made Reagan's case for new leadership an easy one to drive home. And Carter's failure to secure the release of fifty-two hostages held by Islamic revolutionaries at the U.S. embassy in Tehran played to Reagan's saber-rattling strengths.

Reagan's greatest challenge was to win the trust of Americans, to persuade them that he was no Goldwater—no erratic, potentially dangerous fanatic. A series of blundering remarks he let loose on the stump didn't help his cause. In a speech to the Veterans of Foreign Wars, he claimed that Vietnam had been a noble cause, leading to blaring headlines, REAGAN DEFENDS VIETNAM WAR. Speaking with a reporter from a religious publication, he agreed that creationism should be taught in public schools right alongside Darwinian evolution. Another "clarification" followed.

But Reagan was able to neutralize such lapses by presenting a persona that was commanding yet reassuring. Like John Kennedy, Reagan benefited from his celebrity, but his image was strikingly different from JFK's— heroic in the Western style, rugged yet softened by age, calm and plainspoken, idealistic and sincere. He was no intellectual—his gaffes showed that—but he wrapped far-reaching right-wing principles in simple, commonsensical terms.

Reagan's strongest appeal was to a constituency that had backed Jimmy Carter in 1976, evangelical Americans. Even as mainline or liberal Protestant congregations were shrinking in the 1970s and 1980s, millions of Americans in the South and West were joining evangelical churches. Christian conservatives had long been active in right-wing causes, but it was only in the 1970s, on the strength of their rising numbers, that they became organized as a political movement. They mobilized in opposition to civil rights, to Supreme Court decisions that barred prayers in public schools and legalized abortion, to the social and sexual "permissiveness" that emerged in the 1960s. In 1965, Reverend Jerry Falwell, a Virginia fundamentalist, had condemned Martin Luther King Jr.'s activism on the grounds that, "Preachers are not called to be politicians, but soul-winners." In 1979, Falwell himself became a very effective politician when he founded the Moral Majority in response, he claimed, to a call from God to bring "the good people of America" together to "stop the moral decay in America that is destroying our freedoms." By 1980, the Moral Majority was mobilized nationwide to back candidates that met its Christian standards, including Ronald Reagan.

With his Hollywood career, divorce and remarriage, and inconspicuous piety, Reagan seemed an unlikely hero to fundamentalist Christians. Yet as early as 1975, evangelical leaders united behind his presidential ambitions. In Reagan, fundamentalists at last were hearing a leader who spoke their language. He vindicated their conservative moral values and preached the gospel of anti-communism, believing that God's hand was guiding America's special destiny. They were hearing a man who, avoiding the abrasiveness of Goldwater and the naked opportunism of Nixon, seemed to be trying to bring people together rather than to divide them, a man who promised strong, committed, transforming leadership, rather than the endless concessions of transactional leaders.

This mobilized conservatism showed its power on the first Tuesday of November 1980, when Reagan won a landslide—44 states and 489 electoral votes, with a popular-vote margin of more than 8 million. Republicans captured control of the Senate with fifty-three seats, a net gain of twelve, while Democrats held the House, but only with a much-reduced majority. Reagan rolled up the predicted big majorities of Protestant voters but also almost a majority of Catholics. Astoundingly, he carried New York. But Reagan's biggest gains, compared to Ford's 1976 results, came in the South, signaling a potential expansion of the Republican base. The South was also the only region where turnout rose.

∽

ON JANUARY 20, 1981, Ronald Reagan did not have to ask "Marvin" what to do now. He knew what he wanted and he claimed a mandate to do it, though the meager national turnout—only 53 percent of eligible Americans had cast ballots—and much evidence that voters had rejected Carter's ineffectual leadership rather than embraced Reaganism, cast doubt on that claim. Still, he had a big advantage in the undoubted goodwill of most Americans, the boisterous support of grassroots conservatives across the nation, and copious advice from established Republicans who wondered how in the devil Reagan had done it.

One who didn't wonder was Richard Nixon. He admired—even envied—Reagan's ease and skill on the campaign trail and saw in his triumph a strong first harvest from the political transformation he had helped set in motion. Even better, while Reagan's fellow right-wingers still viewed Nixon with deep mistrust, the president-elect welcomed advice from the disgraced ex-president. And Nixon was not diffident. In an eleven-page memo hand-delivered to Reagan two weeks after the election, he laid out a detailed political strategy the new president should pursue, beginning with "decisive action on the home front."

"Decisive action" was what Reagan had in mind. A report drafted during the transition warned that, "No American president since Franklin D. Roosevelt has inherited a more difficult economic challenge." And Reagan meant to meet it as FDR had confronted the Depression. Even as Reagan set out to dismantle the New Deal, Roosevelt remained his political model, especially for courageous leadership in an emergency.

Like FDR, Reagan considered himself president of all the people. He designed his inaugural address to reassure Americans that he could pull the country through. Like FDR, he wanted to move quickly on sweeping legislation, to rival the "Hundred Days" of 1933. Like FDR, Reagan had a single, simple idea to guide him and the country. But where Roosevelt fervently believed in the active power of government to do good, Reagan—well, Reagan had been saying it since his General Electric days, but never more plainly than in his inaugural address: "In this present crisis, government is not the solution to our problem; government is the problem."

The economic crisis in combination with Reagan's convictions led to an extraordinary demonstration of creative presidential leadership—and to a profound and enduring transformation of the Republican party. Reagan sought to fashion a broad consensus in Congress and the nation to put through the radical economic measures at the top of his agenda. "We've come to a turning point," he said shortly after his inauguration. "We're threatened with an economic calamity of tremendous proportions, and the old business-as-usual treatment can't save us."

MUCH OF the planning for the president's program had been achieved during the transition with teams of economic and political experts fleshing out Reagan's broad goals and strategies. Though often depicted as a passive president—almost a bystander to his own presidency—Reagan organized the White House to keep himself in the game on the major direction of his policy and politics. He welcomed conflict, though not acrimony, among his advisers, and even institutionalized it. "The whole Cabinet argues in front of me," he said in 1981, describing the process he favored. This gave him "the benefit of the thinking of all of them." And "when there's been enough argument and enough discussion . . . I make the decision."

Content to delegate wide areas of responsibility, he was nonetheless careful that no single aide assumed too much authority. To head his staff, he appointed a troika of men who reported directly to him. Two were long-time California aides: Ed Meese, a hard-line right-winger, and Michael Deaver, the keeper of the president's image. But the memory of his first year in Sacramento, when, as he wrote later, "nothing went according to my plan," encouraged him to reach beyond old California loyalists to men with wider political and governmental experience. Most notably, he named James Baker as his chief of staff, the troika's third member. Baker had opposed Reagan twice—with the Ford campaign in 1976 and as manager of his friend George Bush's effort in the 1980 primaries. But Baker was what Reagan badly needed: an honest broker who ensured that the president was exposed to the full range of options on an issue and that Reagan's directives were carried out. Almost immediately, Baker became the first among equals in the troika.

Though Reagan filled his government with conservative businessmen and right-wing activists, Baker's appointment angered the ideologues, who feared that his relative moderation and acute political realism would sway Reagan in the wrong direction. They were right to worry, but only because the president shared Baker's pragmatism. Indeed, one of Reagan's distinctive contributions to the advance of the conservative movement was the tough competitiveness masked by his geniality. He was never one to "go off the cliff with all flags flying," as he remarked disdainfully of one true believer. He was convinced that winning—even at the cost of tactical compromises—would build the long-term strength and success of the movement.

The economic crisis gave the new president the chance for a very big win with small need to compromise. Within a month of his inauguration, he presented a "program for economic recovery" to a joint session of Congress. It was a sweeping expression of his conservative beliefs. He asked Congress to cut more than 40 billion dollars from the last Carter budget by reducing or eliminating scores of federal programs and by attacking "waste and fraud" that he claimed cost taxpayers 25 billion dollars a year. He demanded a 30 percent income tax reduction over three years.

"The new president," wrote the *New York Times* the day after the program was introduced, "is staking the Republicans' future on achieving a philosophical sea change in American politics." A poll showed that two-thirds of Americans agreed with Reagan's course of action—even if many couldn't make sense of his figures. Neither could many members of Congress. The Democratic leadership introduced its own, more modest tax cut proposal, weighted to benefit working- and middle-class Americans. But the president—riding a surge of public affection after he survived an assassination attempt in March—never flinched.

Late in July, with the final vote on the tax cut near and the White House proposal trailing in the House, Reagan went on a lobbying blitz, combining a televised appeal for public support with phone calls and meetings with more than eighty members of Congress, many of them conservative Democrats—mainly Southerners—under pressure to back their party's alternative. The president made these Democrats an enticing offer: He would not campaign against them in 1982 if they bucked their party and supported the administration's proposal. When Reagan's bill won in the House, 238-195, Democrats—forty of them—made the difference.

By August, Congress had given Reagan almost everything he had asked for: the biggest tax cut in American history and deep spending reductions, except for a large jump in defense outlays. It was the most dynamic display of principled presidential leadership since the early years of Lyndon Johnson. Like LBJ, Reagan had seized the moment for dramatic action and had orchestrated a broad and unrelenting collective effort to achieve it. Even more than Johnson's Great Society, though, Reagan's 1981 economic program altered the landscape of American politics. Somewhere, Barry Goldwater might have glowed.

PURE CONVICTION as well as crass politics propelled these bills through Congress, trumping widespread pessimism—even within the White House—that the plan would actually work, that it would produce economic growth and that economic growth plus reductions in spending could offset the revenue lost by the tax cuts and keep the federal budget balanced. Reagan's vice president, George Bush, had called this "voodoo economics" in the 1980 primaries. The president himself, though, was an optimist as perhaps only a true believer can be. This was in part the reason that even so many of his faithful followers could not take Reagan seriously as an ideological thinker. He seemed so simplistic, even guileless. The famous Goldwater speech in 1964 was, after all, an eloquent restatement of old right-wing truisms. Reagan had warned of creeping socialism marked by burdensome taxes and profligate spending and promoted by that "little intellectual elite" in Washington who thought they could "plan our lives for us better than we can plan them ourselves." How did Reagan get from there— a hackneyed speech on behalf of a doomed candidate—to a revitalized, modernized conservatism that by the 1980s had become the spearhead of what he was proclaiming as a "Republican revolution"?

In producing what historian Ted McAllister called the "transformation of American conservatism," Reagan drew on his experiences as governor and his campaigns across the country to glimpse new possibilities. He also benefited from the ferment among conservative thinkers and the institutionalization of conservative ideas during this period. Heavily financed think tanks were emerging to refine and advance conservative policies. Well-edited journals were attracting broader audiences. A host of writers were gaining access to the big metropolitan press. What came to be called "Reaganism" embraced a diversity of conservative creeds, ranging from free-market radicalism and antigovernment libertarianism to a religious fundamentalism that sought to erase the boundary between church and state. Reagan contributed little to the development of these doctrines. His crucial role was as a unifier. He united the right in part by promoting polarization, by distilling the ideological and political conflict between "us" and "them."

Reagan needed not merely to mediate among the different strains of modern conservatism—all transactional leaders must do that—but also to transform the right-wing coalition at its foundations. Above all, this meant completing the process that began decades earlier and accelerated in the 1960s and 1970s: bringing conservative Southern Democrats solidly and permanently into a broadened right-wing Republican movement. For years, the Southerners had been streaming into the GOP in presidential elections while voting Democratic in local, state, and congressional contests.

How then could Reagan Republicans persuade them to desert the old Democratic pols who had delivered so much to their states and localities? Mainly by preaching timeworn Southern dogmas—states' rights, lower taxes, "traditional" values—in refurbished terms. The racial appeals of Reagan Republicans, for instance, reached new heights of subtlety, turning liberal arguments on their heads. Reaganites were the first to admit that discrimination based on race was morally wrong. But they were also the first to insist that it was entirely a thing of the past. African Americans now played on a level field of freedom and opportunity with whites, Reaganites claimed. If government were to give them special advantages such as affirmative action, it would be institutionalizing a "reverse discrimination"—against whites.

Even as Reagan's economic policies tilted heavily to the benefit of the well-off and corporate interests, his social and cultural populism—the hostility to big government, the opposition to abortion and support of school prayer, the appeals to patriotism and condemnations of vulgarity and immorality in popular culture—positioned the GOP as the natural home of white Southern conservatives. Reagan invited them to become the vital center of a conservative takeover of the GOP rather than continue as the scorned rump of a Democratic party dominated by Northern liberals.

But did the Reaganites really mean it? Could converts to the GOP trust Reagan to stay the course? Or would he exploit and desert them, as Nixon had done? No fear—Reagan would stand fast. He would do so because he was a would-be transforming leader, not simply a skillful, self-serving broker like Nixon. Unlike Nixon—and most of his other recent predecessors—Reagan made a real commitment to strengthening his party, to making it a vehicle for something more than his personal ambitions. He had consistently supported his fellow Republicans. Even in his first California race for governor, he had persuaded other Republican candidates to run together as a team. In 1980, he joined GOP candidates for Congress on the Capitol steps to indicate that his was a *party* campaign.

But Reagan did not aim to integrate himself into the center of the Republican party. Rather, he intended to pull the entire party with him to the right, to integrate the conservative movement—the activists in their citizens' and lobbying groups and think tanks—as the dominant force within the party. Reagan went far in transforming the GOP, replacing old party professionals with conservative loyalists and creating an effective leadership that united the political operations of the White House, the congressional campaign committees, and the Republican National Committee. Still, an ambitious eight-year initiative to renew the party at the grass roots—targeting all 3,000 local GOP organizations—had mixed results by the end of the 1980s. And not all right-wingers followed Reagan into the new, conservative heart of the party. Many preferred the freebooting headiness of movement politics to the hard, disciplined work of party building.

Much—probably too much—depended on one man's continuing popularity and leadership. For a time, Reagan's public support appeared only to increase, as he received credit for an economic recovery from the depths of the early-1980s recession. He benefited too by the emergence of a remarkable new reformist Soviet leader, Mikhail Gorbachev, whose efforts to wind down the Cold War allowed Reagan to play the role of peacemaker after his decades-long turn as anti-communist militant.

But in his second term, Reagan yielded to the same temptation to overreach that had afflicted his predecessors after years in office. For Johnson, it was Vietnam; for Nixon, Watergate. For Reagan, it was the convoluted and secret Iran-Contra deal—the illegal sale of arms to Iran in exchange for the release of American hostages held in Lebanon and then the use of profits from that deal to fund counterrevolutionaries in Nicaragua, despite an explicit congressional ban on such aid. This abuse of power brought hearings in Congress and criminal indictments. Reagan escaped the worst only by pleading that he had not understood what was being done in his name. It was the low ebb of his leadership—and the effective end of his conservative thrust.

IN THE LAST analysis, did Reagan pull off a realignment of historic proportions, a fundamental reassembly and reorganization of party bases rivaling the great political transformations of the past? Underlying electoral and attitudinal changes beyond his control gave traction to Reagan's strategy. Indeed, to a significant extent, he rode the crest of a massive self-transformation of the South.

FDR's attempted purge of Southern conservatives in 1938 had failed mainly because the New Deal had put down few electoral roots in the South. Poor whites, who truly needed a new deal, remained unorganized, and black Southerners were politically disempowered. FDR had not conducted the long and heavy preparatory work at the grass roots. Instead, he tried to force change with a single blow from the top down.

Four decades later, Southerners were in the midst of purging themselves out of the Democratic party from the bottom up. And Reagan's role, which he performed masterfully, was to deepen and accelerate that process by offering Southern refugees from the Democratic party a comfortable and radically refurbished new home.

Still, the Grand Old Democracy retained a strong electoral grip on many of its historical constituencies. By 1987, Republicans held only 39 of 116 Southern seats in the House and 6 of 22 in the Senate. At the grass roots, Democrats dominated all the Southern state legislatures; the best the GOP could do was 37 percent of Tennessee's lower house. By the test of earlier realignments, the 1980s fell short as a realigning era. The persistent gap in those years between Republican presidential preferences and Democratic voting on the other ballot lines meant that the loss of confidence in the Democratic party had yet to translate fully into broad support for Republicans below the presidential level.

Years earlier, right-wing Republicans such as Goldwater appeared to be "running alone" without allies. By the 1980s, that was no longer true. Because of Ronald Reagan's leadership, Republicans now found themselves engaged with vast numbers of Americans North and South. Republican leaders looked around—was there another Ronald Reagan in sight?

THE CARTER-CLINTON
CONNECTION

In December 1978, as Jimmy Carter was completing his first two years as president, he granted me an interview in the White House. It was not an easy time for the president or for the American people. As Carter moved into the third year of his presidency, he had not yet secured his leadership. With both inflation and unemployment rising sharply, conservative Republicans had made strong gains in the midterm elections, even while Democratic liberals battled the president over economic policy. Already there were stirrings of a "Dump Carter" movement within the party.

Over a small luncheon table in the Oval Office, I reminded the president of crucial turning points in midterms of the past. Franklin Roosevelt had inaugurated his "second Hundred Days" in 1935—the radical Second New Deal. Abraham Lincoln had issued the Emancipation Proclamation on the eve of his third year in office. At his midterm Woodrow Wilson was starting to shift the Democratic party toward a more urban base. John Kennedy in his third year had begun to move boldly toward a strong posture on civil rights and a détente with the Soviet Union.

I looked expectantly at Jimmy Carter. The Washington pundits were talking about a fundamental shift in his leadership, from the moralistic idealism they saw in his campaign and early presidency to the acceptance of a brokerage role, a descent into the politics of reciprocity and compromise. Did he see it that way?

Yes and no. He ticked off a number of major problems and his efforts to resolve them. But it was wrong, he said, to find an artificial cohesion in all this, a single thrust. He did not want to discuss his "strategy" or "vision." He did not have—he did not want—a neat little catchword like New Deal or New Frontier to oversimplify his presidency. He did not want, really, to tell me what kind of president he intended to be.

As GOVERNOR of Georgia in the early 1970s, Jimmy Carter had provided few indications of what kind of chief executive he would be. He had resisted efforts to define him as a conservative or a liberal or centrist. "I'm more complicated than that," he had insisted. Of course he was a Democrat, a Southern Democrat, but how much did that tell about him? Carter was rather conservative in some ways, but in others he was a populist, a progressive businessman, social gospeler, technocrat, even a modern liberal.

But could he really be all these things? Politically, he became a centrist by default as much as by design, as he shifted and adjusted the conflicting strains in his thought. What held it all together was a higher faith in rationality. As governor, he often presented himself not as a politician but as a practical-minded planner. He believed that change should be rational and orderly, guided by intelligent and flexible management, the union of theoretical concepts and practical implementation. He liked to point to his early experience as chair of a regional planning commission in Georgia. "We tried to assess what our rural counties and people possessed in natural and human resources," he recalled, "what we would like to be in years to come, and the alternative courses of action open to us." They learned as planners, he said, to take the roles of servants and not masters of the people whose needs they sought to meet.

All very rational. But Carter's high-minded approach—a stance above the political fray, above the conflict of ideologies—made him intolerant of the disorderliness inherent in the conversion of plans and promises into policies. It encouraged him to question the motives of those who opposed him and to blame setbacks on the selfishness of special interests. From the beginning of his political career, when he ran for the Georgia state senate as an innocent taking on the old boys, Carter deliberately set himself apart from conventional politics.

JIMMY CARTER brought that mistrust of ordinary politics and practicing politicians to his run for the presidency. It became the cornerstone of his campaign, the heart of his promise to Americans of new, moral leadership.

Though Carter formally launched his presidential campaign late in 1974, two years before the 1976 election, he had begun laying plans for it much earlier, in the aftermath of Nixon's 1972 landslide. It was an audacious ambition for an obscure governor from the Deep South, a region that had not given the country a president since the Civil War. Carter had no experience of Washington and few ties to the Democratic party's national leadership. That led him to an equally audacious strategy: He would run *against* Washington, as an outsider to the political establishment.

The kernel of that approach came in a November 1972 memo from Carter's closest political adviser, Hamilton Jordan. "Perhaps the strongest feeling in this country today," Jordan wrote, "is the general distrust of government and politicians at all levels." And with Nixon's reelection, Jordan surmised, "the desire and thirst for strong moral leadership" would only grow.

Two deepening, overlapped lines of fracture within the Democratic party helped open Carter's path to the nomination. First was the ancient division between North and South, which had widened as national party leaders like JFK and LBJ adopted the goals of the civil rights movement. Nixon had already begun to draw Southern Democrats over to the GOP. Carter embraced his Southern roots—his strategy presumed that he would be the only Democrat in the primary race capable of holding the Southern base for the party—but he came as the herald of a *new* South. As governor, he had pledged to end racial discrimination and arranged for the installation of the first portrait of a black Georgian in the State Capitol—Martin Luther King Jr.

A second fissure within the Democratic party had its origins in the harsh conflict between party regulars and the insurgents who had helped topple LBJ in 1968. This division gave Carter another opportunity to seek out a middle course between party factions. After taking control of the party, the insurgents had suffered a severe setback in 1972 with George McGovern's crushing defeat. Centrist Democrats called for more moderate leadership and began a search for candidates who might appeal to an electorate that seemed to be growing more conservative.

In 1969, the insurgents had pushed through a change in party rules that also helped set Carter's course in the race for the presidency. To reduce the influence of party bosses on the selection of delegates to presidential nominating conventions, liberals had revised the rules so that all convention delegates now had to be selected through state primaries and caucuses. This change made it much more possible for a little-known outsider to the party establishment like Carter to break through. The governor had only to concentrate his efforts in small early battlegrounds—caucuses in Iowa, the New Hampshire primary—where the premium was on labor-intensive but inexpensive retail politicking. A respectable showing—an improvement on low expectations—would give Carter the credibility—meaning media, money, momentum—to go on to larger contests.

As JIMMY CARTER hit the road near the end of his gubernatorial term in 1974, campaigning almost alone with a few aides and a couple of reporters, the Watergate scandal engulfing Richard Nixon's presidency gave a powerful lift to his promise of inspiring leadership. Encouraged by a media adviser to flash "that Kennedy smile," Carter not only welcomed comparisons to the late president but embroidered them a bit. Like Kennedy, he would say in speeches, he was an outsider to the political establishment who had to overcome doubts about his electability and leadership. Like Kennedy, he was running at a time of uncertainty and drift on the vow "to get the country moving again" with "new ideas and a new generation of leadership."

And like JFK, Carter was running less on these "new ideas" than on personality. Carter's blurred stances on issues, his determination to balance appeals to right and left, led historian C. Vann Woodward to remark on the candidate's propensity "for fusing contradictions and reconciling opposites," producing "an unusual assortment of unified ambiguities and ambiguous unities." Accused of fuzziness and flip-flopping on the issues, Carter gave a Kennedyesque reply: "I'm not an ideologue and my positions are not predictable."

But while JFK's image was one of cool glamour, toughness, charisma, Carter offered a humble plainness, stubborn integrity infused with Baptist piety. "I'll never lie to you," he told voters. "I'll never make a misleading statement. I'll never betray your trust." He promised "a government as good and honest and decent and truthful and fair and competent and idealistic and compassionate, and as filled with love, as are the American people."

Carter's message fell on willing ears as he gained traction through the succession of primaries, parlaying wins in Iowa and New Hampshire into success in Southern states and an impressive triumph in Pennsylvania, where he drew support from a broad range of Democratic constituencies. Throughout the primary season, he concentrated his fire on Washington, represented by the Democratic members of Congress opposing him in the race. The issue, Carter insisted, was "the division between the insiders and the outsiders." His opponents and critics, he said, were those who sought "to maintain at all costs their own entrenched, unresponsive, bankrupt, irresponsible political power."

Even as he accepted the Democratic nomination at Madison Square Garden in July 1976, Carter maintained his posture as an outsider. While proclaiming, "I have always been a Democrat," he took a direct shot at the Washington establishment: "We have seen a wall go up that separates us from our own government," he said. "Too many have had to suffer at the hands of a political and economic elite."

IN THE GENERAL election, Carter gained only a slim mandate against President Gerald Ford, a supreme Washington insider after decades in Congress. A midsummer lead in polls of better than two-to-one almost disappeared by election day, and Carter squeaked by with just over half the votes cast. His edge in the electoral college was the narrowest since 1916. And he owed that margin to a strong get-out-the-vote drive by the much-scorned Democratic National Committee and labor unions, whose members put Carter over the top in a number of crucial Northern states.

Carter preferred to believe that he had won as an outsider, running alone—that, as he often said during the campaign, he owed nothing to anyone, and therefore that he had no need to come to terms with the Democratic party. But now, when he no longer enjoyed the luxury of running against Washington, if he was to achieve anything as president, Carter *had* to be a political broker, wheeling and dealing with senators, members of the House, and governors, as well as with despised "special interests."

From the beginning of his presidency, Carter had to battle with a Congress that was reasserting its authority against presidential power in the wake of Vietnam and Watergate. And Congress itself was also changing, as a new breed of entrepreneurial politicians, much like Carter himself, filled the ranks. They were less responsive to party discipline than their predecessors had been. As he coped with the fragmenting forces of the dispersed constitutional and political system, Carter was forced to descend from his lofty perch.

But the president did not have the heart for it. From the first days of his administration, Carter tested the patience of the Democratic caucus that controlled both House and Senate by his disregard of congressional practices and proprieties. He neglected to consult Democrats before appointing people from their states to federal offices—even when those appointees were Republicans. He cut nineteen water projects from a budget bill; members from the affected districts learned about it from their local newspapers. A proposal to reorganize government was stalled when Carter refused to compromise with the chairman of the relevant House committee. The president had to turn to Republicans to put the bill up.

The liberal *Washington Monthly* reported a particularly telling incident in 1978, when Carter met with one of those special interests that had had much to do with his election to the presidency—the AFL-CIO's top leadership—to parley over labor's role in fighting inflation. The unions had promised concessions in specific areas such as health care costs, but they were wary of the White House request that they make an all-out promise of "wage deceleration." At the meeting, Carter asked the union leaders for their cooperation and then began to depart. George Meany, the union's head, spoke up. "Wait a minute, Mr. President. I want you to hear our response."

Carter listened to Meany, who reiterated his opposition to deceleration. Then the president stood up, declaring, "If you can't support me I'd rather not talk," and strode out of the room.

∽

THOUGH HE LACKED John Kennedy's eloquence, President Carter was, like JFK, far more comfortable when he could address national interests that transcended party politics, when he could summon Americans to meet shared challenges. And with his engineer's mind, Carter relished the chance to craft comprehensive solutions to complex problems. The energy crisis of the 1970s seemed tailor-made for Jimmy Carter's leadership style.

America's consumption of oil had long outgrown the country's capacity to produce it, making the United States critically dependent on foreign sources. When Arab countries, angered by American backing of Israel in the Yom Kippur War, cut off oil shipments, it was a staggering blow to the economy—and to the psyche of Americans.

In early 1977, Carter made the enactment of a comprehensive plan to move the country toward energy self-sufficiency his highest priority as president. The energy crisis was, he declared, the "moral equivalent of war," a test of "the character of the American people and the ability of the President and Congress to govern this Nation." Carter chose to develop his energy plan in great secrecy. The public and Congress, as well as members of the administration apart from the small group devising the plan, were kept in the dark. Rumors swirled about the president's intentions, but he would not let on, telling reporters at a press conference, "I don't know how to answer your questions about specifics of the proposal."

The questions were answered when, after three months of preparation, the president unveiled his program on April 18, 1977. If the goal was simple—to increase energy production and reduce consumption—the package was staggeringly complex. There were 113 separate provisions: a gasoline tax, incentives for conservation, accelerated licensing of nuclear plants, efficiency standards for new buildings, and much more. Even administration officials contradicted one another when trying to explain the plan's intricacies. Yet the White House insisted that Congress pass it whole.

The energy proposal was "vintage Jimmy Carter," a close aide remembered. In the aide's words, the president was telling Congress, "We know what the answer is, we're going to present it to you and we're not going to try to cajole you. . . . It's very evident to you and everybody else that it has to be done."

Tip O'Neill, the Speaker of the House, enthusiastically backed the president's initiative but predicted "the toughest fight this Congress has ever had." He was amazed when Carter couldn't see that. The president told O'Neill that because his plan was "the right thing, the rational thing," the American people would understand and support it, and Congress would obediently follow. "This is politics," the Speaker replied sharply. "Not physics. We need you to push this bill through."

O'Neill did his part with a clever stroke—he routed the entire package through an ad hoc "Committee on Energy," a fast-track alternative to the usual gantlet of myriad committees and subcommittees. Carter's proposals rolled through the House in just a few months, only to roll up against the Senate, which did not believe in expediting gimmicks, and where Carter had no resourceful ally like O'Neill. The upper chamber duly cut the program into six separate bills, which subjected them to raging special interests. Piece by piece, the package unraveled.

After standing by with rising indignation for weeks, Carter finally fought back, surprising senators with the first personal lobbying he had done as president. But nothing moved the Senate. The plan was put over to 1978, when it met with the same obstacles, as well as flagging public interest. Only with compromises to oil and gas interests Carter had earlier disdained and a furious last-minute White House lobbying push, did Congress, in October 1978, after eighteen months, approve the National Energy Act.

It was a long, messy, costly battle—and it was renewed just eight months later when OPEC, the international oil cartel, announced another round of price increases in June 1979—the fourth in five months—igniting fury at the pump and fears of rationing. The president, who had made energy the centerpiece of his leadership, absorbed much of the public's anger.

Carter rushed back from a summit in Tokyo to address the nation. But he abruptly canceled the broadcast and retreated to Camp David for eleven days of reflection on the wider problems facing his administration.

With inflation soaring while unemployment grew, two-thirds of Americans believed that the nation was "in deep and serious trouble." There was a remarkable unanimity about the root of the problem: a profound failure of leadership. There had been no midterm shift in Carter's leadership, no broader strategy. James Fallows, a former Carter aide, described a "passionless presidency," incapable of inspiring people or mobilizing committed followers. Carter, Fallows wrote in 1979, was a leader who "fails to project a vision larger than the problem he is tackling at the moment," who "has not given us an *idea* to follow." Journalist Nicholas Lemann saw many of the same qualities in Carter: a "small-picture soul" sitting in the Oval Office "checking off dozens of Option Ones and Option Twos," an isolated man unable to develop close and supportive relationships with other leading Democrats. The president's followership, Lemann concluded, didn't extend "much beyond his immediate family and his four or five closest advisers." It was a rather smallish power base. "Why does it always have to be Carter against the world?" one staffer asked.

Up at Camp David in July 1979, the president was reevaluating his entire administration. He reached beyond his circle of advisers to invite a large range of people to the mountaintop to talk with him—people from academia, the media, unions, interest groups, as well as governors and members of Congress—134 in all. It was "a highly personal, anti-institutional method" of consultation, wrote a *Newsweek* columnist who attended, "circumventing (or fleeing or ignoring) the machinery of government itself."

Carter later recalled that his many guests told him in various ways that "the country was waiting for stronger and clearer leadership from me." Pragmatists among his advisers suggested that this meant he should propose decisive measures to address the hardships facing Americans. But the president took a different meaning.

What he had realized, Carter said when he finally addressed the country, was that "all the legislation in the world can't fix what's wrong with America." A crisis of "the American spirit," a loss of faith in the ability of Americans to shape their future, was the real problem. But when people looked to Washington for leadership, they found only "paralysis and stagnation and drift." The president pointed to the energy crisis as "the immediate test of our ability to unite this Nation." It was an opportunity to begin "the restoration of American values."

Carter's bleak candor impressed most Americans and won him some breathing room. But then, a few days later, he abruptly fired five Cabinet members and reshuffled the administration.

The goodwill evaporated. Now the speech and the purge in combination seemed less an assertion of leadership than an attempt to deflect blame elsewhere, anywhere—the American "spirit," members of his Cabinet—and away from Carter's failure to cope. The public's view, his pollster noted that fall, was "that events dominate us, that we react to, not lead events." The president was right that Americans were desperate for leadership, but they were now looking for it elsewhere.

THE CHALLENGE to Carter's leadership would come in the showdown campaign of 1980, and first of all from within Carter's own party. Senator Ted Kennedy would make that challenge, the man who had been dismissed by Carter's pollster after the 1976 election as among those "traditional Democrats" who were "as antiquated and anachronistic a group as are conservative Republicans." Kennedy's road to political apostasy was smoothed by the conviction that he, not Carter, represented the true Democratic faith, the liberal legacy Carter had cast away. Far more than his brothers John and Robert, Edward Kennedy, first elected to the Senate in 1962, had become a figure of stature and substance in the Democratic caucus. And far more than they, he had a long and impassioned commitment to the principles and causes of liberalism. Where Carter's backers saw naked ambition and a sense of entitlement in the senator's revolt, Kennedy saw a battle for the soul of the Democratic party, a battle with roots in the 1960s, when the party began to break apart over civil rights, the Great Society, and Vietnam.

It was a contest of great portent, mirroring and widening the cleft in the party as it struggled to find a leadership strategy. Carter stood for the South and the border states that were slowly slipping out of the old Democracy's grasp. Kennedy spoke for the "Northeast party" that had dominated progressive politics for decades and against which Carter had defined himself. Its reformist heart lay in Massachusetts and other New England states that had spawned abolitionist, suffragist, and other causes, but it reached across the northern tier of the Midwest, the Northwest, and to California, where progressive "missionaries" from the East had had their impact. It was this party that would make a stand against the Republican surge—the party that would comprise the "blue states" of the early twenty-first century.

But in 1980, Carter bested Kennedy at the Democratic convention, rolling up huge delegation majorities from his native region. This support was deceptive, though. Carter could not hold his Southern base in the fall against a conservative with a determined appeal to evangelical

Christians. Those voters had given the devout Baptist from Georgia better than half their ballots in 1976. Four years later, they went almost two to one against him.

And the "Northeast party" fell away from the president too. In 1976, union families and other elements of the traditional Democratic base had given him the edge against Gerald Ford in several key states. Not so in 1980. "A lot of working Democrats," a Carter pollster warned the president on election eve, "are going to wake up tomorrow and for the first time in their lives vote Republican." Many others—unable to pull the lever for Ronald Reagan—stayed home.

༂

FOR MANY DEMOCRATS, the prospect of Ronald Reagan in the White House was a shock and an omen. What had seemed unthinkable in 1964 had come to pass. And was that only the beginning? The organized and aggressive conservative movement vowed to overturn the entire political order the Democratic party had defined and dominated since the 1930s.

Democrats had lost control of the Senate for the first time in twenty-six years, and while they still controlled the House, they lost thirty-three seats there in the 1980 election. There were worrying signs that the party's base was eroding, and not only in the South but among a broad swath of middle- and working-class Americans. It appeared that Nixon's plan to disassemble the old Democratic coalition and use its pieces to construct a permanent Republican majority was bearing fruit. President Carter's share of the popular vote in 1980—41 percent—was the lowest of any Democratic incumbent in history. A third of self-identified Democrats voted against him. Republicans were claiming many of these as part of their own new base: Reagan Democrats.

The right-wing challenge, far from uniting liberal and conservative factions in the Democratic party, divided them even more deeply. The split was ideological but also strategic: How best could Democrats meet the intensifying Republican threat? To moderates, Jimmy Carter's win in 1976 proved the electoral power of centrism. To liberals, his defeat in 1980 proved its weakness.

The case for centrism became acute in the 1980s, as Reaganism appeared nearly unstoppable to many moderates. Vindicated by Reagan's rout of liberal Walter Mondale in 1984, when the Republicans made even deeper inroads in traditional Democratic constituencies, centrists established the Democratic Leadership Council as a meeting place for so-called New Democrats, who styled themselves rebels against the old liberal establishment. These New Democrats wanted a new strategy—a winning strategy. The DLC quickly became a formidable organization. It was nationally organized, well funded, and highly vocal. Its prestige soared when an attractive young presidential hopeful, Governor Bill Clinton of Arkansas, became its head in 1990.

The DLC had strong intellectual credentials too. In a monograph issued that same year, "The Politics of Evasion," political scientists William Galston and Elaine Kamarck took the liberal establishment to task for clinging to three basic misconceptions. One they called "the myth of mobilization": the notion that low voting turnout, especially on the part of African Americans, Hispanics, and women, was the main cause of Democratic defeats, rather than the party's loss of support from the middle and working classes, from Southern men and Northern ethnics. Those voters *were* turning out—for Republicans. Another was "the myth of liberal fundamentalism": the idea that the Democrats had to move left to win, despite evidence of an increasingly conservative electorate. The third was "the myth of the congressional bastion": the claim that it didn't matter whether Democrats lost the presidency because they had a "lock" on the Congress and on so many state and local offices. On the contrary, Galston and Kamarck claimed to find "a slow-motion, trickle-down realignment in which, over time, Republican presidential strength is inexorably eroding Democratic congressional, state, and local strength."

And the DLC's solution? To reverse its decline, the Democratic party had to win back mainstream Middle America by transforming its issues agenda. In economic policy, this meant turning away from government as an agent for change to a new emphasis on individual initiative and the private sector. In a 1991 manifesto, the DLC proposed market-oriented policies pitched at the middle class around themes of opportunity, responsibility, and choice. That manifesto also urged Democrats to embrace the social issues that had proven so profitable to Republicans. These "moral and cultural values that most Americans share" included "traditional"—heterosexual, two-parent—

families, tough positions on law-and-order, and opposition to so-called "reverse discrimination"—civil rights policies that favored African Americans and other minorities at the expense of whites.

To liberals, the DLC appeared to be proposing a massive shift of the party's agenda rightward, toward corporate interests and religious conservatives and antigovernment zealots, away from its commitments to workers and the economically dispossessed, to equal opportunity and social justice, to civil rights and health care and the environment. In short, to stop Democrats from becoming Republicans, the DLC was urging the Democratic party to become like the Republican party, only moderately less so.

AS AN AMBITIOUS young politico, Bill Clinton had managed the Carter campaign in his native Arkansas in 1976, and few Southerners could have taken a more special satisfaction in Carter's victory than he. The Georgian had proved that a moderate Southern governor could seize the Democratic nomination and then win the presidency.

In his own campaign for the office sixteen years later, Governor Bill Clinton followed much of the Carter recipe. He too fought a long, hard slog up from relative obscurity through the primaries against a fragmented field. And like Carter, Clinton exploited the vulnerabilities of a floundering Republican incumbent to win the general election.

Unlike Carter, though, Bill Clinton did not run entirely alone. Two years earlier, when he was considering a presidential race, he had formed an alliance with the Democratic Leadership Council. Clinton's relationship with the DLC was symbiotic. For the DLC, whose founder, Al From, according to a colleague, considered the Arkansas governor "the most attractive political animal he had seen in his life," a Clinton candidacy would make his group a prominent player in Democratic politics. The DLC's hope was that, much as Ronald Reagan had, Bill Clinton would run from outside his party's establishment and succeed in pulling the whole party in his—and the DLC's—direction, forging a new, more conservative center. For Clinton, the DLC offered resources for a presidential race—staff, strategy, money. Its chairmanship gave him a national platform. The DLC also gave him a message.

Bill Clinton's boundless political ambitions had first been triggered by a handshake with John Kennedy in the Rose Garden in 1963, when Clinton had visited the White House as a delegate from Boys Nation. It was a transformative experience for the hero-worshipping teenager. Clinton's political blooding came in the turbulent Vietnam era as an antiwar protester and, in 1972, an ardent supporter of George McGovern. Yet even then, Clinton's activism already was being tempered by his ambition to run for governor back in Arkansas and ultimately for the presidency. While managing McGovern's hopeless Texas campaign, he realized that the fatal problem of McGovern's insurgency was its lack of "a core, a center, that was common to a great majority of the country." To win in Arkansas—and beyond—Clinton would need just such "a center core" that people could "understand and relate to and trust."

That lesson was reinforced by his first term as governor. Like his idol, JFK, Clinton relished the game of politics and cherished the independence from factional ties that allowed him to practice the arts of maneuver. Though he lacked Kennedy's vast personal resources, he had a similar gift for attracting loyalists—old school friends, local activists, political technicians, and a sprinkling of savvy vets. For his 1978 gubernatorial run, in which he challenged Arkansas' Democratic establishment, Clinton had constructed a political network of his own by drawing on hundreds of contacts whose names he had entered on index cards. It was called by an editor "the best organization ever put together in Arkansas without machine support."

Clinton won the office on a sweeping platform of reform. But by feverishly pushing his reform agenda—fifty items in all—the governor confused voters and offended every powerful interest in the state. In 1980, the year of the Reagan surge, Clinton was voted out of office. When he made his successful comeback two years later, he began his campaign with an extraordinary televised apology for the mistakes of his first term. He ran now with scaled-down ambitions and a chastened promise to listen more closely to what people wanted. His governorship became a permanent campaign, with constant attention to the political utility of his policies. He went on to win reelection four times.

BY THE TIME he began his run for the presidency in 1992, Bill Clinton had honed his political style—a moderate stand on issues colored by populist rhetoric—to a keen edge. He adopted the DLC's strategy of aiming to win over the broad middle class, the Reagan Democrats, and the growing number of suburban voters who considered themselves independents. And Clinton adopted the DLC platform, favoring balanced budgets and middle-class tax cuts, the death penalty, and "personal responsibility"—centrist code for less government activism in social welfare and a tougher line on crime. He wrapped the platform up in the soft populist slogan "Putting People First." He underlined his New Democrat ties by picking a fellow Southern centrist, Senator Al Gore of Tennessee, as his running mate and creating TV ads that represented them as "a new generation of Democrats" who "don't think the way the old Democratic party did."

Still, while echoing Republican attacks on "tax and spend" big-government liberalism, Clinton could not renounce that old party base. He proposed expanded public investment in education and worker training and, most ambitiously, promised a national health care system to provide insurance for every American. Still, he largely took the support of liberals for granted, counting on their eagerness to end twelve years of Republican rule.

The election results revealed the limits of Clinton's New Democrat appeal. Clinton took only 43 percent of the popular vote against George Bush's 37 percent. Ross Perot, a populist conservative who exploited frustration with both parties, took 19 percent, winning the largest total vote of any third-party candidate in American history. While Clinton made incremental gains in the South and among Reagan Democrats, there was little sign of a realignment of the Democratic base. The old party coalition, weakened though it was, put Clinton in the White House.

BILL CLINTON'S early presidency was hardly a model of New Democracy. It was, rather, a remarkable display of chaos in government as an overweeningly ambitious but inexperienced chief executive sought to make a powerful mark in his first hundred days. Besieged by Democratic policy entrepreneurs eager to promote their agendas after twelve wilderness years, and confronted by the irreconcilability of many of his own campaign pledges, Bill Clinton did what he had done in his first term as governor—he tried to embrace them all. At first, Clinton seemed to be making an abrupt swerve leftward, though that appeared to be less the result of calculation than of confusion. The president quickly offended key New Democratic constituencies with a proposal to lift the ban on gays in the military—the outcry forced a quick retreat—and with executive orders that loosened federal restrictions on abortion.

Most contentious—and chaotic—was the debate over the administration's economic program. The challenge was to reconcile four promises Clinton had made in the campaign: an economic-stimulus package, ambitious investments in infrastructure, a middle-class tax cut, and a reduction in the budget deficit. Each had its fervent advocates, with liberals pushing for the stimulus and investments and conservatives wanting to aim at the deficit, which new estimates indicated would be much larger than expected, while middle-class tax cuts were a proud centerpiece of the New Democrat agenda. Debates raged interminably through the early weeks of his presidency as Clinton deferred hard choices while hunting for a formula that would satisfy everyone. The fracas reinforced the image of the Democratic party that New Democrats hoped to overcome—that of a collection of feuding interest groups.

And, in the end, the president pleased no one, except the conservative deficit hawks. The middle-class tax cut was dropped as unaffordable. Instead, there would be tax increases to reduce the deficit. The meager stimulus Clinton finally proposed was a third the size of what he had promised in the campaign and would be offset by spending cuts needed to reduce the deficit. Clinton satisfied himself, perhaps, least of all. Frustrated by his own decision to emphasize budget reduction in the economic program, he lashed out at aides. "Where are all the Democrats? I hope you're all aware we're all Eisenhower Republicans. We're Eisenhower Republicans here, and we are fighting the Reagan Republicans. . . . Isn't that great?"

The Democrats on Capitol Hill were no better pleased. The party's caucus was more liberal than it had ever been. Republican gains in the South had eroded the power of the Democrats' conservative wing, and New Democrats had not yet won many converts in Congress. At the outset, with the government under unified Democratic control for the first time since 1980, expectations for action ran high. Quickly, Congress passed and Clinton signed bills that George Bush had vetoed: a family- and medical-leave law and a measure to make voter registration easier. These early acts added to the impression of a liberal tilt by the president and raised expectations for more. And Bill Clinton was a willing partner, inviting members of Congress into his administration's deliberations.

But in the case of his economic program, Clinton's inclusiveness backfired, as members of Congress, all with their own agendas, added to the confusion of pressures on the president. And when the economic program finally emerged, many felt that their wishes had been ignored. Even worse, once the stimulus bill was killed by a Republican filibuster in the Senate, all that remained was an unappetizing menu of tax hikes and spending cuts. That budget bill passed the House by a single vote, with dozens of Democrats opposed, and was fought to a tie in the Senate, which was broken by Gore's "aye." Clinton's early efforts to unite Democrats behind his economic program ultimately left the party more divided than it had been before.

On two other important measures of that first year, the president again won, but his successes fractured his party. A crime initiative that mixed tougher penalties and beefed-up enforcement with new prevention strategies was meant to display Clinton's New Democrat credentials and steal a march on Republicans. But when many House Democrats rejected the bill, it was hijacked by Republicans who stripped out much of its New Democrat innovation—and funding—before delivering it to the president for his signature.

The North American Free Trade Agreement was opposed by a majority of Democrats in both chambers. Liberals and labor unions denounced NAFTA as a sellout to corporate interests that would cost hundreds of thousands of American workers their jobs. The DLC embraced it with fervor, though, and called its passage—with essential Republican backing—"the president's finest hour."

Thus was the stage set for the issue on which Bill Clinton would stake his presidency: health care.

SURELY THE TIME for action was now. In earlier eras—the 1930s, the 1960s—Democratic presidents had taken leadership to respond to dire needs. Now was the time for a grand third act. The health care system in the United States was by far the costliest in the world, while almost 40 million Americans had no medical insurance—a number that was growing by a million a year—and 40 million more were underinsured, with little coverage in case of serious illness.

Elected on the promise of a "national system" that would "cover everybody," the new president immediately set a task force to work writing a plan. Led by First Lady Hillary Rodham Clinton, specialists of diverse backgrounds met in small and large groups to flesh out the president's goals. Months passed as the task force toiled over the formidable complexities.

The plan that slowly emerged was ambitious, but hardly revolutionary or even radical. It was not a government takeover of the European or Canadian sort, where public health systems provided effective care at reasonable cost. There was no chance at all that Congress would approve such a measure for the United States. The Clinton proposal sought to achieve the great liberal purpose of guaranteed coverage for every American. But it also would attempt to satisfy the core New Democrat principle of creating partnerships between the public and private sectors. It would establish a system of "managed competition" that required employers to insure workers, mostly through large regional purchasing alliances that would induce the private insurance companies to compete on both the cost and the quality of care. Federal and state programs would subsidize coverage for the jobless.

It was not until September 1993—far beyond the "one hundred days" Clinton had promised in his campaign—that the plan was ready to be unveiled, with a powerful address by the president to Congress. The talk almost became a disaster at the very start —was it an omen?—when Clinton found the text of a completely different address on the teleprompter at the rostrum, but he improvised skillfully until the correct speech was loaded. After praising his wife's work as leader of the task force, the president eloquently urged Congress to seize this "magic moment" when "for the first time in this century, leaders of both political parties have joined together around the principle of providing universal, comprehensive health care." At the core was "health security"—benefits "that can never be taken away." Brashly, Clinton challenged lawmakers: "Before this Congress finishes its work next year, you will pass and I will sign legislation to guarantee this security to every citizen of this country." Initial public reaction was broadly positive—if uncertain about the plan's details—and Clinton won praise for arousing a bipartisan commitment to health care reform.

But the hour was fearfully late. The delayed health bill was crowded from the congressional agenda by the divisive fight over NAFTA and other pending measures. The relevant committees would not get to serious work on it until the following spring, which would run up to the 1994 midterm elections. What could the White House do to speed action? Other presidents—Franklin Roosevelt and Lyndon Johnson—at times overrode delays and opposition, using bombast, bullying, and bribery of the legal sort.

But Clinton lacked the discipline and sense of timing of his great predecessors. Consumed by the battles over his economic program, he had done little to prepare a national campaign of public education and mobilization to follow his speech. Then the plan had been introduced into the midst of the bitter NAFTA battle, which absorbed the president's attention for months. Foreign crises—Somalia, Russia, Haiti—also distracted Clinton. After an initial flurry in September 1993, he spoke sparingly on health care until he re-launched the proposal in his State of the Union address in January 1994, and then again he let the momentum ebb as public support drained away. Hillary Clinton sought to fill the gap, sallying forth to Capitol Hill and to meetings across the country. But there was no substitute for determined presidential leadership.

Nor was the administration message direct and compelling. Clinton had decided to conduct a *marketing*—not a public education—campaign. The president was a master simplifier, but perhaps he simplified too much. To a public baffled by the proposal's complexity, uncertain about what it would mean for them, such slogans as "Health care that's always there" sounded hollow, even evasive.

Politics, like nature, abhors a vacuum, and the leadership void extended to the Democratic leaders in Congress. They set up no omnibus committee that might have helped Democrats unite around a single approach. Instead, myriad rival plans emerged, producing disarray among the president's putative allies. Moderate Democrats decided that the Clinton proposal was too ambitious and too reliant on government controls and, with DLC encouragement, gravitated to a cheaper scheme that failed to ensure universal coverage. Liberals turned away from Clinton's plan as too timid and too reliant on market forces and pushed for a Canadian-style single-payer system.

Into the void of the health care debate streamed the combined forces of the Republican party, conservative think tanks and pressure groups, and the medical and insurance lobbies. In marketing the plan, the administration downplayed—even obscured—its most sensitive element, the role of government in regulating and funding the reformed system, emphasizing that health care would remain fundamentally private. To no avail. Ideologues and insurers rolled out a massive fear campaign, raising the specter of health care rationing, bureaucrats making medical decisions, businesses and jobs taxed out of existence. A brilliant television ad, "Harry and Louise," portrayed a white middle-class couple worriedly picking the plan apart. Opposition spread into sectors to the right of the GOP and into the surging ranks of evangelical conservatism, whose leaders seized on the opportunity to widen their agenda beyond "core family issues." The conflict became personalized; Hillary Clinton, initially the angel of reform, was attacked to the point of demonization.

The end of the health care plan a year after Clinton introduced it was hardly anticlimactic—there had been no climax. It never came squarely before Congress. It did not even have the honor of being voted down by the House or Senate, which at least might have given it a chance to come back on a better day. The most far-reaching liberal initiative since the Great Society just faded away.

"GREAT INNOVATIONS should not be forced on slender majorities," Thomas Jefferson had warned. Bill Clinton defied this common-sense adage when he proposed his sweeping health care plan. Like Clinton, Abraham Lincoln and Woodrow Wilson had won only pluralities against several contenders, but each had embarked on strong action—Lincoln to save the Union and Wilson for his "New Freedom" reforms. The crucial difference was forceful and persistent leadership. Earlier presidents had persevered, while Clinton dropped health reform like a live hand grenade.

Even without the bruising battles of the first two years, Clinton and his political advisers knew that they faced one of the most predictable outcomes in American politics: presidential loss of support in midterm elections. But not even Bill Clinton, an election buff, could have predicted his party's disaster of 1994. For the first time in four decades, Democrats lost control of both houses of Congress as Republicans gained fifty-two new House seats and eight in the Senate. The GOP also carried a host of state and local contests. Most gallingly, the shocking results were seen as a judgment on the president. Crowed a right-wing senator, "Bill Clinton won this election for us."

⌁

ANOTHER YOUNG Southerner, who now became Speaker of the House, could—and did—take credit as the architect of the 1994 Republican triumph. But Newt Gingrich had ambitions far beyond winning elections for his party. He planned to reshape an institution that historically seemed resistant to institutional change—John Kennedy's den of "worms," the House of Representatives—and turn it into the seat of national policymaking. He would use it to enact a conservative program that the Republican right had dreamed of since Goldwater but that had eluded them under Nixon and even Reagan. This self-described "transformational figure" wanted to produce a "genuine revolution" that would, as he put it, "renew American civilization." A former history teacher at West Georgia College, he had long been fascinated by the lives of strong leaders such as Winston Churchill. He had also talked with managers from Ford Motor Company, Coca-Cola, and the Army about the art of leading—and disciplining—large bodies of people.

When Gingrich launched his campaign against Democratic domination of the House in the 1980s, he ran practically alone. He was rising through the House rank-and-file using his newly acquired leadership skills. As he gained seniority, he recruited young and conservative members, gave them advice and money, and brought them into sub-leadership positions in the lower chamber.

His target was almost as much his own party's established leadership as the Democrats. Those Republicans were old pols of the go-along, get-along school, seemingly resigned to permanent Democratic control. Most of those who backed Gingrich's revolt did not imagine that they were taking part in a radical reformation; they were mainly intent on winning power so they could put through bills that would benefit business and farm interests back home. Yet in the weeks before the 1994 election, 367 Republican congressional candidates pledged loyalty to a ten-point party platform Gingrich had devised, the Contract with America. "Our government operates on the party system," Gingrich announced to reporters. "We are a team. And we're offering you a contract on what our team will do."

Suddenly, almost unexpectedly, he was the Speaker, with, he believed, a mandate for change that he could impose on the other branches of government. He was now ready with a leadership team of the sort he had seen in the big corporations. A key player was the new majority whip from Texas, Tom DeLay, alias "the Hammer." He was Gingrich's disciplinarian, and his writ ran beyond the Republican caucus to corporate executives and lobbyists hopeful for favorable legislation. DeLay enforced a strict policy of pay-to-play. Another important figure was Majority Leader Dick Armey, also a Texan and a fanatical advocate of removing "the invisible foot of the government" from the economy and taking apart the whole welfare state. Other members of the top team specialized in tax cutting, dismantling environmental regulation, undermining abortion rights.

Gingrich's leadership team—and most of the rank-and-file—ranged between the right and the hard right. They differed in emphasis on many issues—how much federal money should be dished out to one of their key constituencies, farmers; how much attention should be paid to the agenda of another, fundamentalist Christians. But they agreed on their core beliefs—the defense of individual and corporate liberty against government oppression.

For a time in spring and summer 1995, the new Speaker was the toast of Washington. With Clinton on the defensive, Gingrich was indeed a kind of prime minister, the source of ideas and initiatives in the government, leading from the legislature. His "gang" passed bill after bill to enact their Contract, on issues ranging from welfare reform to tax cuts to crime.

After some months, though, the "revolution" began to falter, slowed more by constitutional realities than by its liberal foes. Whatever mandate the Speaker claimed, however thoroughly he dominated the House, he could not force his will on the Senate, even when it was in the hands of fellow Republicans. The upper chamber still stood in all its very deliberate majesty. Gingrich had formed a working relationship with Bob Dole, the Senate Republican leader, but Dole was more cautious, and the Senate far slower to act, than the House revolutionaries wished.

But the Constitution had also established another separate power center—the presidency. Amazingly, Bill Clinton found himself having to assert to reporters, six months after the election debacle, that "the President is relevant here." But even a beleaguered president remained a dangerous foe. Gingrich grasped this better than some of his followers, who fluttered angrily whenever he parleyed with the president.

Liberal Democrats, who had seen the Republican takeover as a call to battle, were infuriated when Clinton turned his back on them and retreated to the New Democrat centrist strategy, to his defensive instinct for moderation. Even his own vice president, Al Gore, urged him to stand for something positive. But Clinton decided that an aggressive occupation of the center was the key to his own political survival. Indeed, he became a crusading centrist, a militant defender of popular entitlements like Medicare and Medicaid, school lunches, job training, and environmental programs—all targets of Republican antigovernment assaults.

A showdown was inevitable, and it came in the fall of 1995 over the annual federal budget. The Speaker was confident that Clinton would ultimately have to surrender to Congress. Clinton was sure that Gingrich had finally overplayed his hand. Though the president accepted the broad Republican goal of reaching a balanced budget over a period of years, he was unyielding on the details. He flatly rejected Republican demands for deep cuts in myriad programs that benefited the middle and working classes and the poor. "If you want to pass your budget," Clinton told the Speaker, "you're going to have to put somebody else in this chair."

President and Congress became so stalemated that the government, unbelievably, simply ran out of money and shut down. Gingrich and his troops could not overcome the power of the White House. As the deadlock continued into 1996, after another shutdown, with the public blaming Republican extremism for the crisis, the Gingrich revolution reached its dead end. Its leader agreed to a compromise.

So president bested Speaker. Why? Gingrich was confronting more than a resourceful antagonist fighting for political survival. The Speaker was confronting a *system*—a constitutional dispersal of power. With his vaunting ambition, Gingrich had believed he could govern from his perch in the House. He had wanted to be a transforming leader like Theodore or

Franklin Roosevelt, one who created major changes. In the final traumatic test, he ended up as a failed transactional leader, still governing the House but governing alone in a separated institution.

CLINTON'S DRAMATIC comeback from the edge of political extinction raised the curtain for his reelection bid in 1996. He continued to pick his spots, sometimes challenging the Republicans, sometimes giving in—most notably, by reversing himself to sign into law a drastic rollback to welfare after he had vetoed two earlier versions passed by Republicans. Liberals were aghast that a Democratic president would join with right-wing Republicans to destroy a signal expression of the party's historic values. But Clinton exploited their fury as effectively as he had that of Republicans, as proof of his political independence. "It's not about moving left or right," he liked to say, "but moving forward."

The president was lucky, too, in his Republican opponent. While Clinton claimed to be building "a bridge to the 21st Century," Senator Bob Dole seemed to offer one back to the middle of the twentieth. As majority leader, Dole had served as Gingrich's sidekick during negotiations with the White House, though often uncomfortably. The Kansan was no right-wing revolutionary, but an old Senate wheelhorse. He had been Gerald Ford's running mate two decades earlier, picked then because the Reaganites couldn't stand Nelson Rockefeller and Ford couldn't stand Reagan. Now Dole's main claim to the GOP nomination was that it was his turn.

Considering the tumult of Clinton's first term, the 1996 campaign was remarkably dull. On the president's part, the deadening effect was intentional. He had become a master of moderation, running strictly on the New Democrat line. Liberals might charge him with "neo-Republicanism," but he was determined never again to find himself far from the mainstream of public opinion. Close examination of polls turned up little somethings to promise everyone while Clinton crafted the ultimate feel-good campaign. His buoyant energy was the sharpest contrast he offered to his mordant and lethargic opponent.

Republicans eyed Bob Dole with dread. Few better than Dole exemplified the old GOP order Gingrich and his cohorts had supposedly overthrown. Few were less likely to excite the right-wing activists who had become so crucial to the party's success. The last, desperate hope was that the party's congressional surge of 1994 would persist into 1996 and, in an unprecedented reverse-coattails effect, drag Bob Dole into the White House. It didn't happen.

Bill Clinton's win, impressive as it was after the catastrophe of 1994, was sharply limited. In the first place, voter turnout was the lowest since Calvin Coolidge's 1924 landslide over John W. Davis. Scarcely half of eligible voters voted, and, as in 1992, Clinton failed to win even half of those votes. Ross Perot, running a second time, inspired much less fervor than he had in 1992 but still took 8 percent of the vote, enough to deny the president a majority.

Worse, Clinton failed to lead the Democrats to recovery in Congress. To do so, the president would have had to identify himself closely with a party many voters still saw as too liberal. His New Democrat strategy led him in the opposite direction. Some in his party suspected that the president almost preferred a Republican Congress. After all, he had floundered badly in his first two years, when Democrats had controlled Capitol Hill, as he negotiated the tricky cross-pressures between his party's centrists and liberals. After the 1994 collapse, Clinton had discovered a clear role for himself. He could serve as a check on right-wing extremism, while also holding the Democratic left at bay. And soon he would be trying to convert that survival tactic into a governing philosophy called the Third Way that combined a concern for social justice and opportunity with an abandonment of "big government" approaches of the past. It was a refinement of the New Democrat strategy, an attempt to lift it above its origins in Democratic party infighting and opportunistic compromises with conservatism. The Third Way would lead not between but above the old left-right divisions—a lofty dream of transformative politics beyond partisanship.

It was that kind of time. The Gingrichites too, of course, had promised something altogether new. But a year into Clinton's second term, in 1998, reality kicked in, with a swell of old-style gutter politics, when Republican extremists turned a tawdry White House sex scandal into an opportunity for impeaching a president and dragging him to trial in the Senate.

BILL CLINTON was the first Democrat since Franklin Roosevelt to win two presidential elections. He not only survived impeachment, but as his years in office came to a close, his public approval ratings were higher than those of Eisenhower and Reagan at the end of their terms. Some Democrats regretted that he was constitutionally barred from seeking a third term, as FDR had done. His great predecessor had bequeathed his party a clear liberal direction and an electoral coalition that, despite much fraying, retained potency six decades later. But what was Bill Clinton's legacy?

Vice President Al Gore had, like Clinton, been one of the brightest lights of the Democratic Leadership Council. His most visible role in the administration was as leader of the grandly named "Reinventing Government" project, which aimed to reduce bureaucratic red tape—a classic New Democrat initiative. So in 2000, Gore was ideally positioned to run as Clinton's heir who would set the Democratic party firmly on the Third Way.

Then an interesting thing happened. As Gore's campaign struggled to gain ground against what his Republican opponent, George W. Bush, was calling his "compassionate conservatism"—itself a concession to the political appeal of centrism—the vice president suddenly decided to ditch Clintonism for the embrace of old Democracy. He emerged as a populist crusader. "They're for the powerful," he said of Republicans in his speech accepting his nomination at the Democratic convention in Los Angeles. "We're for the people." To "those who need a voice, those who need a champion, those who need to be lifted up so they are never left behind," Gore vowed that "I will work for you every day, and I will never let you down."

It is true that Gore didn't lose at the polls in 2000, but the agonizing denouement of that election made the recriminations within the Democratic party bitterer yet. Centrists predictably blamed Gore's old-fashioned class warfare for his defeat. "The New Deal political philosophy that defined our politics for most of the 20th century has run its course," the DLC announced one more time. But progressives argued that Gore's liberal turn had pulled his candidacy out of a tailspin. The campaign surged when Gore "successfully defined Bush as a candidate of the wealthy and privileged." It fell short because Gore failed to bind his red-meat rhetoric to tough policy sinew; he remained a centrist sheep beneath that wolf's clothing. Imagine, they said, what a *real* fighting liberal might do.

In the end, two presidential victories and eight years of Clintonism settled nothing for the Democratic party. The party had suffered badly under his leadership. It had not only lost control of Congress, it had sacrificed nearly half the governorships it had held in 1992, as well as a fifth of state legislative chambers. The Democratic National Committee had become a scandal-tarred fundraising machine for the president.

In the common phrase of that time, the Democratic party at the turn of the millennium was still in search of its "soul." Bill Clinton had not given it one. Two decades earlier, Ronald Reagan had run and won as an outsider to his party's moderate mainstream and had then succeeded in transforming the GOP, making the conservative movement he led its new soul. In 1992, New Democrat Bill Clinton had run and won as an outsider to his party's liberal establishment, but he failed to convert the party to centrism. A crucial difference was in the convictions the two leaders espoused. Reagan's conservatism was a polarizing ideology, offering a stark contrast to moderate and liberal ideas that mobilized and empowered followers. But Clinton's New Democracy was constructed as a carefully compromising array of policies, designed to *reduce* conflict with competing ideologies. It was a soulless exercise in opportunism worthy of Richard Nixon, tailored to reach targeted groups, assembling superficial, transient coalitions rather than a lasting followership mobilized by a coherent, meaningful set of principles.

Bill Clinton proved to be a genius of entrepreneurial politics—of the politics of personal survival—not of collective political action. Setting himself at the center—against both left and right—he too often found himself alone there, in search of something to stand for beyond his own ambition.

Chapter 7

THE BUSHES:
STANDING TOGETHER
ALONE

Over the past half century, the Republican party has undergone one of the most remarkable transformations in American history. The GOP has survived the loss of anti-communism as its great rallying cry and deftly substituted terrorism as the enemy. It has converted the South from a Democratic to a Republican bastion. Republicans have flipped ideologically from an antigovernment and pro–states' rights party to one that champions a powerful national government—a government, moreover, that promises to enforce conservative moral values. They have renounced the isolationism of the 1930s to embrace global adventurism, leading a crusade to spread·American values. Above all, the GOP has transformed itself from a sharply fragmented party into a strong and disciplined national organization. By doing so, it has become the party of government.

We vaguely connect these momentous changes to a host of right-wing leaders, especially to Goldwater and Reagan and Gingrich. But the basic transformation of the GOP was actually the work of millions of voters who gave up old loyalties to forge a new Republican base. Southerners who had for generations voted straight Democratic tickets became alienated by the liberalism of their party and gulped and embraced the party that precipitated the War Between the States. Working-class Americans turned away from the economic liberalism of the party of Franklin Roosevelt for the social conservatism of the party of Herbert Hoover. Millions of Roman Catholics abandoned their historic ties to the party of the Kennedys and voted for the party of the presidential Protestants, including George Bush I and George Bush II.

Political bases come in various forms and sizes. The original political base of the Bushes took the form of hundreds of Christmas and other family cards in Barbara Bush's "shoebox," the file she began to keep in the 1950s. Letters she received, persons she encountered at meetings, correspondence among the big Bush family—all were duly recorded, sometimes with her comments. The hundreds grew into thousands and eventually, by the time the names were computerized, close to a hundred thousand contacts were on file. When any Bush ran for office, the campaign began with a huge mailing to people whose names were drawn from Barbara Bush's lists. She became both archangel and archivist of the Bush dynasty.

The Bushes were related to fifteen former presidents, including Washington, Lincoln, and both Roosevelts, according to a genealogist. But the family did not play up the dynasty idea and disliked comparisons to other dynasties. Such as the Kennedys. The first President Bush told the *New York Times* in 2000, "That really irks me. We're not like them. We don't do press about everything."

In fact, the Bush dynasty thrived on discontinuities. Each generation seemed born anew. The family had New England roots and grew rich on Wall Street, in investment banking. Senator Prescott Bush, George H. W. Bush's father, was a moderate Republican from Connecticut. But his son abandoned the Northeast for Texas and oil prospecting. He remained a Republican, but his political coloration took on some of the local conservatism. Yet Bush I's lack of deep ideological roots in the right wing later sealed his failure as Ronald Reagan's heir in the presidency.

His son, George W. Bush, though he was sent back east for schooling, prided himself as a native-born Texan. In the Lone Star State, he told the *Times*, "you were judged apart from your pedigree." Yet for most of his life, little more than his pedigree distinguished Bush II. It was only when he struggled free of it and was born again into the faith of Barry Goldwater and Ronald Reagan, offering himself as their true heir, that he became more than his father's son and carried the Bush dynasty into the next generation.

GEORGE H. W. BUSH has often been viewed as the classic insider. He entered politics early, excited by his father's election to the Senate in 1952. George Bush represented a Houston district for two terms in the House of Representatives, then served as chairman of the Republican National Committee under Nixon and as envoy to Communist China, followed by a stint as head of the CIA. He jousted for the Republican presidential nomination in 1980 with Ronald Reagan, who neatly balanced his winning ticket with this "moderate" Republican as his running mate.

In a longer perspective, though, Bush was more an outsider, even a loner. For one thing, he lost almost as many races as he won. He ran for United States senator from Texas in 1964, was defeated, then ran for the same seat six years later and was beaten again. Even more, Bush was never clearly identifiable in the Republican party. He was not a Reaganite—that was one reason he was chosen to balance the ticket. But he was too conservative to be at ease with moderates in the East—that was one reason he decided to make his political fortune in the Lone Star State. Yet even there he was caught in crosscurrents. In his 1964 Senate race, hoping to capitalize on Goldwater's popularity in Texas, he ran to the right, opposing the Civil Rights Act and Medicare. But as the national Republican campaign sank in the fall of 1964, Bush ran away from it. His Democratic opponent taunted him: "You can find everything on those billboards except the word 'Republican.' He's got it there so small you've got to . . . get out of your car, and look for it with a magnifying glass." After his defeat, Bush told his minister, "I took some of the far right positions to get elected. I hope I never do it again. I regret it."

He did not like to be pinned down ideologically. His fierce drive for office was not motivated by an overriding philosophy or "vision." He scoffed at the idea. Bush viewed himself as a problem solver, a negotiator, a political trader. In office or out, he was fascinated by the processes of government, the mechanics of politics. Indeed, presidential scholars Kerry Mullins and Aaron Wildavsky called his administration a "procedural presidency" that emphasized rules, order, and hierarchy. Bush saw processes not as the tools of purpose and policy but as the essence of politics and government. Thus the president must, above all, be a manager.

These views separated Bush intellectually as well as politically from the ideas and movements that were dominating American and even world politics during the 1970s and 1980s. These were times of ferment, revolution, bloodshed. But when Bush ran for the presidency in 1988, he ran as the candidate of the status quo. He perceived no mandate for fundamental change in his election, so why should he initiate it?

How had this "loner" won the presidency in the first place? Serving as Reagan's vice president had given him access to a national rostrum, which he exploited indefatigably. But history had not been kind to vice presidents hoping to move into the Oval Office, except after the death of the incumbent. They had usually been chosen because of their appeal to a different constellation of interests than that of the presidential nominee and often found themselves at odds with their chief—and with his most fervent followers. As vice president, Bush had been absolutely loyal to Reagan in policy and politics for eight years and had kept free of major controversies. Yet such fealty to an ideology he had earlier scorned suggested to reporters that he was "a man of no discernible political passions beyond a passion to win political office." To claim Reagan's mantle for his own run, Bush would have to do more.

Above all, he would have to be sound on taxes. Reagan's "voodoo economics" had helped produce a recovery in the 1980s but at the cost of budget deficits so threatening that Reagan himself had had to agree to a series of large tax hikes disguised as "reforms" of the tax system. Still the deficit—and pressures for more tax increases—grew. Here Bush saw an opportunity to leave no doubt about his conservative bona fides. He would outdo his boss with a flat vow *never* to raise taxes. When he delivered it to delegates at the 1988 Republican national convention, they came to their feet, stamping and roaring. "The Congress will push me to raise taxes," he trumpeted, "and I'll say no, and they'll push, and I'll say no, and they'll push again, and I'll say to them, 'Read my lips: no new taxes.'"

"I have to become more like Ronald Reagan," Bush told a campaign aide, "but I can't go all the way." At the convention, Bush promised a "kinder, gentler nation." While this was to be achieved through voluntarism, not by new government social programs, his call for a "new harmony" was a muted rebuke of the hard right's harshness.

But if Bush couldn't be Ronald Reagan, he could at least persuade conservatives that he was no Michael Dukakis. There was nothing kind or gentle in the Bush campaign's onslaught against the Democratic party's nominee. Bush painted the Massachusetts governor as a dangerous liberal elitist "born in Harvard Yard's boutique." In a classic conservative assault, Dukakis was mauled as deficient in patriotism, cowardly on national security, a slave to outdated big-government dogmas who had turned his state into "Taxachusetts." So vicious was the Bush attack—and so lame Dukakis's response—that the very term "liberal" became an epithet of abuse. Democrats ran away from what Republicans jeeringly called "the L word."

It was a dispiriting campaign. By election day, two-thirds of Americans who intended to vote wished that they had other candidates to choose from. Voter turnout reached new lows. The Reagan base gave Bush his victory, but he ran 5.4 million votes behind their hero's numbers four years earlier. To conservatives, Bush had proven little more than that he was no Michael Dukakis.

I F I T had been out of character for Bush to cry out "read my lips," it would also have been out of character for the American political system to leave this daring shout of leadership unchallenged. Months into his presidency, Bush faced the dilemma he cannot but have anticipated—to sink more dangerously into debt or to break his pledge and raise taxes. Compromises with the congressional Democratic leadership in 1989 allowed him to push the day of reckoning into the second year of his presidency. But with estimates of the budget shortfall growing almost daily, Democrats would not let him escape a second time. If there was to be a tax increase, they were unwilling to take the fall all by themselves and allow Republicans to castigate them for tax-and-spend liberalism.

The president was also pushed by his closest aides. His trusted budget director, Richard Darman, was a deficit hawk who had made himself "anathema to movement conservatives," as the president himself noted, by his widely known disdain for Bush's convention pledge. Bush had chosen John Sununu for chief of staff, mainly because as Republican governor of New Hampshire, Sununu had given him a crucial boost in the presidential primary there. Sununu terrorized his staff, alienated even friendly members of Congress, and epitomized the expediency of Bush's administration. "Look, you want a strategy," Sununu replied to an aide who complained about the lack of one, "my strategy is to maintain maximum flexibility so that I can take advantage of opportunities as they arise."

Facing a stalemate over the budget, the president finally yielded in May 1990 to the key Democratic precondition for budget negotiations—that there be no preconditions. This was a vague concession, but the mere implication that tax hikes were on the table was enough to alarm conservatives. Still, Democrats insisted on a more explicit statement and, in June, Bush acknowledged that he could not keep his campaign pledge. There would have to be, he announced publicly, tax increases to reduce the deficit. Conservative reaction was fierce. The *New York Post* ran a glaring page-one headline: READ MY LIPS: I LIED. Vice President Dan Quayle, a young Indiana senator Bush had picked for his ticket to appease conservatives, thought that the president had squandered the Republicans' best issue, "the one that had, more than any other, made the Reagan revolution possible."

Bush's abandonment of his pledge set off months of contentious negotiations over a deficit-reduction plan, with Bush trapped between Republicans infuriated by his betrayal of the Reagan legacy and Democrats eager to erase that legacy. The White House drew more fire from the right for its ineptness at the bargaining table—where Darman and Sununu led for the administration—and for Sununu's threats of political retribution against Republicans who resisted cooperation with the president. Bush had to suffer the ultimate embarrassment when the federal government shut down, however briefly, in October 1990, until an emergency spending bill could be passed. Unlike Bill Clinton later, George Bush absorbed most of the blame from press and public.

To conservatives, the budget crisis revealed Bush as a weak and opportunistic president, moving right or left as changing political pressures dictated. "Why can't they be more supportive," he complained in his diary at the time. "The right wing is giving me lots of fits." Indeed, some ambitious conservatives used the president's vacillations to sharpen Republican party divisions between traditionalists and radicals. No one attacked the tax increase more hotly than a rising young Republican star in the House, Newt Gingrich, who instead of mobilizing congressional support as minority whip, undermined the efforts of Bush allies to win backing on the Hill.

ONE OF the recurring phenomena in twentieth-century America was the role of war in rescuing presidents caught in political mires: Woodrow Wilson regenerated after his narrow reelection in 1916; FDR transformed to "Dr. Win the War" from "Dr. New Deal" after his second-term setbacks; Harry Truman in Korea, even LBJ in Vietnam—all found that war boosted their popularity, however briefly.

Rarely has a president's image shifted as abruptly as George Bush's in the wake of "Desert Storm," the operation to expel Iraq from Kuwait. For him, it appeared to be the "perfect war." The crisis erupted amid the interminable budget wrangle, where the president was pictured in the press as the chief of a "Bush League of stumblebums," and it played to his strengths—his long experience and main interest in foreign policy.

Diplomatically, he did almost everything right. Immediately after Saddam Hussein's forces invaded Kuwait, Bush began to work the phones to build a coalition of world leaders. He turned swiftly to the United Nations, securing from the Security Council a prompt resolution that called for Iraq's immediate withdrawal and imposed sanctions.

For Americans too it seemed a perfect war, after Vietnam and other misadventures abroad. Using Saudi Arabia as its staging base, the Pentagon began with weeks of bombing across Iraq, including Baghdad. Then ground troops from the American-led coalition struck into Kuwait with overwhelming force and speed. After one day of fighting, Saddam's army was decimated, with soldiers surrendering in masses. Coalition casualties in the three-day war were remarkably light—148 Americans killed, 458 wounded—compared with tens of thousands of Iraqi casualties.

And Bush knew when to stop the war. Millions of Americans (including this writer) wanted to "finish the job" by driving on to Baghdad. Why leave Saddam in power? Mindful of the Vietnam experience, Bush reckoned the costs of escalation: a bloody fight to take the Iraqi capital, a long-term military commitment while the country was stabilized, its government and economy reconstructed. The president wanted no part of that. "Kuwait is liberated. Iraq's army is defeated," Bush announced to the country the day he ended the war. "Our military objectives are met." He told an aide that night, "No second thoughts."

In his solo performance, Bush showed a firmness and assurance in stark contrast to his handling of domestic issues. That skill enabled him to escape the hazards of governing alone. Like Lyndon Johnson in the early years in Vietnam and like his son later, the president operated with extraordinarily little restraint from his fellow Americans or from abroad. Decisionmaking was confined to an inner circle of like-minded men, with little serious consideration given to options beyond the hard line that led to war. Congress was kept out of the loop. It did not pass its own war resolutions until a few days before the air assault was launched in January 1991, and Bush said later that he would have sent troops into combat without congressional approval if he had had to.

IN THE AFTERMATH of Bush's triumph, nearly nine of ten Americans said they approved his work as president, giving him the highest rating ever recorded. How then could he lose reelection just twenty months later, taking only 38 percent of the popular vote? How could he lose states that had been Republican strongholds for decades? How could he lose to a virtual unknown, a mere Arkansas governor?

The Bush strategy for reelection, masterminded by John Sununu, was simply to ride the Gulf War wave of public approval. But the economy dipped sharply in 1991, and Americans sensed little concern in the White House about their plight. Denying that there was a recession and constrained by its commitment to deficit reduction, the administration beat back efforts by congressional Democrats to put together a stimulus package of tax cuts and spending increases. But it offered no alternative of its own. Even Sununu's resignation that December, as the president's poll numbers were in free fall and political panic began to set in at the White House, failed to overcome the drift and inaction.

The problem was the president. Bush "had no clear idea where he wanted to go," a former aide said. "We conveyed no certainty, and we had no credibility with regard to our own principles" after the broken tax pledge. Bush could be remarkably candid in acknowledging how far opportunism motivated him. Asked by a reporter during the 1992 primaries why he was pushing welfare reform after neglecting it for three years, he replied, "The politics drives some things. . . . they get much more clearly focused every four years, and then you go ahead and try to follow through and do something about them." By that time, three quarters of Americans were convinced that their country was headed in the wrong direction.

Among those who most fervently agreed was the conservative base of the Republican party. Bush was embarrassed in the primaries by the right-wing populist Patrick Buchanan, a former Nixon and Reagan aide whose strident denunciations of "King George" attracted a shocking 34 percent of New Hampshire's Republicans. In an act of rank opportunism—and ineptitude—the president gave "Pitchfork Pat" a starring role at the GOP national convention in Houston in exchange for his endorsement. From the platform committee to the podium, the convention was dominated by Reaganites who turned what was supposed to have been George Bush's coronation into a parade of implicit attacks on his moderate leadership. Buchanan delivered the biggest thrill to the right-wing faithful when he summoned them to a "religious war" for "the soul of America," shouting, "Take back our country!"

However demagogic, Pat Buchanan was speaking for an escalating force that probably was the decisive factor in Bush's defeat. To secular-minded politicians of the old school, the issues and intensity of the surging religious right represented a new, even bewildering challenge. Bush had embraced the Episcopalianism of his grandfather and father, but religious politics in America had changed drastically over the course of his career. The Texas where he had solicited votes as a young man was increasingly becoming the land of the fundamentalist devout. A few years after he left the presidency, a study reported that "fully 92% of Texans believe that religion is 'important' in their lives," and seven of ten believed that "the Bible is God's word and that all its prophecies will transpire."

Whatever private reservations Bush had about religious extremists, as president he said and did most of the right things to curry their favor. Why then did they not back him wholeheartedly in 1992? For all Bush's efforts, conservative Christians could not identify with him. He could not *lead* them. Where Ronald Reagan was a persuasive spokesman for religious conservatives, Bush's embrace of their issues—his renunciation of his earlier support for abortion rights, his sudden championing in 1992 of "family values"—appeared to be transparent pandering. More than his highchurch, Eastern, establishment roots, Bush was a man who—even proudly—lacked "the vision thing" that Ronald Reagan had in such abundance, the principled purposefulness evangelical conservatives looked for in leaders.

But then, few Americans could identify with the president or experience the fruitful engagement with him that is the essence of leadership. Bush seemed awkward in many settings but never more so than when he tried to identify with the needs and struggles of working people and the poor. He was reduced to blurting out, as he did one cold winter's day in New Hampshire in 1992, "Message: I care." He had compromised enough, evaded enough, switched enough to avoid stereotyping. But that had cost him the kind of following, the kind of base, that sticks to a man through victory and defeat. Essentially he was an outsider, running alone.

Ꮽ

BUSH HAD LOST the base. To Republican conservatives, that was the message of 1992. The president had hemorrhaged votes among Reagan Democrats and suffered losses across the South. He was beaten decisively among independents Reagan had attracted to the fold. Over a quarter of Republicans rejected Bush. His 38 percent share of the popular vote was 16 percent lower than his share in 1988, when he was clutching Reagan's coattails. Only twice in six decades had a party's support in successive elections dropped so steeply. It took the GOP half a century to claw back from Hoover's 1932 catastrophe. Democrats still had not recovered from Humphrey's 1968 defeat. Republicans feared Bush had lost more than an election.

Even his son, George W., recognized his father's failure as Reagan's heir. In the aftermath of 1992, he told writers, "The messenger was unable to carry the message." At that time, though, Bush II appeared to be little more than the fiercely loyal heir to a political loser.

Upon entering Yale in 1964 after graduation from Andover, George W. Bush joined a fraternity, was tapped for Skull and Bones like his father, coasted along as a gentleman-C student—unlike his father, who had made Phi Beta Kappa. George won hundreds of friends and contacts, partied rowdily, drank excessively. Later, he told his family that he had not learned "a damn thing at Yale."

But this was the 1960s, a time of political trauma and polarization for the United States. Yale was no refuge. William Sloane Coffin, the university chaplain, was a Yalie who had been initiated into Skull and Bones in 1948 by none other than George Bush I. So George W., who paid little attention to campus politics—ignoring the Young Republicans and the more radical anti-faculty conservatives—mistook Coffin for an old boy when he went to the college chapel to meet him in 1964. Instead, he found a liberal activist who had cheered Bush I's recent loss in his Senate race as a setback for Goldwater extremism. Bush II was shocked and wounded when Coffin told him his father had lost to a better man. To the younger Bush, the confrontation signified the arrogance and righteousness of Eastern liberalism as he found it at Yale. "They thought they could create a government that could solve all our problems for us," he said thirty years later. They were privileged people who felt so guilty about their advantages that they were driven to "overcompensate by trying to give everyone else in life the same thing."

Bush II went on to Harvard Business School and then, emulating his father, settled in Texas as an oil dealer and entrepreneur. Business was so unrewarding that three years later, in 1978, he followed his father into a different venture, running for Congress. His family standing helped him win the Republican nomination in his West Texas district, but not the general election. He returned to the oil business, only to see his firm founder amid the collapse of world oil prices. In 1986, he managed to sell it to a company eager for the association with a vice president's son and came out with a bottom-line profit of around a half million dollars.

At Yale and after, following closely in his father's footsteps, Bush II could not ignore the contrast between his lackluster performance and Bush I's accomplishments. The father had made his mark in the oil business and an even grander one in politics. The son identified closely with these achievements. Fiercely loyal, he demanded the same from all who worked for Bush

I. During his father's administration, he shuttled between Texas and Washington to serve as enforcer, pushing out John Sununu when the chief of staff became an embarrassment. "He knew what his father wanted without being asked," a colleague recalled. Bush I's defeat in 1992 was probably as much a blow to the son as to the father, especially since the loss was to a man both Bushes thought unworthy of being president of the United States.

The son was infuriated by the disloyal Republicans who had deserted the president in the pinch. Still, he felt that his father too had been guilty of inconstancy—too moderate, too centrist. Bush II had served as emissary to the right for Bush I, assuring one activist in 1988, "You'll be astounded at how conservatively he will govern." The lesson of 1992 was clear. The "vision thing" mattered. Republicans must stick rigidly to conservative doctrine. They must be continuous and disciplined campaigners. And they must hang tough. Two years after his father's defeat, Bush won the governorship of Texas after, yes, a very disciplined, very tough campaign.

How could it happen that this long-unfocused man, no longer young but still in his father's shadow, the scion of Eastern moderate Republicans, the half-educated product of Andover and Yale, embarked on a course that would carry him within a few years to the White House as a committed conservative? Bush governed Texas from the Reagan playbook. He admired the former president's ability to blend personal amiability, undiluted conservatism, and political ruthlessness into a winning strategy. For all his family ties, Bush was, like Reagan, a relative late-bloomer in electoral politics, with an outsider's attitude to the establishment his father embodied. As with Reagan, his genial, down-home persona softened the hard edges of his conservatism. And like Reagan, he concentrated on a handful of signature issues from his campaign—pro-business economic policies, law and order, welfare reform, education—where his skill in reaching out to conservative Democrats in the legislature allowed him to claim a decent record of achievement.

To the state's growing flock of religious conservatives, the governor could offer a compelling personal story of redemption. A heavy drinker since Yale, Bush woke up in a hotel room one morning in 1986 with a mighty hangover and looked into the bathroom mirror. A friend who was with him recalled that he was thinking of Bush I's presidential ambitions—"Someday, I might embarrass my father." But the son was in the midst of a profounder realization. That same year, he underwent a "renewal of faith" that led him into fundamentalist Christianity. In a curious way, his new faith gave him some separation from the elder Bush. Later, as president, asked whether he had sought advice and strength from his father before he decided to invade Iraq, Bush II replied that that was the "wrong father" to appeal to. "There is," he said, "a higher father that I appeal to."

His readiness to invoke his faith publicly gave the governor the credibility with the evangelical community that had always eluded his father. Bush II promoted the takeover by religious groups of such public services as drug rehabilitation, adoption, and even the operation of state prisons. Calling it "compassionate conservatism," he wrapped his campaign to gut the state's welfare system in the mantle of "personal responsibility," suggesting that the poor might better look to Christian charity—and to God—than to government for relief. Under Governor Bush, Texas ranked last among the states in per capita government spending, while one in six Texans lived in poverty, a rate 25 percent higher than the national average.

Even as he ran for reelection in 1998, the governor was greeted with "Bush for President" signs across the state. Though he turned aside talk about his intentions, he created an informal strategy group and made trips to primary states and fundraising meccas. His Texas landslide that year—he took 70 percent of the vote, bringing millions of conservative Democrats into his fold—made him the frontrunner for the GOP nomination. He was deluged by pleas to make the race.

After two defeats to Bill Clinton, Republicans were desperate for an "electable" candidate, and Bush offered undeniable advantages. First, of course, was the name, but as important was the elder Bush's huge network of moneymen, which enabled the son to harvest tens of millions almost effortlessly. Above all, to those longing to reconstitute the Reagan coalition of economic and social conservatives that had faded with the candidacies of Bush I and Bob Dole, George Bush II, with his skill in playing Reagan politics proven in two elections, seemed heaven-sent. "I haven't seen a candidate like this in my life," said Harry Dent, a key architect of Nixon's "Southern strategy."

When he began his campaign in 1999, Bush II made clear that he would be "a different candidate than the previous George Bush who ran for president." He called his father's agreement to increase taxes, the violation of his convention pledge, a mistake, and promised that there would be new people in his campaign, "conservative-minded people." Most important among those people was Bush's chief strategist, Karl Rove, though he was not really new. Rove's political education went back to the Watergate era, when he was chairman of the College Republican National Committee. It was then, when Bush I was serving as Nixon's party chairman, that Rove met the Bush family. Rove went on to win a reputation among Republicans as an immensely knowledgeable election expert with a taste for very dirty tricks and an attacking style. He had orchestrated Bush II's brilliant gubernatorial races, and his job now was to bring that skill at mobilizing voters across a wide range of constituencies to the national level.

For the Republican primaries, though, where conservative activists dominated, a narrower approach was needed. The Bush-Rove strategy was a flexible blend of hard, Christian-tinted conservative doctrine with thick draughts of what reporters called "slaughterhouse politics." Ineffective in New Hampshire—Bush was trounced by Arizona senator John McCain—the campaign struck back in ultraconservative South Carolina by stealing McCain's "reformist" mantle and mounting an all-out assault on the senator as a corrupt tax-and-spend Washington insider. The campaign spread rumors that McCain's wife was a drug addict and that the couple had a black child. In vain McCain protested, "He comes from a better family. He knows better than this."

The governor's play to the hard right paid off in South Carolina and elsewhere. Though McCain himself had a strong conservative record, he departed from orthodoxy on some issues and shied from making much publicly of his personal faith. Not so George Bush, who rolled up a two-to-one margin over McCain among conservative Republicans who voted in the primaries and a better than three-to-one edge among evangelicals.

IN THE FALL CAMPAIGN, though, Bush faced a very different set of challenges than he had in the primaries or than his hero Ronald Reagan had in 1980. Opposing him was the vice president of a popular incumbent who presided over a strong economy. Among conservatives there was a passionate desire not only to recapture the presidency but also for united government in the form of GOP control of both White House and Congress. Unlike two Southern governors before him—Carter and Clinton—Bush had no intention of running against his party's base. He was eager to accept the mantle of Reagan's heir.

But in the country, there was no appetite for a radical turn. How could Americans be convinced to throw out the incumbent's heir? First, Bush had to overcome doubts that he was up to the job. Like Reagan, he had committed blunders that gave him the appearance of a lightweight. Like Reagan, Bush could counter by pointing to his record as governor.

Equally important was his unusual choice of running mate. Dick Cheney was a former Nixon and Ford aide and House minority whip, then Bush I's Defense secretary who had overseen the brilliant Gulf War strategy, and later head of Dallas-based Halliburton, a vast oil and gas conglomerate. A tough partisan, Cheney had remained through the Clinton years at the center of a web of hard-right veterans of Republican administrations.

Cheney did not bring the conventional balance to Bush's ticket. He was at least as conservative as Bush and, though a Wyoming native, he made his home in Bush's Texas. What he did offer was balance to Bush's perceived lack of gravitas. Cheney's visible discomfort with—even disdain for—the frothy rituals of domestic politicking only enhanced his wise-man aura.

Cheney was also the classic Washington insider, balancing the outsider thrust of Bush's campaign. Here too Bush stuck to the Reagan script, playing the common man from the heartland who vowed to bring plain common sense and integrity to the capital. Bush took aim at the partisan bickering in Clinton's Washington. Pointing to his success in Texas at reaching across to conservative Democrats, Bush promised to be "a uniter, not a divider." And he painted Gore as a typically opportunistic insider—"someone who will say anything to get elected"—while presenting himself as a man of stubborn convictions.

But to capture the center, Bush had to blur those convictions. "Compassionate conservatism" seemed the ideal tool, a variation on Clinton's Third Way, centrism with a conservative twist. To reinforce the impression, Bush adapted popular pieces of Clinton's agenda. While offering few details, Bush promised progress on education, health care, Social Security. The status quo—this was the point—would be safe in his hands. A quarter of the electorate was persuaded that Bush was a moderate.

That was not quite enough to win the popular vote. Bush lost a big midsummer lead when Gore embraced a populist message, appealing to Reagan Democrats on economic issues. When the votes cast on November 7 were counted, Bush was down half a million out of the 104 million total. He had overwhelming support from fellow Republicans and won 80 percent of conservative evangelicals' votes, compared to Bob Dole's 65 percent four years earlier. And he won every state in the South, except one. That was Florida. Bush would have to wait five weeks before the Supreme Court gave him that state and with it the presidency.

∽

ON HIS FIRST visit to Washington after the Supreme Court voted, Bush claimed a mandate: "I believe I'm standing here because I campaigned on issues that people heard."

But while Bush radiated an outward optimism reminiscent of Reagan, from the start he governed like a man teetering on the edge of a political precipice. "Compassionate conservatism" had not, after all, given him a Reaganesque mandate. It was the hard-core base that had put him in position to seize the presidency—the GOP right-wing coalition, backed by the corporate interests that had bankrolled the massive effort to turn out conservatives on election day. If Bush had a mandate, it was from them. To keep it, he would out-Reagan Reagan.

As a first step, Bush made his presidency a permanent campaign. Within a week of Bush's inauguration, Karl Rove was hosting meetings to plan for the 2004 election. Politics dominated this White House to a remarkable degree, with Rove as strategist-in-chief and disciplinarian, ensuring that the departments and agencies followed the White House's political playbook. In fact, as John DiIulio, the president's adviser on "faith-based initiatives," discovered, there was "a complete lack of policy apparatus" in the Bush administration. Everything—"and I mean everything"—was "being run by the political arm." DiIulio's own brief was to siphon billions of dollars out of federal funds and deliver them to key religious constituencies perform-ing charitable work.

Bush's top priority was a huge tax cut, introduced to Congress the day after his inauguration. With the country enjoying a budget surplus after years of anxiety about deficits triggered by Reagan's 1981 tax cuts, Bush had promised new cuts in the campaign. The surplus, he would say, wasn't the government's money. "It's the hard-working people of America's money and I want to share some of that money with you." But a vast majority of Amer-icans—over 80 percent—opposed Bush's tax cuts, asking that the surplus be used for purposes such as paying down the national debt or shoring up So-cial Security.

But tax cuts were at the heart of the conservative revolution. They were the keys both to liberating individual initiative and to "starving the beast" of big government. They were the issue that made Reagan and later unmade Bush I. The new president was eager to leave his mark as Reagan had. In fact, his $1.35 trillion cut over ten years would outdo his mentor's achieve-ment. The president was delighted. "It's going to be a heck of a lot bigger than anybody thought," he boasted.

Congressional Republicans also were thrilled. They still controlled Con-gress, but with majorities reduced in 2000. Indeed, the Senate was split evenly, 50-50, with Vice President Cheney in position to cast a deciding vote. Conservatives in this politically precarious position were eager to co-operate on such a base-pleasing venture. Pushing for rapid action, White House and Congress brushed aside objections to the tax cut's cost and its lack of fairness—it would give 40 percent of the benefit to the richest 1 per-cent of Americans. When the plan came to a vote in the spring, not one Re-publican in the House opposed it and only two did in the Senate.

It was a triumph of collective action that aligned White House, Congress, activists, and the base. On the tax cut and other issues, the administration was determined to control the agenda. "Our strategy," Bush's chief lobbyist said, "is to always stay on offense and keep moving." The Bush team worked closely with congressional Republicans, most of all with the president's ide-ological soul mates in the House. With its bigger contingent of GOP mod-erates, the Senate was more troublesome, and by the summer of 2001, the president's initiatives were stalled there. The limits of his mandate were becoming all too clear, especially after Senator James Jeffords of Vermont handed control of the Senate to the Democrats by resigning from the GOP caucus in protest against the White House's hard-right line and its bullying of party moderates. He had warned Bush, Jeffords said, that "he'll be a one-term president if he doesn't listen to his moderates."

AFTER THE TERRORIST attacks of September 11, 2001, Bush quickly won acclaim for rallying the country. As with Bush I after his successful Gulf War, the public perception of the president was transformed almost overnight. Gone was the aura of illegitimacy that had clung to him. His polls shot up astronomically and stayed high for months. Even more profound was the transformation in Bush's self-perception. He now saw himself as a man with a mission on which he would stake his presidency, with a mandate from Americans to lead a war on terror. He told advisers that little they had done before 9/11 mattered now. He was fighting a new war from the battlements of a new presidency. Borrowing from Reagan, the reborn president spoke out in stark and moralistic terms, vowing to "rid the world of evil" in a conflict that "will end in a way and at an hour of our choosing."

As war leader, Bush established—and extended—his authority. The president chaired meetings of the National Security Council, leading discussions of a plan to attack the terrorist threat at its source in Afghanistan. Bush had learned from the disarray, indiscipline, and indecision of his father's administration. An exceptionally orderly man, Bush II had created an orderly government that had power and control centered in the White House, with himself playing the role of "decider." After 9/11, aides remarked, Bush made his decisions with a new earnestness and relish.

The 9/11 attacks also transformed Bush's domestic agenda, making internal security the new focus. Within weeks, the administration pushed through the Patriot Act to give the executive branch vastly increased investigative and surveillance authority. Democrats and even conservatives worried about this surge of new federal power and the threat to civil liberties, but they were cowed by fears of appearing weak on national security. The bill was voted through the Senate by 98-1 and the House by 357-66.

To coordinate domestic security, Bush proposed a new Cabinet department that would combine twenty-two federal agencies and 17,000 employees—a massive centralization of power in the executive. No one doubted that this meant White House control. After 9/11, Bush kept his Cabinet on an even shorter leash. "It's a very tight team," a White House aide said in December 2001, "very regimented, very tight message discipline."

As before, that message was developed and enforced by Karl Rove. After 9/11, the White House political team focused on the off-year elections of 2002. Bush and Rove wanted not merely to stem the traditional loss of seats by the president's party, but to reverse it, above all to recapture the Senate. They started early, recruiting attractive candidates and building a $150 million war chest. As few presidents had done for midterms—Reagan most recently—Bush put his prestige on the line by making ninety campaign visits to crucial districts.

In 2002, the messenger *was* the message. With his approval ratings still high—90 percent among Republicans—Bush's war leadership held center stage. Democratic issues—the weak economy, Social Security, health care—could gain little traction against the GOP's relentless focus on the terrorist threat. In January 2002, Rove made the strategy clear to the Republican National Committee: "We can go to the country on this issue because they trust the Republican Party to do a better job of protecting and strengthening America's military might and thereby protecting America."

As the election campaign heated up, so did Bush's push for regime change in Iraq. The administration linked Saddam Hussein to the 9/11 attackers and claimed that he possessed weapons of mass destruction that posed an immediate threat to the United States. The president's mid-campaign demand that Congress authorize the use of force against Iraq offered a lose-lose proposition to Democrats. If they supported the use of force, they would endorse Bush's war leadership and alienate their own supporters. If they opposed it, they would be accused of putting politics ahead of national security. The vote in Congress, late in October, left Democrats trading recriminations on election eve.

Bush won Congress's authorization and also the election. The latter was a personal win. Forty-three percent of those who voted said theirs was a vote for Bush; only 17 percent said they cast their vote against him. Most impressive were the party's gains in state legislatures, and not only in the South. Karl Rove said he detected a "fundamental" shift to the GOP, and even Democrats conceded Bush a big win. "He got his mandate," said Al Gore's campaign manager.

Still, the GOP's gains in Congress were modest. The party added two Senate seats and now held a single-vote edge there. In the House, the GOP gained six seats, but their majority remained smaller than it had been in 1995. And after shunning domestic-policy commitments in the campaign, apart from another tax cut, what mandate could Bush claim? He had, as a Democratic operative noted, rolled the dice in 2002 and won his electoral gamble. But he had staked all on his war leadership.

THAT WAR leadership would be the main issue again as the most critical election of all—2004—approached. But in the aftermath of Bush's March 2003 invasion of Iraq, it was no longer unassailable. As American troops struggled to contain an insurgency in Iraq long after the president had declared victory, controversy erupted over the administration's use of intelligence to win support for the war, and, even more, whether the White House had ignored warnings in advance of the 9/11 attacks that might have prevented them. Add to this the loss of millions of jobs as the numbers of impoverished Americans rose annually and a budget deficit bloated by another round of tax cuts, and a nightmarish memory hung over Republicans—of the failed reelection campaign of Bush I in 1992.

Even so, Bush and Rove were scarcely unprepared. For four years they had been laying a most ambitious plan—to win a party victory up and down the ballot, not merely Bush's own reelection. Such a wide and deep party triumph would solidify the base, reaching down to the state level and the grass roots. It would require a massive effort. Campaign manager Matthew Dowd described a painstaking search for unregistered, nonvoting, and potential Republicans. With a field operation five times larger than in 2000, the campaign "micro-targeted" such likely supporters. They were identified via consumer databases, voting files, sample polls, and computer modeling, and then pursued by mail, phone, and face to face. All of this would climax in an unprecedented turnout drive on voting day.

In time for the campaign, "compassionate conservatism" was pulled out of the icebox, linking a small blizzard of ill-defined proposals. But the president's main domestic planks—where he showed a measure of commitment—were pitched to the right: making the tax cuts permanent, reforming the tax code by enacting a flat tax or national sales tax, and partially privatizing Social Security. And Bush also lent support to a frenzied campaign by the religious right to ban gay marriages—by constitutional amendment, if necessary.

But Bush's central appeal remained his war leadership, and that in turn rested on his own character, especially in contrast to that of his opponent, John Kerry. The president would offer no plan to defeat terrorism or to extricate the country from Iraq. He made no apologies for mistakes in strategy or execution. He promised more of the same, what he called the continued spread of freedom and peace around the world. The issue was simple: In troublesome times, who was to be trusted, Bush or Kerry? Much as his father had done so effectively to Michael Dukakis in 1988, the Bush campaign savaged John Kerry as an elitist, a liar, an equivocator, an opportunist, a flip-flopper, spoiling his credit as a potential leader. Meanwhile, Bush adopted the Reaganesque figure of a tough but humble man, a man of moral clarity and deep conviction. "Even when we don't agree," Bush said accepting his party's nomination in September, "at least you know what I believe and where I stand." By election day, Bush had an overwhelming edge over Kerry in voter judgments on such traits as "strong leader" and "honest and trustworthy."

Yet Bush proved again that he was no Reagan at the polls. In 2004, the president scraped by. He won a majority of the popular vote this time—barely, with 51 percent—but a lead of a mere 120,000 votes in Ohio spared him defeat in the electoral college. With both parties focused on turnout, 17 million more Americans voted than in 2000. Here the GOP had a decided advantage. Bush's micro-targeted mobilization paid off as the GOP made gains at the base. As many as 4 million new evangelical voters turned out for Bush. But the president had done nothing to expand the base into fresh constituencies.

The Republicans strengthened their grip on Congress, especially the Senate, with further gains in the South. But Bush's strategy failed to shift the partisan balance in the states—indeed, Democrats made slight gains—reflecting the fact that the base the Bush Republicans mobilized was deep rather than broad, compared to the sweeping victories of FDR, LBJ, and

Reagan. As a party victory, the election confirmed that the GOP was now the party of the hard right.

∽

IN HIS FIRST TERM, George Bush emerged from an election that gave him the narrowest conceivable legitimacy and proceeded to fashion a remarkably cohesive government. Before and especially after 9/11, Bush and his team turned presidential government into a power structure that more resembled the British parliamentary system than the American model of checks and balances. Authority radiated through the executive branch into Congress. The president was at the center, at the head of the team, leading from his conservative convictions. The task of his White House staff was to enforce loyalty and discipline, to ensure that the president's will reached into the departments and agencies. Careful to avoid losing battles, willing to compromise as a last resort and claim victory, Bush continued to command the legislative agenda. After 9/11, when national-security issues predominated, Democrats became more docile while Republican loyalty intensified. In his first two years, the president had the highest level of support in Congress of any president since Lyndon Johnson.

Vice President Cheney served as a kind of deputy prime minister in Bush's collective leadership. From his service in the Ford administration, Cheney had unrivaled knowledge of how the executive branch worked. He assembled his own powerful staff and planted loyalists in key posts to maximize his influence. Within months of the inauguration, reporters noted Cheney's central role in the White House. Nicholas Lemann wrote in May 2001 that already Cheney had "gone far past the boundary of influence of any previous Vice-President in American history." His imprint was evident on economic and energy policies and, above all, on foreign policy, where the new president had little experience. Unlike most vice presidents, this one had the president's ear. Cheney saw Bush every morning and several times each day. If Bush believed his father had failed because he was wishy-washy, Cheney's advice for a successful presidency—stay on the offensive and push back hard against critics; be assertive and decisive and never waver—strengthened his own instincts.

Cheney himself rarely wavered. Told early in 2001 by a press aide that reporters were calling him a hard-liner, he replied, "I *am* a hard-liner." After 9/11, Cheney presided over an informal war cabinet of hard-liners that included Defense Secretary Donald Rumsfeld and other experienced power-wielders. This small group drove the administration's aggressive response to terrorism and, above all, the president's determination to stay on the offensive by invading Iraq. Cheney's group rode herd on the military, intelligence agencies, and the bureaucracy, determined to push the president's authority through the government and to project American power around the world.

After his reelection, Bush was confident that he had secured a mandate for his collective leadership and power. "I earned capital in the campaign," he said, "political capital, and now I intend to spend it." Bush's doggedly partisan leader in the House, Majority Whip Tom DeLay, was even more exultant. On election night 2004, he saw the GOP as "a permanent majority" that would "lead this country in the direction we've been dreaming of for years."

YET ALMOST from the outset of the president's second term, the collective power fashioned by Bush, Cheney, and their fellow Republicans faced the harshest tests of governance. Despite months of intensive campaigning, Bush was unable to draw on his new "political capital" to win support for his top priority, the dismantlement of the Social Security system. Other major proposals fell by the wayside. A White House push for a radical overhaul of the tax code got nowhere. In late summer 2005 came Hurricane Katrina, which devastated the Gulf Coast. Collective leadership that might have united the action of federal agencies and pulled together national, state, and local efforts was utterly lacking. With the administration reeling from the Katrina backlash, a Bush nominee for the Supreme Court who was a White House functionary and close friend of the president was greeted with derision by the administration's own conservative loyalists, amid cries of crony government.

Within a year, under the pressure of these failures and of mounting investigations of the Bush team's actions, the fabled discipline of the White House was breaking down. Dissenters spoke—usually anonymously—to reporters; rumors of feuds and power struggles swirled. The president himself was not immune. Insiders pictured an isolated man, alone within a small circle of loyalists who feared to bring him bad news that would puncture hopeful illusions and provoke outbursts of irritation and rage.

Bush's popular support melted away. The mandate for his war leadership—based on trust in his character and purpose, as well as public insecurity after 9/11—faded. More and more he appeared to be governing alone. What went wrong? Bush's cascading failures revealed that from the beginning of his presidency his collective leadership and power were both less and more than they seemed.

BUSH AND CHENEY came into office in 2001 determined to expand presidential powers. They were convinced that since Vietnam and Watergate there had been, in Cheney's words, "an erosion of the powers and the ability of the president of the United States to do his job." In their view, even the assertiveness of the Reagan presidency had failed to clear obstacles to presidential leadership. Their aim was to resurrect in full the "imperial presidency" they thought Congress had dismantled after Nixon's abuses of power. Moreover, to compensate for his weak political position, the new president was determined to stay on the offensive, to assert his authority in every possible way against low expectations.

Though Congress was in friendly Republican hands, the president was intent on redefining the balance between the branches. He had a duty, Bush said in 2002, "to protect the executive branch from legislative encroachment." The administration's refusal to cooperate with inquiries marked its rejection of Congress' traditional oversight functions, its right and duty to scrutinize presidential actions. Frustrated by a Bush claim of executive privilege, one right-winger in the House complained to Justice Department attorneys, "This is not a monarchy. . . . Your guy's acting like he's king."

While Bush did not cast a single veto during his first five years in office, he quietly attached qualifying statements to bills that came to him for approval, indicating that though he was signing them into law, he was not bound to execute them as Congress intended. Bush was not the first president to employ such "signing statements," but he used them far more frequently and cast them in far more sweeping terms than any of his predecessors had. The statements—ultimately there would be hundreds—often flatly declared the laws he was signing unconstitutional. Usurping the functions not only of Congress to define the law but also of the courts to interpret it, the president intended to govern alone.

The administration's most sweeping and ominous thrust for power came in the "war on terror." Other presidents in times of crisis had reached—and overreached—for expanded authority. But few have made such big and explicit claims for unchecked powers. In an analysis delivered two weeks after 9/11, a Justice Department lawyer concluded that Congress could place no limits "on the President's determinations as to any terrorist threat," even a threat "that cannot be demonstrably linked to the September 11 incidents." And decisions as to how he would respond to such a threat "are for the President alone to make." This was not mere constitutional theorizing. It became the administration's charter for action, covering a host of secret, often illegal exertions of unlimited powers.

Dick Cheney was the most aggressive advocate of "robust" and "unimpaired" presidential power in wartime. Defending the administration's secret and illegal program of warrantless surveillance in late 2005, he dismissed concerns about the absence of congressional or judicial oversight and the risk to civil liberties: "Either we're serious about fighting the war on terror or we're not." For Cheney, the 9/11 attack and the wars that followed were an opportunity he gladly seized "to restore the legitimate authority of the presidency."

"If there's anything improper or inappropriate in that," the vice president insisted, "my guess is that the vast majority of the American people support that." Yet Cheney was outraged that the American people had found out what the administration was doing. Mere knowledge of the spying program's existence "damages national security," he said.

The war on terror gave Bush and Cheney a rationale to govern alone, to exercise powers in the name of national defense whose limits, in their view, only the commander-in-chief—not Congress or the courts—could define. Bush spoke as though he alone bore responsibility for the country's security.

YET EVEN as the president claimed such responsibility—and such power—he and his team were strenuously avoiding accountability for their actions. Accountability is the keystone of true collective leadership in a democracy. By enabling citizens to know who is doing what and when and for which reasons and to hold the leadership responsible for its actions, accountability serves as a check on power. But it depends on the openness and honesty of the leadership.

From its beginnings, the Bush administration asserted such sweeping prerogatives to keep knowledge from Congress and the public that, as one historian said, they "would make Nixon jealous in his grave." The White House struck strongly at administration leakers, rejected congressional requests for information Bush's predecessors had routinely granted, and issued executive orders that curtailed public access to presidential records.

Much as in Nixon's day, policymaking was secretive, dominated by small circles within the White House. A former State Department official recalled Cheney's powerful war cabinet as a "little cabal" that "made decisions that the bureaucracy did not know were being made," resulting in what he called "aberrations, bastardizations, perturbations." As not only Nixon but JFK and others had shown, a closed decisionmaking process, impervious to outside voices and alternative information, too often led to misjudgments and flawed or incompetent execution.

Even more, the Bush team used its control of information to manipulate public discussion of its proposals and policies. More aggressively than any of its predecessors, the administration provided information that backed up its message and withheld information that did not. Nowhere was this more consequential than in the president's conduct of war. Rising public mistrust of a secretive administration that repeatedly asked Americans to "trust us on this" had its roots in the Bush team's most striking violation of democratic governance: its abuse of classified intelligence to mislead the people about the threat Iraq posed to the United States, including making claims that Iraq was complicit in the 9/11 attacks, that Iraq possessed stores of chemical and biological weapons, and that Iraq was obtaining the means to build and deliver a nuclear bomb. Once the war began, the Bush White House compounded these failings by persisting in falsifications even after they had been disproved, savaging critics and dissenters within and outside the administration, and, with the aid of congressional Republicans, stifling inquiries into the motives and conduct of the war.

Invoking his extraordinary wartime powers, the president ordered that alleged terrorists and insurgents apprehended by American forces in Afghanistan, Iraq, and elsewhere be held outside the protection of American due process or international law. As evidence of the mistreatment of these detainees mounted, the administration shrouded the issue with intense secrecy and denials, again campaigning to block inquiries. Blame was deflected down onto the lower echelons, despite evidence of the authorization of systematic torture at the highest levels. The Senate at last forced debate in the fall of 2005 by approving a ban on cruel, degrading, and inhumane treatment of prisoners. The White House fiercely opposed the measure, and Vice President Cheney was described by the *New York Times* as "a prime mover behind the attempts to legalize torture."

Although the Bush team had successfully misled the country into war, its continued lack of candor, its refusal to acknowledge mistakes, its rejection of accountability, drained public support for its warmaking as the Iraqi insurgency entered its fourth year. Increasingly, the president was making war alone. Now the dread Vietnam analogy was unavoidable: Could a presidency whose credibility was so deeply compromised regain the public trust needed for a harsh struggle against tenacious foes?

By the sixth year of his presidency, that fading trust in Bush's leadership was reaching the base. The mandate from the right that Bush had nurtured through successive elections and on which he had grounded his collective leadership was eroding. The president was at risk of losing the base, and even more dramatically than his father had. Paradoxically, it was Bush II's obsessive attention to the base that pushed him to govern alone and that led to his failures to expand beyond it.

Apart from the war on terror, the right-wing agenda—and so Bush's agenda—was never the agenda of a majority of Americans. A January 2001 survey had asked Americans what they considered the top national priorities. Apart from education, the results had little in common with the incoming president's legislative agenda. That was heavy with inducements to the base—huge tax cuts, faith-based programs, new outlays for defense. Even in 2002, as Bush campaigned on his war leadership and prepared to invade Iraq, he scarcely addressed the issue most on the minds of Americans: not terrorism but the economy. The top priority of his second term, apart from tax cuts, was Social Security privatization. Three quarters of Americans opposed it.

Having played consistently to the hard right from the beginning of his presidency, Bush was disconnected from the broad mass of Americans. He could not fashion a true collective leadership, as Reagan had, when he was unable to reach beyond a minority of supporters. Even a sympathetic Congress could not routinely push through measures that most Americans opposed. To placate the base, Bush resorted to unilateral powers of the presidency. He made dozens of recess appointments of hard-right conservatives whose nominations Congress would not confirm. He issued orders to send federal funds to religious groups when Congress refused to authorize doing so. Another executive order banned federal support for research on new embryonic stem-cell lines vehemently opposed by the religious right. Bush ordered rule changes that rolled back a vast array of environmental regulations. He ordered a reevaluation of the science behind workplace health and safety laws with the intent to weaken them.

In these ways and countless others, Bush ran together with his base by governing alone. But by 2006, rebellion was flaring at the base. The religious right was angry that its causes were being neglected, especially its demands for a constitutional amendment banning same-sex marriages and even stiffer limits on abortion. James Dobson, a leading Christian rightist who had played a central role in mobilizing evangelicals in 2004, accused Republicans of "just ignoring those that put them in office." He threatened to withhold his support from the party in the midterm elections. Bush understood the ingratitude and insatiability of specialized interest groups. From his father's experience, he wrote in 1999, he had learned "how quickly a constituency can forget success."

But conservative doubts about the president and his team were running deeper than that. They ran even deeper than his *lack* of success—his sinking poll numbers and the Iraq quagmire. Some on the right were asking if the

Bush people were conservatives at all. A prominent Reagan-era official fired from his right-wing think tank for criticizing the president described Bush as an "impostor," a "pretend conservative" who rivaled Richard Nixon for opportunism and ruthlessness in pursuit of political gain. Many on the right scorned Bush's "big-government conservatism" as a contradiction in terms, pointing to the administration's vast spending increases—the largest since Lyndon Johnson's—as well as the creation of a gigantic new bureaucracy, the Homeland Security Department.

At the core of Reaganism was shrinking government. Reagan was a strong president, of course, but for the purpose of weakening the government. Now there was Reagan's heir, Bush II, bulking up government and his own powers. His series of tax cuts weren't "starving the beast" but—to the mounting horror of fiscal conservatives—ballooning the national debt. States' rights conservatives—that first wave of refugees from the Democratic party—saw power shifting from local and state governments to Washington. Libertarians saw an executive branch claim sweeping authority to intrude into the lives and thoughts of citizens. Old-fashioned conservatives heard a president declare that he was above the law.

Congressional Republicans, derided as a rubber stamp for the administration, were beginning to rediscover checks and balances, pushing back against the president's assertions of power. Desperate to keep their hold on Congress, they faced a crucial question in 2006: to run together with Bush or away from him? Karl Rove, at least, had no doubt of the answer. In January, he told the Republican National Committee that the "war on terror" would again be the central issue. It was the one polarizing issue that would unite the party around the president and his "post-9/11 worldview."

To all appearances, Rove was confident. The Democrats were wrong on national security—"deeply and profoundly and consistently wrong." And he gloated over the GOP's "stunning political achievement" across four decades. But Republicans couldn't have done it alone, he admitted. The Democrats had given them a big helping hand, and therein Rove found "a cautionary tale of what happens to a dominant party" when "an entitlement mentality takes over and when political power becomes an end in itself rather than a means to achieve the common good."

To many Democrats, and not a few Republicans, this seemed a fair accounting of the GOP late in the age of Goldwater and Reagan and Gingrich and Bush. But would the Democracy find the leadership—and the followers—as the Republicans had, to seize the opportunity, to transform the party into a disciplined national organization, united by shared values, committed to collective action?

Chapter

8

NEEDED:
PARTY POLARIZATION

O n the morning of November 5, 1956, Democrats across America
were in despair. Dwight Eisenhower had done it again. His first victory, in 1952, had been understandable—memories of his military leadership in World War II were still fresh. But after four years of his bumbling
presidency, as the Democrats saw it, Americans should have been turning
back to the party of Roosevelt and Truman. But they didn't. Even worse, Ike
had improved his margin over Adlai Stevenson since 1952, this time beating
him by almost 10 million votes.

Five decades after Eisenhower's reelection triumph, Democrats once
again were in despair. In 2004, the Bush II Republicans had beaten them
cleanly in the electoral college, without recourse to the Supreme Court.
Even worse, they had strengthened their hold on Congress. For the first
time since the 1950s, Americans had chosen Republicans to control both
the presidency and the legislature. And with a cooperative Senate, Bush
could use his appointment power to tighten right-wing domination of the
third branch, the federal courts.

Desperately, gloomily, Democrats searched for explanations and scape-
goats. The answer was simple, said some—Bush's naked exploitation of 9/11
and its aftermath. No, others said, John Kerry ran a weak campaign—he
took too long to answer the brutal Republican attacks on his character or he

was too unfocused or too leftist or too rightist or too elitist. Still others blamed the Democrats for failing to appeal to low-income voters, or to suburbanites or farmers, or to those who opposed Bush's war in Iraq or to those who supported it. Explanations unsurprisingly reflected the complainers' ideological or factional positions held long before election day.

Scholars found more nuanced reasons for the Democratic decline, noting trends and movements that stretched back to the days of Robert Taft and Barry Goldwater and even earlier. Fundamental among them were the long decline of the class-based politics that had welded the New Deal coalition together for decades, and the steady rise of both national security anxieties—from the Cold War to the "war on terror"—and sociocultural consciousness as deciding issues in politics. Even as income inequality had risen, race, gender, and religious conflict had sharpened. Overall, the shifting conflict lines had favored the Republicans.

And, indeed, the Democratic defeat in 2004 was no aberration. JFK and LBJ had won two terms in the White House, beating Goldwater in 1964 by 16 million votes. But this was the high-water mark for the Democrats. For the next four decades, they served mainly as the opposition. Their three presidential victories—Carter's one and Clinton's two—were hardly testaments to the party's fighting power; Carter probably would not have won without Watergate, and Clinton never gained a majority of the votes cast. During those four decades, the Grand Old Party would thrice win the grandest prize in American politics—the reelection of a sitting president.

And so passed the most splendid era of American political leadership since the Founding. From the 1930s to the 1960s, it was the era not only of great Democratic presidents, but of brilliant *collective* leadership. Generations of committed, creative reformers reached from the West Wing of the White House through the departments and agencies down to the grass roots, to the well of that great leadership, the tens of millions of citizens who put them into office and kept them there.

SINCE THAT TIME, the party of Dwight Eisenhower has become the party of Ronald Reagan and Bush II. For decades, conservatives had been the extremist wing of a party dominated by go-along, "bipartisan" compromisers.

Now they were no longer the Republican wing of the Republican party—they *were* the Republican party. They were the victorious heirs of those who had fought the lonely battles against all-conquering "radical" Democrats. They could boast too that their early promotion of college political clubs, think tanks, conservative associations, and right-wing magazines and books was now paying off at the polls. Once treated as outsiders, hard-core conservatives now were the heart, the base, of *their* party.

Through decades of Democratic political domination, the Republicans had struggled with a practical question: How break the Democratic grip? In the Reagan era, the GOP made its grand decision—to become the solidly conservative party we know today. It worked. What the GOP base lacked in breadth, it made up for in depth, in fervor and cohesion. Republicans replaced the Democracy as the party of government in part because voters knew where they stood.

And the Democrats? Far more divided than the GOP, they comprised not a base but multiple bases—a liberal base, a centrist base, a labor base, an African American base, and more. Whereas Republicans had largely resolved their differences, the clefts among Democrats had only deepened. Not that Democrats had ignored their internal disunity—for decades they had studied it, debated it, agonized over it. But the dispute remained frustratingly stagnant, a ceaseless debate. It was refreshed each time a new flock of candidates appeared in the primaries to compete for the party's presidential nomination, each touting his or her electability. Where ambitious Republicans had potent incentives to run *with* their party—to exploit its unified base, its organization in depth—the disunity and core weakness of the Democrats encouraged its candidates to run alone, as freelancers piecing together personal electoral coalitions in the hope of breaking through. This made the party's primaries a free-for-all, a bazaar where a half dozen or more candidates bid for specialized fragments of the Democratic electorate. The winner was the candidate who picked up the largest number of pieces, without unifying the party, much less *leading* it.

Lacking the force multiplier of a mobilized, unified base, Democrats played the politics of incremental addition in general election campaigns, casting for available independent or swing voters with opportunistic appeals that bore little resemblance to a coherent party program, scrambling to assemble a transient coalition that would drag them over the November finish line. As Bill Clinton showed twice, running alone could just barely work for a Democrat facing an enfeebled Republican opponent estranged from his own party's base. More often, though, running alone not only ended in defeat, but also reinforced the party's disunity, exposing the weakness at its core and reviving the furious debate between centrists and liberals over its "soul."

Such division is not a new predicament for Democrats. During most of the nineteenth century, the party was divided between its Northern and Southern wings. Later, the conflict between Roosevelt progressives and anti–New Deal conservatives reached a dramatic climax in 1938 when FDR tried to purge reactionary Southern Democrats from the party—and failed. Even so, the power of the New Deal's ideas and of the electoral coalition that united behind them ensured that for several decades the party—and the nation's politics—were dominated by a broad liberal consensus.

The struggle for the "soul" of the Democratic party was reignited with the shattering of that consensus in the late 1960s and came to a head in the early 1990s after Ronald Reagan had won twice and his less glamorous successor, George H. W. Bush, seemed headed to a second term. In 1992, a group of political scientists issued a manifesto, "The Democrats Must Lead," calling for a party that would take strong stands, respond to the needs of women and African Americans, push for more economic and social equality, and "dump Dixie." Instead, Bill Clinton of Arkansas and of the Democratic Leadership Council took over, and rather than revitalize the party, his centrist presidency, in the liberals' view, helped precipitate the two terms of Bush II.

Since Hillary Clinton had for years backed a strong liberal agenda, especially on health care and other social questions, I wondered about her view of her husband's centrist policies, his weaving between right and left. I interviewed her in the East Wing in the last year of his presidency. While stoutly defending the Clinton program in general, she acknowledged that it had been pieced together and that the individual pieces didn't "appear to be related in any thematic way." Still, she insisted, they were part of a larger whole, an effort to give Americans "some reason once again to feel connected to their government." Bill, she told me, "has tried to take positions that were reasonable and prudent and progressive all at the same time." Despite her defense of her husband's centrism, I came away from the interview with the impression, as I wrote at the time with my coauthor Georgia Sorenson, that Hillary was a potential transforming leader dedicated to real change. Clearly by 1999 she was making plans for her own career in electoral politics. Yet she was unable or unwilling to lay out a comprehensive Democratic strategy.

Nor apparently did Hillary Clinton fully recognize what Democrats historically—and Republican conservatives in her own time—had shown, that the most powerful connection people could feel to their government was through a political party that expressed their needs and values and sought political power in order to act in their interests. People felt *dis*connected to government in large measure because they were unconnected to a political party. Tens of millions of Americans were so alienated that they failed to make the simplest, most fundamental connection to their political leaders. They failed to vote.

NONVOTING AT the presidential level today produces an astonishing outcome: After a typically close contest, the winner might be the choice of barely a quarter of the American electorate. The president who speaks sonorously for the whole nation has actually been empowered by a distinct minority. In effect, recent presidents have been running alone, unconnected electorally with the vast majority of the people.

Realistic analysis of nonvoting in America is inevitably depressing and baffling. Why, for example, do so many poor people typically fail to use their vote for their own self-interest, to choose the one leader who is certain to affect their fates and fortunes? The stark fact is that since 1960 voting turnout has fallen in nearly every presidential election, and the rate of turnout at the bottom of the income scale has averaged half that at the top—a differential, political scientist Thomas E. Patterson noted, that "was unheard of in Europe but found also in some less-developed democracies, including India." Even in 2004, when both parties made massive exertions to get their voters to the polls, turnout—though the highest since 1968—still barely scratched 55 percent of Americans of voting age. Turnout falls to even lower levels in congressional races, and lower still for state and local races. Do I sound preachy? Full disclosure: I'm sometimes one of the no-shows in town elections even when I may know personally candidate Mary or Bill or Sally.

Democrats confront an electoral system that is both anti-democratic and anti-Democratic. That system, which distorts and weakens government, is one of the most backward and ineffective among the great democracies. This is not a big problem for the Republicans. Skillful at targeting their mobilization efforts at their own base, they are beneficiaries of a system that depresses broader turnout, and philosophically they don't believe in government anyway. But Democrats for a century or more have pinned their hopes on a strong and effective public leadership backed by the large and wide mass of Americans.

The American electoral system has been so much criticized from the top down that it might be more useful to reappraise it at the grass roots. Consider Minnesotan Steven Schier, voting in his local precinct on November 7, 2000. As a good citizen, Schier had read up on the local, state, and national races in the weeks before election day. He felt well prepared to vote. "Once I received my ballot, though," he wrote, "I discovered I was supposed to cast some twenty-six votes. I was ready to cast my vote for president, congressional offices, and the state legislature, but I was also asked to vote on local soil and water commissioners, on whether or not to retain several state judges, and on several local tax issues." He could recall nothing in the press about these lesser questions and contests. And Schier was not only a good citizen. He was a political scientist whose special field was electoral politics.

Comparing it to electoral contests in other democracies, Schier called the American electoral system uniquely, "baroquely" complicated, producing turnout that was among the lowest in the world. Other analysts were less kind, especially after the 2000 election was decided not by the millions of Americans who like Schier overcame the electoral system's myriad discouragements to voting and cast their ballots on November 7, but by the votes weeks later of five Supreme Court justices who rendered one of the most nakedly partisan decisions in the Court's long history. These analysts saw America politically as a banana republic writ large.

BUT THE MAIN reason for nonvoting is far more basic and portentous. *People don't vote because they don't care.* These tens of millions of nonvoters don't care because they don't see that political leaders care about *them*, their wants and needs. They don't think they can do anything about that. They don't see that their vote will make a difference to their lives. They did care in the 1930s and 1940s and 1950s and 1960s because FDR versus Alf Landon and Truman versus Tom Dewey and Johnson versus Goldwater offered fundamentally different kinds of leadership, compared, say, to Ford versus Carter or Clinton versus Dole. This is true at the grassroots level as well. During the civil rights struggle of the 1960s, African American registration in the South more than doubled, because blacks had struggled for the right to vote and they knew the huge stakes involved. In response, Southern whites flocked to the polls because they too recognized the stakes.

Scholars have found that nonvoting is part of a much broader social phenomenon. Tocqueville's America was a nation of joiners "forever forming associations"—eager participants in every sort of civic activity, solemn or silly. But an epic study by Harvard political scientist Robert Putnam and colleagues, *Bowling Alone*, published in 2000, showed that this is no longer the case. The study showed a startling drop in participation not only in politics but also in churches and charities, neighborhood associations and broad social movements—even in bowling groups. More and more, Americans have become unlinked from one another.

The withdrawal of Americans from politics is the gravest disconnect, weakening the impact of citizens on the life-and-death decisions of their government. Putnam found political activity in decline across the board. People don't sign petitions or write letters to members of Congress or editors, attend public meetings or rallies or join committees, as they did only two decades ago. As millions of potential followers have dropped out, the well of leadership has dried up at the grass roots. Politics has become a spectacle, something to be watched, not practiced. At the same time—and as a result—political leaders have become less accountable. They too are disconnected. Resting on their narrow bases of support, they can in effect run and govern alone, with little fear of being held responsible at the ballot box by an indifferent or disengaged citizenry. All this has bred a vicious circle: As people grow uninvolved, they feel less able to influence decisionmaking; with that loss of self-efficacy, their alienation, mistrust, and cynicism deepen.

A major cause of this drastic decline in political participation is the absence of strong party identity, of clear-cut conflict—"us" versus "them."

Listen to the analysts of voting. In his *Vanishing Voter*, Thomas Patterson offers the results of a recent survey that compares beliefs about politics to voting intentions. The leading discouragement to voting is the belief that "Parties are alike." Other ideas that inhibit voting include "Politics is complicated" and "Candidates say anything to get elected." And, Patterson notes, such beliefs stop people not only from voting but from paying any attention at all to politics.

If, in the era of the highly ideological, polarizing Bush II Republicans, tens of millions of Americans don't vote because they see no crucial choice between the parties that will have an effect on their lives, it is because Democrats are not offering them that choice. They are not rising to meet the Republican challenge squarely.

The Democratic party today is stranded. Faced with the hard question that haunted Republicans for decades—how weaken the opposition's grip on power—Democrats remain deadlocked between centrists who would blur their differences with conservatives and progressives who would intensify them. The party needs to mobilize millions of potential voters but cannot do so for lack of a powerful appeal to them.

If Democrats are to recover their leadership, the party must *un*complicate politics. It must *say something*, take a clear, fighting progressive direction, connect elections with people's lives so that the middle class and the working class and the poor vote for their true self-interest. This in turn will call for the party to make up its own mind and reject centrist programs and strategies. On the overriding questions facing the electorate, from social reform and economic equality at home to war and peace and trade abroad, centrists want to compromise at the start, in the very way they pitch their policies. But concessions should come at the end game, not before the battle is even joined. Democrats must rise above positioning and tactics to a clear and dramatic choice between conservative and liberal action based on explicit values. Political commentator E. J. Dionne Jr. has presented Democrats with a liberal's marching orders—*Stand up, fight back.*

THE TRANSCENDING issue of the twentieth century—from Theodore Roosevelt and Woodrow Wilson to FDR and LBJ and beyond—was persistent economic and social inequality. And on this issue the Democrats have had a decisive advantage, not only in rhetoric and policy but also in *results*. Larry Bartels, at Princeton's Woodrow Wilson School, has shown that under Democratic presidents, 1948 to 2001, income growth was "fairly egalitarian," but that "middle class and poor families have fared markedly worse, on average, under Republican presidents." Under the GOP in that period, working poor people had less than a quarter of the real income growth they saw under Democrats. Under Bill Clinton, the proportion of Americans living in poverty dropped every year. Under George Bush II, it rose every year.

And economic inequality means political inequality. The poor are poor in political as well as economic resources. As Yale political scientist Jacob Hacker has pointed out, in recent years the class divide in political participation and clout has hardened, meaning "a substantial decline in the responsiveness of political elites to citizens of modest economic means."

But what is the Democratic strategy for mobilizing those voters who would appear to have a stake in liberal, egalitarian programs? How overcome their exclusion and alienation from the political process? What has happened to *class* politics? Old-timers can remember Republican denunciations of FDR for his "demagogic" appeals to the "forgotten man." But would class politics work in twenty-first-century America? With the decline of union labor—that old Democratic bastion—ancient class lines have blurred. At the same time, inequalities are deepening and the old promise of opportunity for *all* Americans has crumbled. Millions of middle-class people have lost the hope of upward mobility and struggle just to stay in place. Meanwhile, the number of working poor—people whose jobs pay them so little that they can scarcely support their families, even as the social safety net shrinks beneath them—has grown astronomically.

Socially and economically, Americans already are polarized along various lines of division—above all, the widening income gap. Politically, they are not yet polarized. They await Rooseveltian leadership that will offer them a real choice—a choice not, as FDR said scornfully, between Tweedledum and Tweedledee, but between contrasting leaderships, conflicting values, alternative futures.

To explain American politics to my children, I would use a term they understood well—*team*. A liberal Democratic party team competed with a conservative Republican team to win the top prize, the presidency. This meant that teamwork *within* each party was crucial. You had to work together to beat the other guy, whether on the football field or on the battlefield.

Later on, my children found this analogy more confusing than helpful. The parties appeared more like arenas of every-man-for-himself conflict than unified attackers of a common enemy. Often, factions within each party warred with one another more than with the opposition party. Executives—presidents and governors—jousted with legislators—members of Congress and state legislatures—fighting institutional battles regardless of party. These conflicts were obviously built into our constitutional checks and balances, but they certainly did not encourage teamwork. Also, and annoyingly, the inter-party conflict—indeed, *all* conflict—would suddenly come to a stop when a big threat burst on people—for instance, a war. Well, I explained lamely to my children, that was like a baseball or soccer game being called because of an approaching storm.

Of all the metaphors for American politics, I still consider sports the most useful. The reason is simple: Conflict is as essential to politics as competition is to athletics. It is conflict, not concord, between opposing parties that lies at the heart of democracy—that vitalizes issues, excites people, mobilizes them at the ballot booth, accustoms them to the agony of losing as well as to the thrill of victory. The lack of such direct party combat lowers the incentive of parties to build broad and cohesive platforms and programs, while it encourages politicians to construct their own campaign organizations separate from the party effort, to narrowcast their appeals in pursuit of personal electoral coalitions. This personalism is in stark contrast with the party teamwork and campaign discipline exhibited early in the Bush II presidency.

The Republican right today understands the power of conflict. Even now, as the party of government, conservatives retain an aggressive edge from their origins as the embattled fringe of the GOP. The right-wing team waged uncompromising war against the Republican establishment, just as they fight without quarter now to keep and extend their hold on the government.

Yet there is a long tradition among politicians and editorial writers to deplore conflict, to prate piously about the need for consensus, for "rising above party." Scholars are no different. They study conflict mainly to learn how it can be avoided. Historians tend to treat conflicts as aberrations from an equilibrious norm, even while dwelling on the great transformational moments when political leaders *disagreed* passionately—when Jefferson and Madison built the first opposition political party to the outrage of the Federalists, when Lincoln refused to appease Southern secessionists, when FDR denounced "economic royalists" and cried out to a roaring crowd of Democrats, "They are unanimous in their hate for me—and I welcome their hatred!"

If conflict and controversy are the very lifeblood of democracy, the motive force for change, if polarization offers a meaningful choice between parties, mobilizes an engaged citizenry and brings more voters to the polls, how explain the endless calls for political harmony and consensus? How explain the appeals for a bipartisanship in foreign policy that would cut voters out from the nation's most crucial, life-and-death decisions? Brazenly partisan Bush II Republicans appear to be unbothered by such questions; they simply stake out their right-wing positions. Polarization leaves Democrats more in a quandary, because historically and philosophically the liberal idea has been for tolerance, reciprocity, "seeing the other side." In politics, though, should not liberals lean more toward the simple proposition embraced by FDR that people deserve a real choice between leaders and between policies that shape the future of their nation?

Today, after years in the political wilderness, the Democrats must take their stand. But the question is not simply moving to the left. The question is how party ideology will affect voting turnout and decisions, how adopting a comprehensive, controversial, and strongly progressive program will generate support at the grass roots that will build the party over the long run. Turnout and tenets are intertwined. Can the Democrats dig out their potential liberal vote as effectively as the GOP has mobilized its evangelicals and other conservatives? If so, the enlarging liberal vote will pull the Democrats to the left, just as the Southern voters pulled the GOP to the right.

But to accomplish that, Democrats must do even more than offer clear alternatives to the Bush Republicans. That alone will not deepen their base. They must reach the millions of Americans turned off by politics and reengage them, mobilize them to vote their own interests. Republicans, to pull out their vote, have relied mainly on money and right-wing interest groups.

The Democrats must exploit their own most potent tool, a "people" weapon—face-to-face appeals to families in their homes, followed by a get-out-the-vote effort bigger than any that the party has conducted in the past half century. It will require establishing or revitalizing tens of thousands of town and precinct committees to empower campaign efforts. It will mean keeping party activists active—involved in planning strategy, holding rallies, setting up storefronts, passing out leaflets, registering voters—*between* campaigns.

All this can be hard work, but it also can be fun. I remember riding in an open campaign car on election day in Boston, at the end of John Kennedy's 1952 Senate race. As we approached the three-deckers, someone in the car would call up to Mary or Agnes on the porch, "Have ye voted?" Sure. "What about Susan?" She already had. "And brother Mike?" He was at work. "We'll send over a car to get him to the polls on time." At the end of the day, I think we in the car felt happier to be active at the grass roots than we would have in the corridors of power.

Chapter
9

EMPOWERING
FOLLOWERS

History is written by the survivors, it is said. Actually, for better or worse, it is written by historians. The scholars not only narrate— they rate. Presidents have been special victims, at least since Harvard history professor Arthur Schlesinger Sr. initiated a presidential-ranking poll decades ago. His son, Arthur Schlesinger Jr., updated the survey in 1996. The verdict of his thirty-two-member jury on most of the presidents we have discussed was harsh. After rating FDR "great" and Truman "near great," the scholars graded Eisenhower, Kennedy, and Johnson as merely "above average"; Ford, Carter, Reagan, Bush I, and Clinton as "below average"; and Nixon as a flat "failure." Surely they would rate Bush II today, fairly or not, as another failure. Still, as Schlesinger Jr. warned, reputations, especially for recent presidents, wax and wane.

Meanwhile, presidents rate the raters. "How the hell can they know?," JFK demanded, after he himself was invited in 1962 to join in ranking his predecessors. "They've never had to sit here, reading all the cables, listening to people all day about these problems."

In my view, historians have been too critical of recent presidents. Kennedy was right: Scholars have little grasp of the complexity of the hour-to-hour problems that stream into the White House. But the problem is

189

deeper—it is institutional. "Expectations of what a president can accomplish have escalated dramatically," wrote David Gergen, who worked with several presidents, "while his capacity for action has diminished even more." And why is that? I believe it is because American political leaders are trying to govern through an eighteenth-century constitution that frustrates collective action and diffuses accountability.

Under a system that meticulously divides and fragments power and responsibility, transforming leadership has been extraordinarily difficult, except in crises such as war or economic calamity. And while the institutional stalemates remain the same, the demands facing government have accelerated. The incremental changes presidents and legislators make through transactional leadership is inadequate to the ever-rising flood of dire problems.

Contrast the American system with majority rule in Britain. The British government is formed by one nationwide election empowering the majority party. Because the executive and the legislature are united, with the Cabinet created by the parliamentary majority, the governing party has the power to lead, to pass measures drawn from the explicit party platform voters endorsed in the election. The prime minister and his Cabinet work as a team with their party in the Commons to lead the country. The government is strictly accountable to Parliament. It falls if it loses a vote of confidence. Then a new election typically is called, bringing both the governing party and the opposition to account before the voters. The British have plenty of problems in their politics, but leadership that is both empowered and accountable is not one of them.

The American system was created by a group of men who feared the tyranny of popular majorities as much as unchecked monarchical power. They diffused the popular will through staggered elections of public officials responsible to different and often competing constituencies. Our system has one president elected every four years, plus several hundred representatives elected every two years, plus one hundred senators elected every six years from vastly different-sized populations. Then there is a powerful judiciary with lifetime tenures, nominated by successive presidents over decades. Each of these occupies a separate niche in the structure of government. Each has its powers checked and balanced by the others. Parties evolved quickly after the Founding in an effort to bring some unity to divided government as the Framers planned it. Party government American-style had some success in overcoming obstacles to action. But as the parties have weakened, divided government has had consequences the Framers didn't plan—frequent stalemates, crises of inaction, crucial legislation stalled for decades.

ONCE UPON a time—actually, twice upon a time—American leaders took a long, hard look at the existing governmental system and proposed major institutional changes. This happened in the 1780s when the Framers of the Constitution, viewing the existing Articles of Confederation as weak and ineffective, revolutionized that system by establishing strong national institutions at the top. It happened again in the 1980s, when some American leaders prepared to celebrate the Constitution's bicentennial by proposing major changes to bring it up to date. They created the CCS—the Committee on the Constitutional System.

If the reformers in 1987 could hardly measure up to the geniuses of 1787, the CCS was still an impressive group. The three cochairpersons of the committee were Establishment people—Lloyd Cutler, a distinguished lawyer and adviser to presidents; Nancy Landon Kassebaum, a Republican senator from Kansas and daughter of FDR's 1936 presidential opponent; and C. Douglas Dillon, JFK's secretary of the Treasury. The committee they chaired included seven former members of the Senate or House, two ex-governors, and a bevy of lawyers, academics, and other experts. After much deliberation, committee members proposed a variety of institutional changes, focusing on ways to bridge the gap between Congress and the presidency in order to undergird governmental teamwork and collective leadership. They even discussed holding a new convention to amend the Constitution, as authorized by its own Article Five.

The impact of the 1787 convention? A transformation of government. The result of the 1987 committee? Practically zero. The media provided some coverage; good-government groups such as the League of Women Voters held discussions; the public as a whole ignored the committee and its works. Congress, of course, took no action—why should beneficiaries of the existing system opt to change it? One CCS proposal, a constitutional amendment to abolish the electoral college, did win the support of fifty-one senators, but that was well short of the two-thirds required for submission to the states for ratification.

Popular interest in the electoral college shot up after the 2000 election debacle. Suddenly, concern over this anachronistic institution was not academic. In some future election, a party that wins the popular vote by hundreds of thousands but loses the election may not be as amenable to defeat as the Democrats were in 2000. In 2004, George Bush II beat John Kerry by 3 million votes nationally, but a swing of only 60,000 ballots in Ohio, out of almost 6 million cast in the state, would have lost Bush the electoral college and his presidency.

Apart from the prospect of disaster, the electoral college has an unfortunate impact on leadership. It encourages campaigns to pour resources into a handful of "battleground" states where the competition for crucial electoral votes is fiercest and to ignore the rest of the country, allowing a candidate to win—and hence to govern—with a very narrow base. The people, at least, believe in simple majority rule when it comes to presidential elections. For decades, polls have shown strong support—margins as high as four to one—for direct popular election of the president, a change that would ground presidential leadership in a wider voting base.

The other needed constitutional change considered by the CCS is more radical—the "team ticket." Candidates for the presidency, Senate, and House would run together on party slates, just as the president and vice president presently do. Voters would cast their ballots for these slates, not individual candidates. Such an amendment would discourage politicians from running alone, apart from their parties. Candidates for both executive and legislative offices would have to cooperate in shaping a united campaign strategy and platform. Even more, because presidents and members of Congress would stand or fall together at the polls, they would be compelled to govern together. Each would be interested in the success of the other and in the achievement of their common goals.

A more modest proposal simply would align presidential and congressional elections. Both senators and members of the House would have four-year terms concurrent with the president's. The midterm election, which historically has almost always caused the president to lose support in Congress and increased the chances of deadlock, would be abolished. The present two-year term for House members has become anachronistic, "too brief for the public good," said one who knew, Lyndon Johnson, in 1966. A longer term for representatives and the abolition of off-year elections would lengthen the political horizons of both president and Congress and open a wider window of opportunity for action. And while it would not promote party cohesion as aggressively as the team ticket, synchronization of elections would create stronger incentives for party-wide cooperation than now exist.

Under the aligning proposal, the president would still have a four-year term, but he would be eligible to run repeatedly, like congressional candidates. The 1787 convention first voted that presidents could be elected for only a single term, but delegates argued that "he who has proved himself to be most fit for Office, ought not to be excluded by the constitution from holding it." The post–World War II Republican Congress disagreed, retrospectively defeating the four-term FDR by initiating the amendment that bars *third* terms. This was probably the most feckless amendment passed in modern times. It hands a newly reelected president, who has just received from voters the finest stamp of approval such a leader can have, advance notice of the walking papers he will be given at the end of his second term, no matter how successful. As an instant lame duck, the president for four years becomes less accountable to the public—he faces no accountability at the ballot box—and loses influence with Congress. "One of the strengths of the presidency is that the fellow will be around tomorrow and remember," a close Reagan adviser said. "The threat of running again and being reelected is about the only party discipline we have in this country." In Reagan's first term, Republicans in Congress voted with him almost three-quarters of the time, but in his last two, lame-duck years, support for the president from his own party dropped to 45 percent. Second terms are rarely occasions for leadership.

WHY, WITH all its failings—misrepresentation of the people, pulverized leadership, shameful voter turnout, failure to come to grips with long-festering problems—has the American political system survived virtually intact? Why have the people not junked it, as the American and French revolutionaries abolished their old regimes? (Of course, the Southern Confederates did try.) The answer in part lies in people's ingenuity in making the most fragmented government work, at least for a time. Most American politicians are superb horse traders, fixers, adjusters, dealers—they are brilliant transactional leaders in a system that encourages that kind of leadership.

But at least since the time of Franklin Roosevelt, Americans have come to expect more from their presidents, from the only leaders elected by the whole nation, leaders who operate from the widest political base, with all the legitimacy that base offers. They have come to expect the transforming leadership that John Kennedy and virtually every one of his successors promised but mostly failed to deliver—leadership that mobilizes Congress and the country to achieve deep and enduring change for the common good. Presidents who have run alone and tried to govern alone have been unable to overcome the hobbles and complexities of our constitutional system. Some have sought to evade those restraints by exercising the very power the Framers of the Constitution dreaded: unchecked, unilateral presidential might and authority. For a while, they governed alone with such powers before the hobbles were—often with a vengeance—restored.

In recent decades, scholars have called the American presidency imperial, beleaguered, gutsy, diminished, as well as paradoxical and pragmatic. If these terms reflect uncertainty over the very nature of the office among the most knowledgeable, we can only imagine the confusion at the grass roots and on the cobblestones. We do know that, however checked and balanced, the American presidency at times has been the greatest weapon for the extension of democracy, at other times the greatest potential threat to it. It can be both, but it need not be both. We can amend our institutions to reduce the incentives and temptations for presidents to run alone and govern alone, and instead give them the power to lead *together* with their followers in the government, in the parties, and across the country, together with the people to whom they must ultimately be accountable.

∽

PRESIDENTS AND other political leaders have a special role and advantage in the pursuit of transforming change. Theirs is the power—at least the potential—to set broader goals and mobilize wide support, to make laws and act decisively to achieve those goals. But even as presidents have struggled to satisfy the high expectations they have created, leaders outside Washington have made their own changes. Throughout American history, such leaders have transformed the country without oratory or big promises—inventors, investors, industrialists, unionists, developers, mayors, city planners, even teachers and writers. Political and governmental leaders historically have sought to regulate these changes, with mixed results. Even more consequential—and still less subject to political control—were other leaders, leaders at the grass roots, people who perhaps would scarcely think of themselves as leaders, but who, pursuing their own goals in the American spirit of individualism, transformed their country. Such were the people in motion, those "voting with their feet"—tens of millions of immigrants streaming into the United States from all points of the compass, tens of millions of migrants moving across the continent looking for better opportunities.

It is important to see transforming leadership in this light—reaching through society, across endeavors of all sorts, practiced by people acting individually and collectively—to avoid defining it as simply the work of those at the top of government. If political leaders often fail to bring about major changes, it is usually because they are only part of the action.

The immigrants and migrants, the militant workers and African Americans, the disfranchised women and the enterprising businessmen who transformed America were not only pursuing their individual hopes and interests. They were seeking the freedoms symbolized by the Statue of Liberty in New York Harbor, the freedoms promised by Jefferson and Lincoln and the Roosevelts, the freedoms proclaimed by the Bill of Rights. What do we call these broader ideas and ideals that have guided followers as well as leaders—doctrines, philosophies, creeds? The fashionable word in recent years has been "values." We were even told after the presidential election of 2004 that "values"—whether conservative moral affirmations or liberal concerns about economic justice and peace—had been the motivating factor in the choice of at least 20 percent of the voters.

Critics quickly leaped on these claims. Most voters hardly knew the word or its meaning, they said. Indeed, critics claimed, Americans had no set of ordered ideas or doctrines. All they had were grab bags of ideas, hodgepodges of likes and dislikes, shifting dogmas and prejudices. Least of all did they have a basic system of ideas, or a transcending ideology, or an enduring national creed.

I have long dissented from this bleak outlook. I believe that Americans have an ordered array of potent values stemming originally and directly from the Western Enlightenment. Analyzing this intellectual and moral powerhouse of ideas that dominated the seventeenth and eighteenth centuries, I have found transcending values that relate closely to people's wants and needs, their fears and aspirations, ideas that influence people's everyday lives and politics. These are not exotic ideas but human beliefs that for centuries have motivated leaders and followers who had only the vaguest notions that they were children of the Enlightenment.

These reigning ideas of the West were superbly articulated and ordered by Thomas Jefferson in the Declaration of Independence. This revolutionary proclamation laid out a set of priorities, brilliantly summarized in the phrase, "Life, Liberty, and the pursuit of Happiness." *Life* must come first, the sheer survival of a people and a nation without which the other two values cannot have meaning. That—saving the Union—was what Lincoln put ahead of the emancipation of slaves, which he delayed until long after the start of the Civil War. But *Liberty*, crowding next to Life, is the supreme moral declaration of the Declaration. Anyone reading through American history must be struck by the constant appeal to liberty, from Patrick Henry's unforgettable "Give me liberty or give me death" to Franklin Roosevelt's Four Freedoms. The *pursuit of Happiness*? This is a more ambiguous term, Jefferson's most distinctive contribution to the Declaration. He had planted the clue to its meaning a few words earlier in the Declaration: "All men are created equal."

These are not separate concepts, like beads on a string. Each modifies the others. Life, as order or security, cannot be pursued to a degree that jeopardizes liberty. Liberty in turn must not be threatened by an egalitarianism that would ignore the needs and nature of a diverse humankind. Jefferson himself embodied the interaction, the balances and imbalances, even the tensions, in the Declaration's famous trinity. As a revolutionary struggling to create a new nation dedicated to freedom, he knew that his weak little country had to be secured against aggression by the big powers. But as a libertarian, he fought John Adams's repressive Alien and Sedition Acts. And as an egalitarian, he held the "greatest degree of happiness possible" for "the general mass" of people to be the "only orthodox object" of government. When serving as American minister in Paris, he urged Americans touring France to step into the hovels of the poor and look into their larders, check the comfort of their beds—to inquire into their happiness.

Seen in this light, the Declaration is not a tidy assemblage of agreed-on ideas. It is a declaration of rational conflict that has raged through two centuries and more of American history. In 1941, Franklin Roosevelt superbly reframed Jefferson's trinity—and the conflicts over its meaning—with a declaration of Four Freedoms. To the liberties of speech and conscience, FDR added the freedom from fear—Jefferson's "Life"—and the freedom from want—Jefferson's egalitarian "pursuit of Happiness." Three years later, Roosevelt went further, charting a "second Bill of Rights" that included economic rights to jobs and fair wages, to decent housing and medical care—all to advance "new goals of human happiness and well-being." Democrats since Roosevelt have embraced his expansive concept of freedom. Like FDR, John Kennedy saw that freedom was woven in with the other values of Jefferson's trinity, that the battle to secure and expand it was a hard fight for people's independence and self-determination, a war against fear and insecurity, poverty and illiteracy, homelessness and hopelessness. Yet JFK confidently foresaw freedom's ultimate triumph. The wave of the future, he said, was "the liberation of the diverse energies of free nations and free men."

Of course, Democrats hold no monopoly on the definition of freedom. Conservative Republicans believe in it too. But whereas to liberals, government has an active role in preserving and widening freedom—ensuring economic security and genuine equality of opportunity for all, regulating private power in the public interest—for conservatives, government is the main threat to liberty—to the freedom of the individual, to private initiative and enterprise. With these fundamentally contrasting visions of the good society, the ideological stage is set for a rational and continuing conflict between the individualistic, free-market liberty of conservatives and the collective freedom that Roosevelt and his followers fought for.

BY KEEPING faith with their values with tax cuts for the rich, cutbacks in services for the middle class and the poor, and promises to destroy programs that provide a minimum of security to the ill and the aged, Bush Republicans have created a new class—potentially a new majority—of forgotten men and women. Can Democrats—keeping faith with *their* values—reach them?

In its essence, leadership is the mobilization of followers who become leaders, an empowering process inspired and tested by transcending values. To mobilize these forgotten Americans—to overcome the class divide that has excluded them from political power—Democrats must modernize and sharpen the durable economic issues of old: jobs, wages, education, women's rights, health. But more than that, they must send a strong, overarching message, with policy proposals set in a larger frame of liberal values, a true *party* program that would mark a commitment by Democrats to these potential followers. They must *run together* on a party platform; they must *govern together* on a party agenda. Only by running together with them can Democrats empower those whose voices have been unheard, those whose needs have been ignored.

We hear much about the needs and values of political leaders because they talk constantly about themselves. We typically know about *followers'* needs and values only indirectly, from polling and elections. This is another form of political inequality: Politicians' views are loud and clear, those of followers muted and murky. To run together means that leaders will hear the needs, the grievances and aspirations, of followers, and, articulating them in a framework of liberal values, use them as the basis for collective political action.

And running together means that the leadership leaders offer meets followers' expectations. Americans, a recent study has shown, want leaders who are forward-looking—steering a definite course, alert to where they are headed. They look to leaders for inspiration, and of course for the competence required to pursue their aims effectively. More than anything else—and significantly—Americans want *honesty* in their leaders. They want leaders to make clear where they stand. They want them to speak the truth. They want them to keep their promises. They want leaders who are worthy of their trust.

These qualities do not inevitably relate to people's real needs. Americans are all too familiar with charismatic leaders who promote glittering prospects that have little connection with people's daily lives. Unlike charismatic leadership, running together is a two-way street, a true engagement between leaders and followers working together with a full appreciation of each other's needs. Followers understand when they must push leaders, but also when they should give them leeway, when to demand and when not to demand specific actions and policies. For this, trust is essential.

Running together means, above all, mutual empowerment. Followers empower leaders with their support and loyalty, with actions they take to help leaders achieve their common purpose. And by mobilizing people to participate in political action, leaders help followers overcome feelings of alienation, cynicism, and helplessness. Participation encourages self-efficacy and collective efficacy. Running together means people are no longer running alone—deprived and powerless—but have joined together to create a transforming force. *They* make change and eventually make history.

These vital processes cannot occur in a void. To overcome the obstacles to change—the organized and entrenched defenders of the status quo, the rigidities of the American constitutional system—they must be seated in an institutional frame. In the past, political parties have been the vehicle for the empowerment of workers, farmers, African Americans, immigrants. Do they empower large masses of people today? Only to a modest degree. But given the challenges that confront any effort to achieve real change, they are the only institutional recourse if tens of millions of the unequal and the unempowered are to run together and ultimately to govern together.

AFTERWORD

We cannot, in the predictable future, change our obstructive, old-fashioned constitutional structure. We *can* change our parties, as the Republicans have brilliantly proved. Democrats can do so at the top, at the state level, and, most crucially, at the grass roots. That will depend on the efforts of local activists to mobilize the party's huge potential.

In my town, Tela Zasloff, as a wife, mother, and horsewoman, has enough to keep her busy. But a year ago, she drove volunteers one hundred miles to New Hampshire to do door-to-door canvassing for a candidate. Her candidate won, but she found the campaign's organization inadequate to mobilize even more volunteers. Recently, she has become a *party* activist, helping to reorganize and empower her county committee. In this way, she can help *all* her party's candidates. She finds the work unglamorous, politically daunting, intellectually exciting. Millions more people like her will be needed if Americans are to bring about the transforming leadership and the far-reaching changes that the country so desperately needs.

Bibliography and Notes

CHAPTER 1 — THE TRIBAL THRUST

Michael R. Beschloss, *Kennedy and Roosevelt: The Uneasy Alliance* (W. W. Norton, 1980).

Joan Blair and Clay Blair Jr., *The Search for JFK* (Berkley, 1976).

James MacGregor Burns, *John Kennedy: A Political Profile* (Harcourt, Brace, 1960).

Robert Dallek, *An Unfinished Life: John F. Kennedy, 1917–1963* (Little, Brown, 2003).

Doris Kearns Goodwin, *The Fitzgeralds and the Kennedys* (Simon and Schuster, 1987).

Rose Fitzgerald Kennedy, *Times to Remember* (Doubleday, 1974).

David E. Koskoff, *Joseph P. Kennedy* (Prentice-Hall, 1974).

Thomas Maier, *The Kennedys: America's Emerald Kings* (Basic Books, 2003).

Ralph G. Martin and Ed Plaut, *Front Runner, Dark Horse* (Doubleday, 1960).

Kenneth P. O'Donnell and David F. Powers, *"Johnny, We Hardly Knew Ye": Memories of John Fitzgerald Kennedy* (Little, Brown, 1972), ch. 2.

Herbert S. Parmet, *Jack: The Struggles of John F. Kennedy* (Dial Press, 1980).

Richard J. Whalen, *The Founding Father: The Story of Joseph P. Kennedy* (New American Library, 1964).

7 ["Third rate district"] : author's interview, March 22, 1959, p. 9.

7 ["A lot of that"] : ibid., p. 10.

8 ["Leader who could lead"] : quoted in Koskoff, p. 43.

8 ["Political leader"] : quoted in Cari Beauchamp, "Two Sons, One Destiny," *Vanity Fair*, no. 532 (December 2004), pp. 362–68, 395–99, at p. 366.

8 [Joe Jr.'s presidential ambition] : see Martin and Plaut, p. 125.

9 ["Flair, action"] : quoted in Kennedy, *Times to Remember*, p. 111.

9   ["Played for keeps"] : quoted in Dallek, p. 43.

9   ["Used to have some fights"] : author's interview, March 22, 1959, pp. 2, 9.

9   ["Comparable to the usual"] : ibid., p. 2.

9   ["Away a lot"] : ibid., p. 3.

10 ["Now Jack"] : letter of December 5, 1934, in Amanda Smith, ed., *Hostage to Fortune: The Letters of Joseph P. Kennedy* (Viking, 2001), pp. 146–47, quoted at p. 147; John Kennedy's letter on "bluffing myself," December 2, 1934, in ibid., p. 146.

10 ["You would be surprised"] : letter of August 2, 1940, in ibid., pp. 453–54, quoted at p. 453.

10 ["Great advantage"] : Kennedy, *Why England Slept* (Wilfred Funk, 1940; reprinted, 1961), p. 225.

11 ["You just do nothing"] : author's interview, March 22, 1959, p. 10.

11 ["He felt he didn't have"] : quoted in Koskoff, p. 405.

11 ["Never was a moment"] : "John F. Kennedy Reflects on His Political Career," ca. 1960, Dictabelt Item #39, President's Office Files, Presidential Recordings Collection, John F. Kennedy Library.

12 ["Very nice organization"] : Joseph Russo oral history, June 2, 1964, pp. 2,3, JFKL.

13 ["Kennedy covered"] : quoted in Martin and Plaut, p. 143.

14 ["Tremendous ferment"] : Mark J. Dalton oral history, August 4, 1964, p. 8, JFKL.

14 ["Really and truly"] : John T. Galvin oral history, May 15, 1964, pp. 8, 11, JFKL.

14 ["I think I know"] : quoted in O'Donnell and Powers, p. 54.

15 ["Not doctrinaire"] : Selig S. Harrison, "Kennedy as President," *New Republic*, vol. 142, no. 26 (June 27, 1960), pp. 9–15, quoted at p. 12. Harrison was the *Crimson* reporter.

15 ["Why I Am a Democrat"] : delivered to the Junior League, October 23, 1946, quoted at pp. 6, 7, Pre-Presidential Papers, House Files, Box 94, JFKL.

15 ["Biggest rallies"] : quoted in Martin and Plaut, p. 143.

16 ["Halfbright"] : quoted in Alonzo L. Hamby, *Man of the People: A Life of Harry S. Truman* (Oxford University Press, 1995), p. 386; see also Lee Riley Powell, *J. William Fulbright and His Time* (Guild Bindery Press, 1996), pp. 47–48.

17 [Rayburn and Kennedy] : see Thomas P. O'Neill Jr. oral history, December 6, 1967, pp. 140–41, JFKL.

17 ["Terrible mistake"] : quoted in Koskoff, p. 393.

17 ["Betrayal" of Poland] : see *Congressional Record*, 80th Congress, 2nd Session, vol. 94, part 6 (June 11, 1948), p. 7867; *Boston Herald* headline quoted in Martin and Plaut, p. 148.

18 ["Squarely with the White House"] : *Congressional Record*, 81st Congress, 1st Session, vol. 95, part 1 (January 25, 1949), p. 532.

18 ["What our young men"] : address delivered in Salem, Massachusetts, January 30, 1949, reprinted in ibid., 81st Congress, 1st Session, vol. 95, part 12 (appendix), p. A993.

18 ["Political point"] : quoted in Parmet, p. 208.

18 ["May have something"] : John P. Mallan, "Massachusetts: Liberal and Corrupt," *New Republic*, vol. 127, no. 15 (October 13, 1952), pp. 10–12, quoted at p. 10.

18 ["Interests of my constituents"] : quoted in Martin and Plaut, p. 149.

18 [Kennedy on labor unions] : quoted in Burns, *Political Profile*, p. 77; Martin and Plaut, p. 152.

19 ["Legislative drummer boy"] : quoted in Burns, *Political Profile*, p. 74.

19 ["Leadership of the American Legion"] : *Congressional Record*, 81st Congress, 1st Session, vol. 95, part 3 (March 22, 1949), p. 2950.

19 ["I guess we're gone"] : quoted in O'Donnell and Powers, p. 75.

19 ["I came back from the Service"] : author's interview, March 22, 1959, p. 4.

19 ["I didn't plan"] : quoted in Martin and Plaut, p. 148.

20 ["No town was too small"] : quoted in O'Donnell and Powers, p. 78.

20 ["Long, long, long labor"] : "John F. Kennedy Reflects."

CHAPTER 2 — PUSHING AND SHOVING

Stephen E. Ambrose, *Nixon* (Simon and Schuster, 1987–89), vol. 1, chs. 24–26.

Kent M. Beck, "What Was Liberalism in the 1950s?," *Political Science Quarterly*, vol. 102, no. 2 (Summer 1987), pp. 233–58.

Nick F. Bryant, *The Bystander: John F. Kennedy and the Struggle for Black Equality* (Basic Books, 2006).

David Burner and Thomas R. West, *The Torch Is Passed: The Kennedy Brothers and American Liberalism* (Atheneum, 1984), esp. chs. 2–3.

James MacGregor Burns, *John Kennedy: A Political Profile* (Harcourt, Brace, 1960).

Thomas J. Carty, *A Catholic in the White House?: Religion, Politics, and John F. Kennedy's Presidential Campaign* (Palgrave, 2004).

Robert Dallek, *An Unfinished Life: John F. Kennedy, 1917–1963* (Little, Brown, 2003), chs. 5–8.

Lawrence H. Fuchs, *John F. Kennedy and American Catholicism* (Meredith Press, 1967).

Alonzo L. Hamby, *Liberalism and Its Challengers: From F.D.R. to Bush*, 2nd ed. (Oxford University Press, 1992), ch. 5.

James W. Hilty, *Robert Kennedy, Brother Protector* (Temple University Press, 1997), pp. 67–73, 92–98, and chs. 6–7.

Doris Kearns Goodwin, *The Fitzgeralds and the Kennedys* (Simon and Schuster, 1987).

David E. Koskoff, *Joseph P. Kennedy* (Prentice-Hall, 1974), esp. pp. 402–39.

Joseph P. Lash, *Eleanor: The Years Alone* (W. W. Norton, 1972), ch. 14.

William E. Leuchtenburg, *In the Shadow of FDR: From Harry Truman to George W. Bush*, 3rd ed. (Cornell University Press, 2001), ch. 3.

Edgar Litt, *The Political Cultures of Massachusetts* (M.I.T. Press, 1965).

Thomas Maier, *The Kennedys: America's Emerald Kings* (Basic Books, 2003), part 3.

John Bartlow Martin, *Adlai Stevenson and the World* (Doubleday, 1977), part 1.

Ralph G. Martin and Ed Plaut, *Front Runner, Dark Horse* (Doubleday, 1960).

Christopher Matthews, *Kennedy & Nixon: The Rivalry That Shaped Postwar America* (Simon & Schuster, 1996), esp. chs. 7–14.

Lawrence F. O'Brien, *No Final Victories: A Life in Politics—From John F. Kennedy to Watergate* (Doubleday, 1974), chs. 1–5.

Kenneth P. O'Donnell and David F. Powers, *"Johnny, We Hardly Knew Ye": Memories of John Fitzgerald Kennedy* (Little, Brown, 1972), chs. 3–8.

Herbert S. Parmet, *Jack: The Struggles of John F. Kennedy* (Dial Press, 1980).

Herbert S. Parmet, *JFK: The Presidency of John F. Kennedy* (Dial Press, 1983), chs. 1–2.

Sean J. Savage, *JFK, LBJ, and the Democratic Party* (State University of New York Press, 2004), chs. 1, 3.

Arthur M. Schlesinger Jr., *Kennedy or Nixon: Does It Make Any Difference?* (Macmillan, 1960).

Arthur M. Schlesinger Jr., *Robert Kennedy and His Times* (Ballantine, 1979), pp. 140–47, and ch. 10.

Arthur M. Schlesinger Jr., *A Thousand Days: John F. Kennedy in the White House* (Houghton Mifflin, 1965), chs. 1–3.

Jeff Shesol, *Mutual Contempt: Lyndon Johnson, Robert Kennedy, and the Feud That Defined a Decade* (W. W. Norton, 1997).

Theodore C. Sorensen, *Kennedy* (Harper & Row, 1965), parts 1–2.

James L. Sundquist, *Politics and Policy: The Eisenhower, Kennedy, and Johnson Years* (Brookings Institution, 1968).

Richard J. Whalen, *The Founding Father: The Story of Joseph P. Kennedy* (New American Library, 1964), chs. 23–24.

Thomas J. Whalen, *Kennedy versus Lodge: The 1952 Massachusetts Senate Race* (Northeastern University Press, 2000).

Theodore H. White, *The Making of the President 1960* (Atheneum, 1961).

21 ["When you've beaten him"] : "Pride of the Clan," *Time*, vol. 76, no. 2 (July 11, 1960), pp. 19–23, quoted at p. 22.

21 ["Blueblood" and "greenblood"] : see Burns, *Political Profile*, ch. 6.

22 ["Four-party" combat] : see James MacGregor Burns, *The Deadlock of Democracy: Four-Party Politics in America* (Prentice-Hall, 1963), esp. ch. 8.

22 [Lodge as Republican moderate] : see Lodge, "Does the Republican Party Have a Future?," *Saturday Evening Post*, vol. 221, no. 31 (January 29, 1949), pp. 23, 81–82; Lodge, "Modernize the G.O.P.," *Atlantic*, vol. 185, no. 3 (March 1950), pp. 23–28.

22 ["Personality state"] : Edward J. McCormack oral history, September 25, 1967, p. 3, John F. Kennedy Library.

22 [Kennedy's "popularism"] : Paul F. Healy, "The Senate's Gay Young Bachelor," *Saturday Evening Post*, vol. 225, no. 50 (June 13, 1953), pp. 26–27, 123–29, quoted at p. 127.

23 ["A dirty word"] : Kenneth O'Donnell, quoted in Martin and Plaut, p. 165.

23 ["Ready-made group"] : John J. Droney oral history, November 30, 1964, p. 18, JFKL.

23 ["Screw it up"] : quoted in Schlesinger, *Robert Kennedy*, p. 101.

24 ["Large numbers"] : Robert F. Kennedy oral history, July 20, 1967, vol. 8, p. 655, JFKL.

24 ["I don't want my brother"] : from an account by John E. Powers, quoted in Peter Collier and David Horowitz, *The Kennedys: An American Drama* (Summit, 1984), p. 185.

24 ["Big as City Hall"] : quoted in O'Donnell and Powers, p. 88.

24 ["Don't get me involved"] : ibid.

24 ["Big debacle"] : Robert F. Kennedy oral history, July 20, 1967, vol. 8, p. 649, JFKL.

25 ["If a real Republican"] : "Stenographic Record: Press Conference of Basil Brewer on His Support of Mr. Kennedy," September 25, 1952, "Endorsements:

Basil Brewer" folder, Pre-Presidential Papers, Campaign Files, Senate Campaign 1952, Box 104, JFKL.

25 [SEES CONGRESSMAN] : *Boston Globe*, September 26, 1952, p. 1, "Newsclips: Basil Brewer Support for Kennedy" folder, Pre-Presidential Papers, Campaign Files, Senate Campaign 1952, Box 116, JFKL.

25 ["Not blinded"] : quoted in Whalen, *Kennedy versus Lodge*, p. 123.

25 ["Though I imagine"] : quoted in Kearns Goodwin, p. 765.

25 ["We had to buy"] : remark to Fletcher Knebel, quoted in Dallek, p. 172.

26 ["More for Massachusetts"] : see Burns, *Political Profile*, p. 111.

27 ["Ruining New England"] : *Boston Post*, quoted in Sorensen, p. 59.

27 [Seaway reversal as career turning point] : see ibid.

27 ["Ever going to be bigger"] : Jack L. Bell, quoted in Parmet, *Jack*, p. 271.

27 ["Legitimate needs"] : *Congressional Record*, 83rd Congress, 2nd session, vol. 100, part 1 (January 14, 1954), pp. 238–40, quoted at p. 240.

27 ["Just keep pushing"] : author's interview, n.d. (1959), quoted at pp. 28, 29.

28 ["Natural resentment"] : Thomas P. O'Neill Jr. oral history, December 6, 1967, p. 119, JFKL.

28 ["Nothing in Jack's hopes"] : letter to John McCormack, August 8, 1951, in Amanda Smith, ed., *Hostage to Fortune: The Letters of Joseph P. Kennedy* (Viking, 2001), pp. 656–57, quoted at p. 657.

28 ["Not involving himself"] : Edward J. McCormack oral history, p. 15.

28 ["Political figure of some strength"] : Richard K. Donahue oral history, November 1966, p. 31, JFKL.

28 ["Constructive, vital"] : "The Case Against Burke," attachment to letter from Kennedy to Judge John Fox, May 9, 1956, p. 2, "Burke, William" folder, Pre-Presidential Papers, Senate Files, Box 498, JFKL.

29 ["Firm stand"] : "Burke Shows His Spots" (editorial), *Springfield News*, May 8, 1956, "Massachusetts State Committee Fight, 1956—News clippings" folder, Theodore C. Sorensen Papers, Subject Files 1953–60, Box 12, JFKL.

29 ["It should not"] : letter to Judge John Fox, May 9, 1956.

29 ["Own unfitness"] : "Block Message," Western Union telegram, May 8, 1956, "Burke, William H." folder, Pre-Presidential Papers, Senate Files, Box 533, JFKL.

29 ["But, you see"] : Donahue oral history, November 1966, pp. 34–35.

29 ["Beginning of a new era"] : quoted in O'Donnell and Powers, p. 116.

29 ["Don't get into the gutter"] : ibid., p. 105.

29 ["Honest intention"] : Donahue oral history, November 1966, p. 40.

30 ["Just not a man of action"] : quoted in Schlesinger, *Robert Kennedy*, p. 146; O'Donnell and Powers, p. 126.

30 ["Real hero"] : letter to Dore Schary, August 31, 1956, in Stevenson, *Papers*, Walter Johnson, ed. (Little, Brown, 1972–79), vol. 6, p. 206.

30 ["Blue language"] : O'Donnell and Powers, p. 122.

30 ["Well, Dad"] : quoted in Kearns Goodwin, p. 788.

31 ["Kennedy's adrenal insufficiency"] : Burns, *Political Profile*, p. 159.

31 [Polls on Catholic presidential candidacies] : Carty, p. 53.

32 ["Not comfortable"] : quoted in Healy, p. 127.

32 ["Get as worked up"] : quoted in Martin and Plaut, p. 204.

33 ["Spending oodles"] : John F. Kennedy to Eleanor Roosevelt, letter of December 11, 1958, "Roosevelt, Eleanor" folder, Sorensen Papers, Campaign Files 1953–60, Box 25, JFKL. The rest of their exchange of letters can be found in this folder.

33 ["Dodged the McCarthy issue"] : quoted in Dallek, p. 233.

34 ["Every now and then"] : quoted in White, p. 90.

34 ["What are our problems"] : quoted in O'Donnell and Powers, p. 160.

34 ["Coldest bath"] : Richard K. Donahue oral history, February 2, 1977, p. 21, JFKL.

34 ["Wasn't the country"] : quoted in O'Donnell and Powers, pp. 166–67.

35 ["Wildest, craziest"] : Donahue oral history, November 1966, p. 74.

35 ["Kinetic people"] : letter to Kennedy, August 26, 1960, p. 1, "Schlesinger, Arthur Jr., 4/26/60–1/23/61 + undated" folder, President's Office Files, Special Correspondence, Box 32, JFKL.

35 ["If you do this"] : Jack Conway, quoted in Schlesinger, *Robert Kennedy*, p. 225.

35 ["Worst mistake"] : Kenneth O'Donnell, quoted in O'Donnell and Powers, p. 192.

35 ["Most indecisive"] : quoted in Schlesinger, *Robert Kennedy*, p. 224.

36 ["Old era"] : July 15, 1960, reprinted in Arthur M. Schlesinger Jr., ed., *History of American Presidential Elections, 1789–1968* (Chelsea House, 1971), vol. 4, pp. 3541–45, quoted at pp. 3543, 3544, 3545.

36 ["Not a set of promises"] : ibid., vol. 4, p. 3544.

36 ["Concrete program"] : Sundquist, *Politics and Policy*, p. 415.

36 ["Most outspokenly"] : James L. Sundquist oral history, September 13, 1965, p. 9, JFKL.

37 ["Intellectual and emotional vacuum"] : letter to Kennedy, August 26, 1960, p. 2.

37 ["What Kennedy believes"] : letter to Kennedy, August 30, 1960, p. 2, "Schlesinger, Arthur Jr., 4/26/60–1/23/61 + undated" folder, President's Office Files, Special Correspondence, Box 32, JFKL.

37 ["Don't give a damn"] : "Little Brother Is Watching," *Time*, vol. 76, no. 15 (October 10, 1960), pp. 21–23, 26–27, quoted at p. 22.

38 ["Project double images"] : quoted in Bryant, p. 171.

38 ["Great secret weapon"] : letter to Kennedy, August 30, 1960, p. 2.

39 ["No-good son-of-a-bitch"] : quoted in Dallek, p. 278.

39 ["Here was a man"] : letter to Mary Lasker, August 15, 1960, in Roosevelt, *It Seems To Me: Selected Letters*, Leonard C. Schlup and Donald W. Whisenhunt, eds. (University Press of Kentucky, 2001), pp. 249–51, quoted at pp. 250, 251.

39 ["Utmost tepidity"] : letter to Kennedy, August 30, 1960, p. 1.

40 ["Carry this campaign"] : July 28, 1960, in Schlesinger, *Presidential Elections*, vol. 4, pp. 3549–58, quoted at p. 3551.

40 ["One of the loneliest"] : Ambrose, vol. 1, p. 557.

40 ["Hadn't done anything"] : Robert Finch, quoted in Matthews, p. 147.

40 ["Most significant"] : John W. Self, "The First Debate over the Debates: How Kennedy and Nixon Negotiated the 1960 Presidential Debates," *Presidential Studies Quarterly*, vol. 35, no. 7 (June 2005), pp. 361–75, quoted at p. 361.

41 [Kennedy "jumpers"] : see White, p. 331; Southern senator quoted at ibid.

41 ["When those boys went out"] : "Whistling Through Dixie," *Time*, vol. 76, no. 17 (October 24, 1960), pp. 25–26, quoted at p. 25.

41 ["Not the Catholic candidate"] : September 12, 1960, reprinted in Schlesinger, *Presidential Elections*, vol. 4, pp. 3559–61, quoted at p. 3561.

42 ["Should be accepted"] : quoted in Matthews, p. 143.

42 [Kennedy on 1960s as revolutionary decade] : see "Questionnaire" prepared for use in the 1960 campaign, n.d., p. 2, "Academic Advisory Group" folder, Deirdre Henderson Papers, Box 1, JFKL.

CHAPTER 3 — THE POWER BROKER

Patrick Anderson, *The Presidents' Men* (Doubleday, 1968), ch. 5.

Irving Bernstein, *Promises Kept: John F. Kennedy's New Frontier* (Oxford University Press, 1991).

Michael R. Beschloss, *The Crisis Years: Kennedy and Khrushchev, 1960–1963* (Edward Burlingame/HarperCollins, 1991).

Taylor Branch, *Parting the Waters: America in the King Years, 1954–1963* (Simon and Schuster, 1988).

Carl M. Brauer, *John F. Kennedy and the Second Reconstruction* (Columbia University Press, 1977).

Carl M. Brauer, *Presidential Transitions: Eisenhower Through Reagan* (Oxford University Press, 1986), ch. 2.

Nick Bryant, *The Bystander: John F. Kennedy and the Struggle for Black Equality* (Basic Books, 2006).

David Burner and Thomas R. West, *The Torch Is Passed: The Kennedy Brothers and American Liberalism* (Atheneum, 1984).

James MacGregor Burns, *Congress on Trial: The Legislative Process and the Administrative State* (Harper & Brothers, 1949).

Stewart Burns, *To the Mountaintop: Martin Luther King Jr.'s Sacred Mission to Save America, 1955–1968* (HarperSanFrancisco, 2004).

Thomas E. Cronin, "Presidential Power Revised and Reappraised," *Western Political Quarterly*, vol. 32, no. 4 (December 1979), pp. 381–95.

Robert Dallek, *An Unfinished Life: John F. Kennedy, 1917–1963* (Little, Brown, 2003).

Bruce J. Dierenfield, *Keeper of the Rules: Congressman Howard W. Smith of Virginia* (University Press of Virginia, 1987), esp. ch. 7.

James Farmer, *Lay Bare the Heart* (Arbor House, 1985).

Lawrence Freedman, *Kennedy's Wars: Berlin, Cuba, Laos, and Vietnam* (Oxford University Press, 2000).

Raymond L. Garthoff, *Reflections on the Cuban Missile Crisis*, rev. ed. (Brookings Institution, 1989).

James N. Giglio, *The Presidency of John F. Kennedy* (University Press of Kansas, 1991).

Hugh Davis Graham, *The Civil Rights Era: Origins and Development of National Policy, 1960–1972* (Oxford University Press, 1990).

David Halberstam, *The Best and the Brightest* (Random House, 1972).

Jim F. Heath, *Decade of Disillusionment: The Kennedy-Johnson Years* (Indiana University Press, 1975), chs. 2–5.

Paul R. Henggeler, *The Kennedy Persuasion: The Politics of Style Since JFK* (Ivan R. Dee, 1995).

Roger Hilsman, *To Move a Nation: The Politics of Foreign Policy in the Administration of John F. Kennedy* (Doubleday, 1967).

Arthur N. Holcombe, *The Foundations of the Modern Commonwealth* (Harper & Brothers, 1923).

Arthur N. Holcombe, *Government in a Planned Democracy* (W. W. Norton, 1935).

Arthur N. Holcombe, "The Political Interpretation of History," *American Political Science Review,* vol. 31, no. 1 (February 1937), pp. 1–11.

Arthur N. Holcombe, "Present-Day Characteristics of American Political Parties," in Edward B. Logan, ed., *The American Political Scene* (Harper & Brothers, 1936), pp. 1–52.

Richard Tanner Johnson, *Managing the White House: An Intimate Study of the Presidency* (Harper & Row, 1974), ch. 5.

David Kaiser, *American Tragedy: Kennedy, Johnson, and the Origins of the Vietnam War* (Belknap Press, 2000).

Barbara Kellerman, *The Political Presidency: Practice of Leadership* (Oxford University Press, 1984), ch. 6.

Peter Kornbluh, ed., *Bay of Pigs Declassified: The Secret CIA Report on the Invasion of Cuba* (New Press, 1998).

William E. Leuchtenburg, *In the Shadow of FDR: From Harry Truman to George W. Bush,* 3rd ed. (Cornell University Press, 2001), ch. 3.

John F. Manley, "Presidential Power and White House Lobbying," *Political Science Quarterly,* vol. 93, no. 2 (Summer 1978), pp. 255–75.

Theodore R. Marmor, *The Politics of Medicare,* 2nd ed. (Aldine de Gruyter, 2000).

John Bartlow Martin, *Adlai Stevenson and the World* (Doubleday, 1977), ch. 3.

Allen J. Matusow, *The Unraveling of America: A History of Liberalism in the 1960s* (Harper & Row, 1984), part 1.

Kenneth R. Mayer, *With the Stroke of a Pen: Executive Orders and Presidential Power* (Princeton University Press, 2001), ch. 6.

Bruce Miroff, *Pragmatic Illusions: The Presidential Politics of John F. Kennedy* (David McKay, 1976).

Richard E. Neustadt, "Approaches to Staffing the Presidency: Notes on FDR and JFK," *American Political Science Review,* vol. 57, no. 4 (December 1963), pp. 855–64.

Richard E. Neustadt, "Kennedy in the Presidency: A Premature Appraisal," *Political Science Quarterly,* vol. 79, no. 3 (September 1964), pp. 321–34.

Richard E. Neustadt, *Preparing To Be President: The Memos of Richard E. Neustadt,* Charles O. Jones, ed. (AEI Press, 2000), part 2.

Richard E. Neustadt, *Presidential Power: The Politics of Leadership from FDR to Carter* (Macmillan, 1986).

Lawrence F. O'Brien, *No Final Victories: A Life in Politics—From John F. Kennedy to Watergate* (Doubleday, 1974).

Kenneth P. O'Donnell and David F. Powers, *"Johnny, We Hardly Knew Ye": Memories of John Fitzgerald Kennedy* (Little, Brown, 1972).

Lewis J. Paper, *John F. Kennedy: The Promise & the Performance* (1975; reprinted by Da Capo Press, 1980).

Richard Reeves, *President Kennedy: Profile of Power* (Simon & Schuster, 1993).

James A. Robinson, *The House Rules Committee* (Bobbs-Merrill, 1963).

Sean J. Savage, *JFK, LBJ, and the Democratic Party* (State University of New York Press, 2004).

Arthur M. Schlesinger Jr., *Robert Kennedy and His Times* (Ballantine, 1979).

Arthur M. Schlesinger Jr., *A Thousand Days: John F. Kennedy in the White House* (Houghton Mifflin, 1965).

Robert Y. Shapiro et al., eds., *Presidential Power: Forging the Presidency for the Twenty-First Century* (Columbia University Press, 2000).

Theodore C. Sorensen, *Kennedy* (Harper & Row, 1965).

Mark Stern, *Calculating Visions: Kennedy, Johnson, and Civil Rights* (Rutgers University Press, 1992).

Daniel Stevens, "Public Opinion and Public Policy: The Case of Kennedy and Civil Rights," *Presidential Studies Quarterly*, vol. 32, no. 1 (March 2002), pp. 111–36.

James L. Sundquist, *Politics and Policy: The Eisenhower, Kennedy, and Johnson Years* (Brookings Institution, 1968).

David C. Warner, ed., *Toward New Human Rights: The Social Policies of the Kennedy and Johnson Administrations* (Lyndon B. Johnson School of Public Affairs, 1977).

Harris Wofford, *Of Kennedys and Kings: Making Sense of the Sixties* (Farrar Straus Giroux, 1980).

Peter Wyden, *Bay of Pigs* (Jonathan Cape, 1979).

43 ["Intrinsic power"] : Holcombe, "Political Interpretation," pp. 11, 9, respectively.

43 ["Organize the thought"] : Holcombe, *Government in a Planned Democracy*, p. 22.

44 ["Generating political power"] : ibid., p. 141.

44 ["Challenging, revolutionary"] : "Text of Senator Kennedy's Speech on Presidency at National Press Club Luncheon," *New York Times*, January 15, 1960, p. 14.

44 ["Alone—at the top"] : Speech to the California Democratic Clubs Convention, Fresno, February 12, 1960, in Kennedy, *"Let the Word Go Forth,"* Theodore C. Sorensen, ed. (Laurel, 1991), pp. 23–28, quoted at p. 24.

45 ["More clearly"] : quoted in Joan Meyers, ed., *John Fitzgerald Kennedy. . . . As We Remember Him* (Atheneum, 1965), p. 174.

45 [Note in Kennedy's pocket] : Reeves, p. 18.

45 ["Exercise the fullest powers"] : "Senator Kennedy's Speech on Presidency."

46 ["This one wants that"] : quoted in Reeves, p. 25.

47 ["I spent so much time"] : quoted in O'Donnell and Powers, p. 234.

47 ["Forget who's the President"] : quoted in Thomas J. Schoenbaum, *Waging Peace and War: Dean Rusk in the Truman, Kennedy, and Johnson Years* (Simon and Schuster, 1988), p. 17.

47 ["President alone"] : "Senator Kennedy's Speech on Presidency."

47 ["Fuck him"] : quoted in Dallek, p. 314.

47 ["Few smart Republicans"] : quoted in O'Donnell and Powers, p. 235.

47 ["Call a few"] : ibid.

47 ["Oh, I don't care"] : quoted in Schlesinger, *A Thousand Days*, p. 135.

48 ["I decided"] : Robert F. Kennedy oral history, February 29, 1964, vol. 1, pp. 18, 16, 20, respectively, John F. Kennedy Library.

48 ["When you people stop"] : quoted in Pierre Salinger, *With Kennedy* (Doubleday, 1966), p. 64.

48 ["In the thick of things"] : quoted in Louis W. Koenig, *The Chief Executive* (Harcourt, Brace & World, 1964), p. 174.

48 ["Loyalty to Kennedy"] : Myer Feldman, quoted in Paper, p. 148.

49 ["Curious atmosphere"] : Schlesinger, *A Thousand Days*, p. 250.

50 ["Perfect failure"] : Draper, *Castro's Revolution: Myths and Realities* (Praeger, 1962), p. 59.

50 ["They couldn't believe"] : quoted in O'Donnell and Powers, p. 274.

50 ["Prisoner of events"] : Schlesinger, *A Thousand Days*, p. 256.

50 ["Every day"] : Robert F. Kennedy oral history, April 3, 1964, vol. 2, p. 144, JFKL.

52 ["Battle for minds"] : Special Message to the Congress on Urgent National Needs, May 25, 1961, in Kennedy, *Public Papers* (U. S. Government Printing Office, 1962–64), vol. 1961, pp. 396–406, quoted at p. 397.

52 ["Last resort"] : quoted in Kaiser, p. 113.

53 ["You two did visit"] : quoted in Hilsman, p. 502.

53 ["My God!"] : quoted in Schlesinger, *Robert Kennedy*, p. 770. The friend was Charles Bartlett.

53 ["Cornerstone of the Free World"] : Kennedy, "America's Stake in Vietnam," address to the American Friends of Vietnam, June 1, 1956, reprinted in Wes-

ley R. Fishel, ed., *Vietnam: Anatomy of a Conflict* (F. E. Peacock, 1968), pp. 142–47, quoted at p. 144.

53 ["Pay any price"] : in Kennedy, *Public Papers*, vol. 1961, pp. 1–3, quoted at p. 1.

53 ["Damned everywhere"] : quoted in O'Donnell and Powers, p. 16.

54 ["Long twilight struggle"] : in Kennedy, *Public Papers*, vol. 1961, p. 2; see also Thurston Clarke, *Ask Not: The Inauguration of John F. Kennedy and the Speech That Changed America* (Henry Holt, 2004).

55 [Democratic losses in Congress, 1960] : see Savage, pp. 88–89.

56 ["One domestic subject"] : Sorensen, *Kennedy*, p. 358.

56 ["Special educational need"] : Special Message to the Congress on Education, February 20, 1961, in Kennedy, *Public Papers*, vol. 1961, pp. 107–11, quoted at p. 108.

56 ["No. 1 priority"] : quoted in Kellerman, p. 57.

56 ["Hawk-like vigilance"] : Gerald W. Johnson, "If a Man Has It," *New Republic*, vol. 145, no. 12 (September 18, 1961), p. 11.

57 ["No reason to weaken"] : Annual Message to the Congress on the State of the Union, January 11, 1962, in Kennedy, *Public Papers*, vol. 1962, pp. 5–15, quoted at p. 9.

57 ["Long-predicted crisis"] : Special Message to the Congress on Education, January 29, 1963, in ibid., vol. 1963, pp. 105–16, quoted at p. 110.

57 ["We will probably"] : quoted in Dallek, p. 632.

57 ["Highest priority"] : quoted in Bernstein, p. 255.

58 ["Hippodrome tactics"] : "Politics and Medical Care" (editorial), *New York Times,* May 21, 1962, p. 32.

58 ["President's performance"] : quoted in Sundquist, p. 311.

58 ["Unprecedented"] : Sorensen, *Kennedy*, p. 344.

58 ["Failure then will not be ours"] : quoted in Dallek, p. 586.

58 ["Fighting mood"] : "Senator Kennedy's Speech on Presidency."

59 ["Reasonable President"] : Neustadt, *Presidential Power*, p. 33.

59 ["Not as aggressive"] : quoted in Paper, p. 262.

60 ["He should wait"] : ibid., pp. 241, 242.

60 ["Extra concerned about"] : Robert F. Kennedy oral history, December 4, 1964, vol. 5, pp. 342, 344, JFKL; see also ibid., December 22, 1964, vol. 7, pp. 598–99.

60 ["Immense moral authority"] : Speech to an NAACP Rally, Los Angeles, July 10, 1960, in Kennedy, *"Let the Word Go Forth,"* pp. 183–86, quoted at pp. 184–85.

61 ["By a stroke"] : quoted in Brauer, *Kennedy and the Second Reconstruction*, p. 43.

61 ["A necessity"] : President's News Conference, March 8, 1961, in Kennedy, *Public Papers*, vol. 1961, pp. 152–60, quoted at p. 157.

61 ["Minimal civil rights legislation"] : quoted in Wofford, p. 133.

61 ["Underplayed it"] : Theodore C. Sorensen oral history, May 3, 1964, p. 122, JFKL; see also press conference of November 20, 1962, in Kennedy, *Public Papers*, vol. 1962, pp. 830–38.

62 ["Call it off!"] : quoted in Wofford, p. 153.

62 ["Been cooling off"] : quoted in Farmer, p. 206.

62 ["Mr. President"] : quoted in Branch, p. 518.

63 ["I have almost reached"] : King, *Letter from the Birmingham Jail* (HarperSan-Francisco, 1994), pp. 15, 16.

63 ["Harmful, wasteful"] : Special Message to the Congress on Civil Rights, February 28, 1963, in Kennedy, *Public Papers*, vol. 1963, pp. 221–30, quoted at p. 222.

63 ["Distance still to be traveled"] : Remarks Upon Receiving Civil Rights Commission Report "Freedom to the Free," February 12, 1963, in ibid., vol. 1963, pp. 159–60, quoted at p. 160.

63 ["Create a situation"] : King, p. 7.

63 ["I am not asking"] : quoted in Schlesinger, *A Thousand Days*, p. 959.

63 ["Justifiable needs"] : President's News Conference, May 8, 1963, in Kennedy, *Public Papers*, vol. 1963, pp. 372–79, quoted at p. 372.

64 ["Gonna make race"] : quoted in Marshall Frady, *Wallace* (New American Library, 1975), p. 140.

64 ["Segregation now!"] : ibid., p. 142.

64 ["They'll never reform"] : quoted in Dallek, p. 600.

64 [Kennedy's civil rights "ExComm"] : see Bryant, pp. 399–400.

64 [May 20 meeting] : partial transcript of tape recording, in Jonathan Rosenberg and Zachary Karabell, eds., *Kennedy, Johnson, and the Quest for Justice: The Civil Rights Tapes* (W. W. Norton, 2003), pp. 116–25; and Bryant, pp. 399–402, and sources therein cited.

64 ["Not only to face up to"] : quoted in Dallek, p. 600.

65 ["Now the time has come"] : Radio and Television Address to the American People on Civil Rights, June 11, 1963, in Kennedy, *Public Papers*, vol. 1963, pp. 468–71, quoted at p. 469; Kennedy's proposals to Congress at ibid., pp. 483–94.

65 ["Political swan song"] : Edwin O. Guthman and Jeffrey Shulman, eds., *Robert Kennedy, In His Own Words* (Bantam, 1988), p. 176.

65 ["Got to get it done"] : quoted in Paper, p. 266.

65 ["Serious fight"] : quoted in Schlesinger, *A Thousand Days*, p. 971.

66 ["What's going on"] : Thomas P. O'Neill Jr. oral history, May 8, 1966, pp. 43–46, JFKL.

66 [White House planning meeting for 1964] : see proposed agenda sent by Steve Smith to Robert Kennedy, October 31, 1963, "Democratic National Committee, 1964 Campaign, 7/1963–10/1963" folder, Robert F. Kennedy Papers, Attorney General's Correspondence, Personal 1961–1964, Box 12, JFKL; memorandum from Smith to the president et al., November 13, 1963, "Smith, Stephen" folder, Robert F. Kennedy Papers, Attorney General's Correspondence, General, Box 56, JFKL; O'Donnell and Powers, pp. 386–87.

67 ["As usual"] : quoted in O'Donnell and Powers, p. 386.

67 ["Loyalty oaths"] : "Memorandum on Party Loyalty in the 1964 Convention and Campaign," November 11, 1963, p. 1, "Democratic National Committee, 1964 Campaign, 11/1/63–11/11/63" folder, Robert F. Kennedy Papers, Attorney General's Correspondence, Personal 1961–1964, Box 12, JFKL.

67 ["Reelection of the President"] : Memorandum from Matt Reese to Steve Smith, November 12, 1963, "Democratic National Committee, 1964 Campaign, 11/1/63–11/11/63" folder, Robert F. Kennedy Papers, Attorney General's Correspondence, Personal 1961–1964, Box 12, JFKL.

67 ["Solid gains"] : "U.S. Voting Patterns: JFK's Gains and Losses," n.d., "1964 Re-Election" folder, David F. Powers Papers, Box 27, JFKL.

67 ["Situation in Virginia"] : Memorandum from Steve Smith to Robert Kennedy, November 15, 1963, "Democratic National Committee, 1964 Campaign, Election Data, 11/15/63" folder, Robert F. Kennedy Papers, Attorney General's Correspondence, Personal 1961–1964, Box 12, JFKL.

67 ["Not gotten himself across"] : Robert F. Kennedy oral history, May 14, 1964, vol. 4, p. 313, JFKL.

67 ["Another tough campaign"] : "J. F. K.—On Re-Election," January 1963, "1964 Re-Election" folder, Powers Papers, Box 27, JFKL.

67 ["Easy one"] : Richard K. Donahue oral history, March 8, 1967, p. 115, JFKL.

68 ["Mutual tolerance"] : Commencement Address at American University, June 10, 1963, in Kennedy, *Public Papers*, vol. 1963, pp. 459–64, quoted at p. 461.

69 ["Not you nor anybody"] : quoted in George Tagge, "Political Lookout," *Chicago Tribune*, July 23, 1960, part 5, p. 8. The boss was Chicago mayor Richard Daley.

70 ["Willing to stand up"] : Address at Barnesville, Georgia, August 11, 1938, in Roosevelt, *Public Papers and Addresses,* Samuel I. Rosenman, comp. (Random

House, 1938–50), vol. 7, pp. 463–71, quoted at p. 466; see also Radio Address on Electing Liberals to Public Office, November 4, 1938, in ibid., pp. 584–93.

CHAPTER 4 — JFK AND LBJ: GOVERNING TOGETHER

Bruce E. Altschuler, *LBJ and the Polls* (University of Florida Press, 1990).

Patrick Anderson, *The Presidents' Men* (Doubleday, 1968), ch. 6.

Edward D. Berkowitz, *America's Welfare State: From Roosevelt to Reagan* (Johns Hopkins University Press, 1991).

Larry Berman, *Lyndon Johnson's War: The Road to Stalemate in Vietnam* (W. W. Norton, 1989).

Larry Berman, *Planning a Tragedy: The Americanization of the War in Vietnam* (W. W. Norton, 1982).

Irving Bernstein, *Guns or Butter: The Presidency of Lyndon Johnson* (Oxford University Press, 1996).

James J. Best, "Who Talked to the President When?: A Study of Lyndon B. Johnson," *Political Science Quarterly*, vol. 103, no. 3 (Autumn 1988), pp. 531–45.

Vaughn Davis Bornet, *The Presidency of Lyndon B. Johnson* (University Press of Kansas, 1983).

Nigel Bowles, *The White House and Capitol Hill: The Politics of Presidential Persuasion* (Clarendon Press, 1987).

Mary C. Brennan, *Turning Right in the Sixties: The Conservative Capture of the GOP* (University of North Carolina Press, 1995).

Stewart Burns, *To the Mountaintop: Martin Luther King Jr.'s Sacred Mission to Save America, 1955–1968* (HarperSanFrancisco, 2004).

Joseph A. Califano Jr., *The Triumph & Tragedy of Lyndon Johnson: The White House Years* (Simon & Schuster, 1991).

Francis M. Carney and H. Frank Way Jr., eds., *Politics 1964* (Wadsworth, 1964).

Robert A. Caro, *The Years of Lyndon Johnson* (Alfred A. Knopf, 1982–), vols. 1–3.

Paul K. Conkin, *Big Daddy from the Pedernales: Lyndon Baines Johnson* (Twayne, 1986).

Robert Dallek, *Flawed Giant: Lyndon Johnson and His Times, 1961–1973* (Oxford University Press, 1998).

Robert Dallek, *Lone Star Rising: Lyndon Johnson and His Times, 1908–1960* (Oxford University Press, 1991).

Ronnie Dugger, *The Politician: The Life and Times of Lyndon Johnson: The Drive for Power, From the Frontier to Master of the Senate* (W. W. Norton, 1982).

Rowland Evans and Robert Novak, *Lyndon B. Johnson: The Exercise of Power* (New American Library, 1966).

Bernard J. Firestone and Robert C. Vogt, eds., *Lyndon Baines Johnson and the Uses of Power* (Greenwood Press, 1988).

Lloyd C. Gardner, *Pay Any Price: Lyndon Johnson and the Wars for Vietnam* (Ivan R. Dee, 1995).

Robert Alan Goldberg, *Barry Goldwater* (Yale University Press, 1995).

Eric F. Goldman, *The Tragedy of Lyndon Johnson* (Alfred A. Knopf, 1969).

Hugh Davis Graham, *The Civil Rights Era: Origins and Development of National Policy, 1960–1972* (Oxford University Press, 1990), part 2.

Alonzo L. Hamby, *Liberalism and Its Challengers: From F.D.R. to Bush*, 2nd ed. (Oxford University Press, 1992), ch. 6.

Jim F. Heath, *Decade of Disillusionment: The Kennedy-Johnson Years* (Indiana University Press, 1975), chs. 6–8.

Paul R. Henggeler, *In His Steps: Lyndon Johnson and the Kennedy Mystique* (Ivan R. Dee, 1991).

Paul R. Henggeler, *The Kennedy Persuasion: The Politics of Style Since JFK* (Ivan R. Dee, 1995), chs. 1–2.

Jerome L. Himmelstein, *To the Right: The Transformation of American Conservatism* (University of California Press, 1990).

Ralph K. Huitt, "Democratic Party Leadership in the Senate," *American Political Science Review*, vol. 55, no. 2 (June 1961), pp. 333–44.

Lawrence R. Jacobs and Robert Y. Shapiro, "Lyndon Johnson, Vietnam, and Public Opinion: Rethinking Realist Theory of Leadership," *Presidential Studies Quarterly*, vol. 29, no. 3 (September 1999), pp. 592–616.

Lyndon B. Johnson, *The Vantage Point: Perspectives of the Presidency, 1963–1969* (Holt, Rinehart and Winston, 1971).

Richard Tanner Johnson, *Managing the White House: An Intimate Study of the Presidency* (Harper & Row, 1974), ch. 6.

David Kaiser, *American Tragedy: Kennedy, Johnson, and the Origins of the Vietnam War* (Belknap Press, 2000).

Michael B. Katz, *The Undeserving Poor: From the War on Poverty to the War on Welfare* (Pantheon, 1989).

Ira Katznelson, "Was the Great Society a Lost Opportunity?," in Steve Fraser and Gary Gerstle, eds., *The Rise and Fall of the New Deal Order, 1930–1980* (Princeton University Press, 1989), pp. 185–211.

Doris Kearns Goodwin, *Lyndon Johnson and the American Dream* (Harper & Row, 1976).

Nick Kotz, *Judgment Days: Lyndon Baines Johnson, Martin Luther King, Jr., and the Laws That Changed America* (Houghton Mifflin, 2005).

William W. Lammers and Michael A. Genovese, *The Presidency and Domestic Policy: Comparing Leadership Styles, FDR to Clinton* (CQ Press, 2000), ch. 4.

Arlene Lazarowitz, *Years in Exile: The Liberal Democrats, 1950–1959* (Garland, 1988).

Chana Kai Lee, *For Freedom's Sake: The Life of Fannie Lou Hamer* (University of Illinois Press, 1999), esp. chs. 4–5.

Mitchell B. Lerner, ed., *Looking Back at LBJ: White House Politics in a New Light* (University Press of Kansas, 2005).

William E. Leuchtenburg, *In the Shadow of FDR: From Harry Truman to George W. Bush*, 3rd ed. (Cornell University Press, 2001), ch. 4.

William E. Leuchtenburg, *The White House Looks South* (Louisiana State University Press, 2005), chs. 8–11.

William S. Livingston et al., eds., *The Presidency and the Congress: A Shifting Balance of Power?* (Lyndon B. Johnson School of Public Affairs, 1979).

John F. Manley, "Presidential Power and White House Lobbying," *Political Science Quarterly*, vol. 93, no. 2 (Summer 1978), pp. 255–75.

John Bartlow Martin, *Adlai Stevenson and the World* (Doubleday, 1977), part 1.

John Frederick Martin, *Civil Rights and the Crisis of Liberalism: The Democratic Party, 1945–1976* (Westview Press, 1979).

Allen J. Matusow, *The Unraveling of America: A History of Liberalism in the 1960s* (Harper & Row, 1984).

Harry McPherson, *A Political Education* (Houghton Mifflin, 1988).

Sidney M. Milkis, *The President and the Parties: The Transformation of the American Party System Since the New Deal* (Oxford University Press, 1993), chs. 7–8.

Herbert S. Parmet, *The Democrats: The Years after FDR* (Macmillan, 1976).

James T. Patterson, *America's Struggle Against Poverty in the Twentieth Century*, rev. ed. (Harvard University Press, 2000), parts 3–4.

Rick Perlstein, *Before the Storm: Barry Goldwater and the Unmaking of the American Consensus* (Hill and Wang, 2001).

Emmette S. Redford and Richard T. McCulley, *White House Operations: The Johnson Presidency* (University of Texas Press, 1986).

George Rising, *Clean for Gene: Eugene McCarthy's 1968 Presidential Campaign* (Praeger, 1997).

George C. Roberts, *Paul Butler: Hoosier Politician and National Political Leader* (University Press of America, 1987).

Dominic Sandbrook, *Eugene McCarthy: The Rise and Fall of Postwar American Liberalism* (Alfred A. Knopf, 2004).

Sean J. Savage, *JFK, LBJ, and the Democratic Party* (State University of New York Press, 2004).

Arthur M. Schlesinger Jr., *Robert Kennedy and His Times* (Ballantine Books, 1979).

Arthur M. Schlesinger Jr., *A Thousand Days: John F. Kennedy in the White House* (Houghton Mifflin, 1965).

Jeff Shesol, *Mutual Contempt: Lyndon Johnson, Robert Kennedy, and the Feud That Defined a Decade* (W. W. Norton, 1997).

Carl Solberg, *Hubert Humphrey* (W. W. Norton, 1984), parts 3–5.

Alfred Steinberg, *Sam Johnson's Boy* (Macmillan, 1968).

Mark Stern, *Calculating Visions: Kennedy, Johnson, and Civil Rights* (Rutgers University Press, 1992).

James L. Sundquist, *Politics and Policy: The Eisenhower, Kennedy, and Johnson Years* (Brookings Institution, 1968).

Irwin Unger, *The Best of Intentions: The Triumphs and Failures of the Great Society Under Kennedy, Johnson, and Nixon* (Doubleday, 1996).

David C. Warner, ed., *Toward New Human Rights: The Social Policies of the Kennedy and Johnson Administrations* (Lyndon B. Johnson School of Public Affairs, 1977).

W. Marvin Watson and Sherwin Markman, *Chief of Staff: Lyndon Johnson and His Presidency* (Thomas Dunne/St. Martin's Press, 2004).

Stephen J. Wayne, *The Legislative Presidency* (Harper & Row, 1978).

Theodore H. White, *The Making of the President 1964* (Atheneum, 1965).

Tom Wicker, *JFK and LBJ: The Influence of Personality Upon Politics* (William Morrow, 1968).

Patricia Dennis Witherspoon, *Within These Walls: A Study of Communication Between Presidents and Their Senior Staffs* (Praeger, 1991), pp. 48–61.

71 ["I want to wind up"] : quoted in Dugger, p. 84. The friend was Otto Crider.

72 ["Beliefs and values"] : quoted in Kearns Goodwin, p. 124.

73 ["System of consultation"] : Stevenson, *What I Think* (Harper & Brothers, 1956), p. ix.

73 ["What do you want"] : quoted in Huitt, p. 337.

73 ["Because he spurned"] : ibid., p. 338.

74 ["Fool the people"] : Roosevelt, "Stevenson on the Civil Rights Bill," My Day column, August 9, 1957, in Roosevelt, *Courage in a Dangerous World: Political Writings*, Allida M. Black, ed. (Columbia University Press, 1999), pp. 280–81.

75 ["They'll gang up"] : quoted in D. B. Hardeman and Donald C. Bacon, *Rayburn* (Texas Monthly Press, 1987), p. 433.

75 ["Flash in the pan"] : quoted in Tip O'Neill, *Man of the House* (Random House, 1987), p. 181.

75 ["Little scrawny fellow"] : quoted in Schlesinger, *Robert Kennedy*, p. 220.

76 ["He's the natural"] : quoted in Dallek, *Lone Star Rising*, p. 575.

76 ["Deep sense of responsibility"] : Schlesinger, *A Thousand Days*, p. 48.

76 ["General supervision"] : quoted in Evans and Novak, p. 308.

77 ["Spectral presence"] : Schlesinger, *A Thousand Days*, p. 1018.

77 ["Filled with trips"] : quoted in Kearns Goodwin, p. 164.

77 ["Where's Lyndon?"] : recounted by Angier Biddle Duke, Kennedy's chief of protocol, in Merle Miller, *Lyndon: An Oral Biography* (G. P. Putnam's Sons, 1980), p. 280.

77 ["So god-damn stupid"] : quoted in Henggeler, *In His Steps*, p. 163.

77 ["My job"] : quoted in Kearns Goodwin, p. 178.

78 ["The ideas and the ideals"] : November 27, 1963, in Johnson, *Public Papers* (U. S. Government Printing Office, 1965–70), vol. 1963–64, part 1, pp. 8–10, quoted at pp. 8, 10.

78 ["Continuously, incessantly"] : quoted in Kearns Goodwin, p. 226.

78 [Johnson's "treatment"] : account drawn from Evans and Novak, p. 104.

78 ["Everything I had"] : Johnson, *The Vantage Point*, p. 159.

79 ["Unconditional war"] : Annual Message to the Congress on the State of the Union, January 8, 1964, in Johnson, *Public Papers*, vol. 1963–64, part 1, pp. 112–18, quoted at p. 114.

79 ["Maximum feasible participation"] : quoted in Bernstein, p. 105.

81 ["Win President Kennedy's program"] : quoted in Henggeler, *In His Steps*, p. 149.

81 ["Hidden majority"] : see Robert Mason, *Richard Nixon and the Quest for a New Majority* (University of North Carolina Press, 2004), ch. 1.

81 ["Growing menace"] : quoted in Goldberg, p. 218.

82 ["Run as Barry Goldwater"] : quoted in White, p. 217.

82 ["Chart a new course"] : quoted in Brennan, *Turning Right*, p. 84.

82 ["I would remind you"] : Acceptance Speech, San Francisco, July 17, 1964, in Arthur M. Schlesinger Jr., ed., *History of American Presidential Elections, 1789–1968* (Chelsea House, 1971), vol. 4, pp. 3664–70, quoted at p. 3669.

82 [IN YOUR GUTS] : quoted in Perlstein, p. 444.

82 ["I want you"] : recounted by Wilbur Cohen, in Livingston et al., pp. 300, 301.

83 ["Most basic right"] : Special Message to the Congress: The American Promise, March 15, 1965, in Johnson, *Public Papers*, vol. 1965, part 1, pp. 281–87, quoted at p. 282.

84 ["They say Jack Kennedy"] : quoted in Evans and Novak, p. 2.

84 ["Bowl with those Congressmen"] : Cohen, in Livingston et al., p. 301.

84 ["These men"] : quoted in Jack Valenti, *A Very Human President* (W. W. Norton, 1975), p. 190.

85 ["Hell of a mess"] : McNamara, "Special Interview I" by Robert Dallek, March 26, 1993, p. 10, Lyndon Baines Johnson Library.

85 ["Some bigger things"] : quoted in Bill Moyers, "Flashbacks," *Newsweek*, vol. 85, no. 6 (February 10, 1975), p. 76.

86 ["Foreign policy was something"] : Goldman, pp. 527–28.

86 ["Asia goes Red"] : Robert McNamara, as quoted by Arthur Krock, memorandum of April 22, 1965, in Gardner, p. 202.

87 ["Deep down"] : quoted in Kearns Goodwin, p. 315.

87 ["We will win"] : quoted in Bornet, p. 266.

87 ["Personalized presidency"] : McCarthy, "Why I'm Battling LBJ," *Look* (February 6, 1968), quoted in Savage, p. 166.

87 ["Growing sense of alienation"] : "McCarthy Statement on Entering the 1968 Primaries," *New York Times*, December 1, 1967, p. 40.

88 [New Hampshire poll] : *Time*, vol. 91, no. 10 (March 8, 1968), p. 22.

88 [Johnson's dreams of paralysis] : Kearns Goodwin, p. 342.

88 ["I shall not seek"] : Address to the Nation Announcing Steps to Limit the War in Vietnam and Reporting His Decision Not to Seek Reelection, March 31, 1968, in Johnson, *Public Papers*, vol. 1968–69, part 1, pp. 469–76, quoted at p. 476.

CHAPTER 5 — NIXON-REAGAN: THE GRAND NEW PARTY

Stephen E. Ambrose, *Nixon*, 2 vols. (Simon & Schuster, 1987–89).

Samuel H. Beer, "Ronald Reagan: New Deal Conservative?," *Society*, vol. 20, no. 2 (January-February 1983), pp. 40–44.

Larry Berman, ed., *Looking Back on the Reagan Presidency* (Johns Hopkins University Press, 1990).

William C. Berman, *America's Right Turn: From Nixon to Clinton*, 2nd ed. (Johns Hopkins University Press, 1998).

Earl Black and Merle Black, *Politics and Society in the South* (Harvard University Press, 1987).

Earl Black and Merle Black, *The Rise of Southern Republicans* (Belknap Press, 2002).

Sidney Blumenthal, *The Rise of the Counter-Establishment: From Conservative Ideology to Political Power* (Times Books, 1986).

Sidney Blumenthal and Thomas Byrne Edsall, eds., *The Reagan Legacy* (Pantheon, 1988).

Nigel Bowles, *The White House and Capitol Hill: The Politics of Presidential Persuasion* (Clarendon Press, 1987), ch. 9.

Carl M. Brauer, *Presidential Transitions: Eisenhower Through Reagan* (Oxford University Press, 1986), chs. 3, 5.

Mary C. Brennan, *Turning Right in the Sixties: The Conservative Capture of the GOP* (University of North Carolina Press, 1995).

W. Elliot Brownlee and Hugh Davis Graham, eds., *The Reagan Presidency: Pragmatic Conservatism and Its Legacies* (University Press of Kansas, 2003).

Steve Bruce, *The Rise and Fall of the New Christian Right: Conservative Protestant Politics in America, 1978–1988* (Clarendon Press, 1988).

William Bundy, *A Tangled Web: The Making of Foreign Policy in the Nixon Presidency* (Hill and Wang, 1998).

John P. Burke, *Presidential Transitions: From Politics to Practice* (Lynne Rienner, 2000), chs. 3–4.

Vincent J. Burke and Vee Burke, *Nixon's Good Deed: Welfare Reform* (Columbia University Press, 1974).

Lou Cannon, *President Reagan: The Role of a Lifetime* (Simon & Schuster, 1991).

Dan T. Carter, *The Politics of Rage: George Wallace, the Origins of the New Conservatism, and the Transformation of American Politics*, 2nd ed. (Louisiana State University Press, 2000).

Jack Citrin and Donald Philip Green, "Presidential Leadership and the Resurgence of Trust in Government," *British Journal of Political Science*, vol. 16, no. 4 (October 1986), pp. 431–53.

Augustus B. Cochran III, *Democracy Heading South: National Politics in the Shadow of Dixie* (University Press of Kansas, 2001).

Robert M. Collins, *More: The Politics of Economic Growth in Postwar America* (Oxford University Press, 2000), esp. chs. 4, 6.

Barry Cooper et al., eds., *The Resurgence of Conservatism in Anglo-American Democracies* (Duke University Press, 1988).

Alan Crawford, *Thunder on the Right: The "New Right" and the Politics of Resentment* (Pantheon, 1980).

Matthew Dallek, *The Right Moment: Ronald Reagan's First Victory and the Decisive Turning Point in American Politics* (Free Press, 2000).

Robert Dallek, *Ronald Reagan: The Politics of Symbolism* (Harvard University Press, 1984).

Ronnie Dugger, *On Reagan: The Man & His Presidency* (McGraw-Hill, 1983).

Paul Duke, ed., *Beyond Reagan: The Politics of Upheaval* (Warner Books, 1986).

Thomas Byrne Edsall and Mary D. Edsall, *Chain Reaction: The Impact of Race, Rights, and Taxes on American Politics* (W. W. Norton, 1991).

John Ehrlichman, *Witness To Power: The Nixon Years* (Simon and Schuster, 1982).

John Ehrman, *The Eighties: America in the Age of Reagan* (Yale University Press, 2005).

Thomas Ferguson and Joel Rogers, "The Myth of America's Turn to the Right," *Atlantic*, vol. 257, no. 5 (May 1986), pp. 43–53.

Thomas Ferguson and Joel Rogers, *Right Turn: The Decline of the Democrats and the Future of American Politics* (Hill and Wang, 1986).

Benjamin Friedman, *Day of Reckoning: The Consequences of American Economic Policy Under Reagan and After* (Random House, 1988).

Michael A. Genovese, *The Presidency in an Age of Limits* (Greenwood Press, 1993), chs. 2, 4.

David Gergen, *Eyewitness to Power: The Essence of Leadership, Nixon to Clinton* (Simon & Schuster, 2000).

Howard J. Gold, *Hollow Mandates: American Public Opinion and the Conservative Shift* (Westview Press, 1992).

John Robert Greene, *The Limits of Power: The Nixon and Ford Administrations* (Indiana University Press, 1992).

John Robert Greene, *The Presidency of Gerald R. Ford* (University Press of Kansas, 1995).

Fred I. Greenstein, ed., *The Reagan Presidency: An Early Assessment* (Johns Hopkins University Press, 1983).

Fred I. Greenstein, "Ronald Reagan: Another Hidden-Hand Ike?," *PS*, vol. 23, no. 1 (March 1990), pp. 7–13.

H. R. Haldeman, *Diaries: Inside the Nixon White House* (G. P. Putnam's Sons, 1994).

H. R. Haldeman, *The Ends of Power* (Times Books, 1978).

Alonzo L. Hamby, *Liberalism and Its Challengers: From F.D.R. to Bush*, 2nd ed. (Oxford University Press, 1992), esp. chs. 7, 8.

Steven F. Hayward, *The Age of Reagan: The Fall of the Old Liberal Order, 1964–1980* (Forum/Prima, 2001).

Paul R. Henggeler, *The Kennedy Persuasion: The Politics of Style Since JFK* (Ivan R. Dee, 1995), chs. 3–4, 7.

Jerome L. Himmelstein, *To the Right: The Transformation of American Conservatism* (University of California Press, 1990).

Godfrey Hodgson, *The World Turned Right Side Up: A History of the Conservative Ascendancy in America* (Houghton Mifflin, 1996).

Joan Hoff, *Nixon Reconsidered* (Basic Books, 1994).

Karen M. Hult and Charles E. Walcott, *Empowering the White House: Governance Under Nixon, Ford, and Carter* (University Press of Kansas, 2004).

Richard Tanner Johnson, *Managing the White House: An Intimate Study of the Presidency* (Harper & Row, 1974), ch. 7.

Charles O. Jones, ed., *The Reagan Legacy: Promise and Performance* (Chatham House, 1988).

Barbara Kellerman, *The Political Presidency: Practice of Leadership* (Oxford University Press, 1984), ch. 8.

John H. Kessel, *The Goldwater Coalition: Republican Strategies in 1964* (Bobbs-Merrill, 1968).

Henry Kissinger, *White House Years* (Little, Brown, 1979).

Henry Kissinger, *Years of Upheaval* (Little, Brown, 1982).

B. B. Kymlicka and Jean V. Matthews, eds., *The Reagan Revolution?* (Dorsey Press, 1988).

Everett Carll Ladd Jr., "Liberalism Upside Down: The Inversion of the New Deal Order," *Political Science Quarterly*, vol. 91, no. 4 (Winter 1976-77), pp. 577–600.

William E. Leuchtenburg, *In the Shadow of FDR: From Harry Truman to George W. Bush*, 3rd ed. (Cornell University Press, 2001), chs. 5, 7.

Robert Mason, *Richard Nixon and the Quest for a New Majority* (University of North Carolina Press, 2004).

Christopher Matthews, *Kennedy & Nixon: The Rivalry That Shaped Postwar America* (Simon & Schuster, 1996).

Allen J. Matusow, *Nixon's Economy: Booms, Busts, Dollars, and Votes* (University Press of Kansas, 1998).

Lawrence J. McAndrews, "The Politics of Principle: Richard Nixon and School Desegregation," *Journal of Negro History*, vol. 83, no. 3 (Summer 1998), pp. 187–200.

David McKay, *Domestic Policy and Ideology: Presidents and the American State, 1964–1987* (Cambridge University Press, 1989), chs. 4, 6–7.

David Mervin, *Ronald Reagan and the American Presidency* (Longman, 1990).

Sidney M. Milkis, *The President and the Parties: The Transformation of the American Party System Since the New Deal* (Oxford University Press, 1993), chs. 9–10.

Iwan W. Morgan, *Beyond the Liberal Consensus: A Political History of the United States Since 1965* (St. Martin's Press, 1994).

George H. Nash, *The Conservative Intellectual Movement in America Since 1945* (Basic Books, 1976).

Richard Nixon, *RN* (Grosset & Dunlap, 1978).

John L. Palmer, ed., *Perspectives on the Reagan Years* (Urban Institute Press, 1986).

Herbert S. Parmet, *Richard Nixon and His America* (Little, Brown, 1990).

Gillian Peele, *Revival and Reaction: The Right in Contemporary America* (Clarendon Press, 1984).

Kevin P. Phillips, *The Emerging Republican Majority* (Anchor, 1970).

Paul Pierson, *Dismantling the Welfare State?: Reagan, Thatcher, and the Politics of Retrenchment* (Cambridge University Press, 1994).

Nicol C. Rae, *The Decline and Fall of the Liberal Republicans: From 1952 to the Present* (Oxford University Press, 1989).

Austin Ranney, ed., *The American Elections of 1980* (American Enterprise Institute, 1981).

Ronald Reagan, *An American Life* (Simon and Schuster, 1990).

Ronald Reagan, *Where's the Rest of Me?* (1965; Karz, 1981).

Richard Reeves, *President Nixon: Alone in the White House* (Simon & Schuster, 2001).

Richard Reeves, *President Reagan: The Triumph of Imagination* (Simon & Schuster, 2005).

A. James Reichley, "The Conservative Roots of the Nixon, Ford, and Reagan Administrations," *Political Science Quarterly*, vol. 96, no. 4 (Winter 1981-82), pp. 537–50.

A. James Reichley, *Conservatives in an Age of Change: The Nixon and Ford Administrations* (Brookings Institution, 1981).

Jonathan Rieder, "The Rise of the 'Silent Majority,'" in Steve Fraser and Gary Gerstle, eds., *The Rise and Fall of the New Deal Order, 1930–1980* (Princeton University Press, 1989), pp. 243–68.

Margaret C. Rung, "Richard Nixon, State, and Party: Democracy and Bureaucracy in the Postwar Era," *Presidential Studies Quarterly*, vol. 29, no. 2 (June 1999), pp. 421–37.

William Safire, *Before the Fall: An Inside View of the Pre-Watergate White House* (Doubleday, 1975).

Lester M. Salamon and Michael S. Lund, eds., *The Reagan Presidency and the Governing of America* (Urban Institute Press, 1984).

Ellis Sandoz and Cecil V. Crabb Jr., eds., *A Tide of Discontent: The 1980 Elections and Their Meaning* (Congressional Quarterly Press, 1981).

Richard M. Scammon and Ben J. Wattenberg, *The Real Majority* (Coward-McCann, 1970).

Michael Schaller, *Reckoning with Reagan: America and Its President in the 1980s* (Oxford University Press, 1992).

Eric J. Schmertz et al., eds., *Ronald Reagan's America*, 2 vols. (Greenwood Press, 1997).

Kurt Schuparra, *Triumph of the Right: The Rise of the California Conservative Movement, 1945–1966* (M. E. Sharpe, 1998).

Patricia Cayo Sexton and Brendan Sexton, *Blue Collars and Hard-Hats: The Working Class and the Future of American Politics* (Random House, 1971).

John W. Sloan, "Meeting the Leadership Challenges of the Modern Presidency: The Political Skills and Leadership of Ronald Reagan," *Presidential Studies Quarterly*, vol. 26, no. 3 (Summer 1996), pp. 795–804.

John W. Sloan, *The Reagan Effect: Economics and Presidential Leadership* (University Press of Kansas, 1999).

James L. Sundquist, "Whither the American Party System?," *Political Science Quarterly*, vol. 88, no. 4 (December 1973), pp. 559–81.

James L. Sundquist, "Whither the American Party System?—Revisited," *Political Science Quarterly*, vol. 98, no. 4 (Winter 1983-84), pp. 573–93.

Martin P. Wattenberg, "The Hollow Realignment: Partisan Change in a Candidate-Centered Era," *Public Opinion Quarterly*, vol. 51, no. 1 (Spring 1987), pp. 58–74.

Joseph White and Aaron Wildavsky, *The Deficit and the Public Interest: The Search for Responsible Budgeting in the 1980s* (University of California Press/Russell Sage, 1989).

Theodore H. White, *The Making of the President 1968* (Atheneum, 1969).

Tom Wicker, *One of Us: Richard Nixon and the American Dream* (Random House, 1991).

Walter Williams, *Mismanaging America: The Rise of the Anti-Analytic Presidency* (University Press of Kansas, 1990), esp. chs. 4–5.

Garry Wills, *Reagan's America: Innocents at Home* (Doubleday, 1987).

92   [FDR's "test"] : Address at Barnesville, Georgia, August 11, 1938, in Roosevelt, *Public Papers and Addresses*, Samuel I. Rosenman, comp. (Random House, 1938–50), vol. 7, pp. 463–71, quoted at p. 469.

93   ["You won't have Nixon"] : quoted in Nixon, *RN*, p. 245.

94   ["Terrible liability"] : quoted in Parmet, *Richard Nixon and His America*, p. 466.

95   ["New alignment"] : "A New Alignment for American Unity," radio speech, May 16, 1968, reported in Donald Janson, "Nixon Discerns a New Coalition," *New York Times*, May 17, 1968, p. 25; "Mr. Nixon's New Alignment" (editorial), ibid., May 21, 1968, p. 46; Safire, pp. 49–50; Mason, pp. 27–28.

96 ["Echoes of the phrases"] : White, p. 131.

96 ["Create the impression"] : Timothy Crouse, *The Boys on the Bus* (Random House, 1973), p. 187.

96 ["McCarthy in a white collar"] : quoted in Fred J. Cook, *The Nightmare Decade: The Life and Times of Senator Joe McCarthy* (Random House, 1971), p. 459.

96 ["Experience, Courage, Integrity"] : quoted in Henggeler, p. 84.

96 ["Not without real dignity"] : Mailer, *Miami and the Siege of Chicago* (World Publishing, 1968), p. 44.

96 [1968 election results] : Richard B. Morris and Jeffrey B. Morris, *Encyclopedia of American History*, 7th ed. (HarperCollins, 1996), p. 517; Parmet, *Richard Nixon and His America*, p. 528; Mason, p. 35; Black and Black, *The Rise of Southern Republicans*, p. 222.

97 ["Emergent Republican majority"] : see Phillips, p. 25.

97 [Nixon's first inaugural address] : January 20, 1969, in Nixon, *Public Papers* (U. S. Government Printing Office, 1971–75), vol. 1969, pp. 1–4.

100 ["From the first days"] : Nixon, *RN*, p. 424.

100 ["Unholy alliance"] : quoted in Parmet, *Richard Nixon and His America*, p. 560.

101 ["Flush it"] : ibid., p. 559.

101 ["Forced integration"] : memorandum to John Ehrlichman, January 28, 1972, in Nixon, *RN*, pp. 443–44, quoted at p. 443.

101 ["Quit bragging"] : quoted in Ehrlichman, p. 227.

101 ["Get their names!"] : quoted in Ambrose, vol. 2, p. 331.

102 [Ambrose on Nixon's enemies] : ibid., vol. 2, p. 624.

102 ["You're out"] : from tape recording of a conversation with H. R. Haldeman and John Dean, September 15, 1972, as quoted in Haldeman, *The Ends of Power*, p. 171.

103 [Nixon's private polling] : Lawrence R. Jacobs and Robert Y. Shapiro, "The Rise of Presidential Polling: The Nixon White House in Historical Perspective," *Public Opinion Quarterly*, vol. 59, no. 2 (Summer 1995), pp. 163–95; see also Jacobs and Shapiro, "Presidential Manipulation of Polls and Public Opinion: The Nixon Administration and the Pollsters," *Political Science Quarterly*, vol. 110, no. 4 (Winter 1995-96), pp. 519–38.

103 ["Simply fed up"] : Annual Message to the Congress on the State of the Union, January 22, 1971, in Nixon, *Public Papers*, vol. 1971, pp. 50–58, quoted at pp. 55, 58.

103 [1972 election results] : Morris and Morris, p. 522.

104 ["Gay libs"] : Jeb Magruder, in Ernest R. May and Janet Fraser, eds., *Campaign '72: The Managers Speak* (Harvard University Press, 1973), p. 235.

105 ["Worst crop"] : quoted in Greene, *The Limits of Power*, p. 162.

105 ["I must build a wall"] : quoted in Reeves, *President Nixon*, p. 29.

105 ["Haven't had the time"] : August 9, 1974, in Nixon, *Public Papers*, vol. 1974, pp. 630–32, quoted at p. 630.

105 ["Watergate bullshit"] : quoted in Monica Crowley, *Nixon Off the Record* (Random House, 1996), p. 149.

106 ["Party will be extinct"] : Robert Teeter, quoted in Mason, p. 212.

106 ["Getting off the floor"] : quoted in Cannon, p. 74.

106 ["From the wrong side"] : news conference of June 16, 1981, in Reagan, *Public Papers* (U. S. Government Printing Office, 1982–91), vol. 1981, pp. 519–26, quoted at p. 526.

107 [Reagan and *The Candidate*] : see Cannon, pp. 47–48.

108 ["Point of a bayonet"] : quoted in Frank van der Linden, *The Real Reagan* (William Morrow, 1981), p. 97.

108 [Cheney on "usurpation"] : Cheney, "The Ford Presidency in Perspective," in Bernard J. Firestone and Alexej Ugrinsky, eds., *Gerald R. Ford and the Politics of Post-Watergate America* (Greenwood Press, 1993), vol. 1, pp. 3–6, quoted at pp. 3, 4.

109 ["Thou shalt not speak ill"] : quoted in Reagan, *An American Life*, p. 150.

109 ["How can you challenge"] : Ford, *A Time to Heal* (Harper and Row, 1979), p. 333.

110 [Reagan on Vietnam] : "Peace," Chicago, August 18, 1980, in Kiron K. Skinner et al., eds., *Reagan, In His Own Hand* (Free Press, 2001), pp. 480–86, esp. p. 481; headline quoted in Hayward, p. 679.

110 [Evangelical church growth] : see Mark A. Shibley, *Resurgent Evangelicalism in the United States: Mapping Cultural Change Since 1970* (University of South Carolina Press, 1996), esp. pp. 27 (table 2.1), 28 (table 2.2).

110 ["Preachers are not called"] : quoted in Hodgson, p. 180.

110 ["Good people"] : ibid.

110 ["Stop the moral decay"] : Falwell, *Listen, America!* (Doubleday, 1980), p. 6.

111 [1980 election results] : Morris and Morris, pp. 539–40; Hayward, pp. 712–13; U. S. Census Bureau, *Statistical Abstract of the United States: 2002* (U. S. Government Printing Office, 2001), p. 254 (table 395).

112 ["Decisive action"] : quoted in Cannon, p. 77.

112 ["No American president"] : ibid., p. 107.

112 ["This present crisis"] : January 20, 1981, in Reagan, *Public Papers*, vol. 1981, pp. 1–4, quoted at p. 1.

112 ["Come to a turning point"] : Address to the Nation on the Economy, February 5, 1981, in ibid., vol. 1981, pp. 79–83, quoted at p. 81.

113 ["Whole Cabinet"] : quoted in Reeves, *President Reagan*, p. 84.

113 ["Nothing went"] : Reagan, *An American Life*, p. 167.

113 ["Go off the cliff"] : quoted in Cannon, p. 185.

113 ["Program for economic recovery"] : February 18, 1981, in Reagan, *Public Papers*, vol. 1981, pp. 108–15.

114 ["New president"] : Hedrick Smith, "Party's Political Future May Depend on Results," *New York Times*, February 19, 1981, pp. A1, B7, quoted at p. A1.

114 [Poll on Reagan's program] : Reeves, *President Reagan*, p. 22.

115 ["Voodoo economics"] : quoted in Herbert S. Parmet, *George Bush: The Life of a Lone Star Yankee* (Lisa Drew/Scribner, 1997), p. 232.

115 ["Little intellectual elite"] : quoted in Reagan, *An American Life*, p. 142.

115 ["Transformation of American conservatism"] : McAllister, "Reagan and the Transformation of American Conservatism," in Brownlee and Graham, pp. 40–60.

118 [Republican representation in the South, 1987] : Paul Allen Beck, "Incomplete Realignment: The Reagan Legacy for Parties and Elections," in Jones, pp. 145–71, esp. p. 167.

CHAPTER 6 — THE CARTER-CLINTON CONNECTION

Henry J. Aaron, ed., *The Problem That Won't Go Away: Reforming U. S. Health Care Financing* (Brookings Institution, 1996).

M. Glen Abernathy et al., eds., *The Carter Years: The President and Policy Making* (St. Martin's Press, 1984).

Bruce Adams and Kathryn Kavanaugh-Baran, *Promise and Performance: Carter Builds a New Administration* (Lexington Books, 1979).

Irwin B. Arieff, "Carter and Congress: Strangers to the End," *1980 CQ Almanac* (Congressional Quarterly, 1981), vol. 36, pp. 3–7.

John B. Bader, *Taking the Initiative: Leadership Agendas in Congress and the "Contract with America"* (Georgetown University Press, 1996).

Kenneth S. Baer, *Reinventing Democrats: The Politics of Liberalism from Reagan to Clinton* (University Press of Kansas, 2000).

232 | Bibliography and Notes

William C. Berman, *America's Right Turn: From Nixon to Clinton*, 2nd ed. (Johns Hopkins University Press, 1998), chs. 3, 7, and passim.

Jeffrey H. Birnbaum, *Madhouse: The Private Turmoil of Working for the President* (Times Books, 1996).

W. Carl Biven, *Jimmy Carter's Economy: Policy in an Age of Limits* (University of North Carolina Press, 2002).

Jon R. Bond and Richard Fleisher, eds., *Polarized Politics: Congress and the President in a Partisan Era* (CQ Press, 2000).

Peter G. Bourne, *Jimmy Carter* (Lisa Drew/Scribner, 1997).

Nigel Bowles, *The White House and Capitol Hill: The Politics of Presidential Persuasion* (Clarendon Press, 1987), ch. 8.

Carl M. Brauer, *Presidential Transitions: Eisenhower Through Reagan* (Oxford University Press, 1986), ch. 4.

James MacGregor Burns and Georgia J. Sorenson, *Dead Center: Clinton-Gore Leadership and the Perils of Moderation* (Lisa Drew/Scribner, 1999).

Andrew E. Busch, "Political Science and the 1994 Elections," *PS*, vol. 28, no. 4 (December 1995), pp. 708–10.

Joseph A. Califano Jr., *Governing America: An Insider's Report from the White House and the Cabinet* (Simon and Schuster, 1981).

Anne Marie Cammisa, *From Rhetoric to Reform?: Welfare Policy in American Politics* (Westview Press, 1998).

Colin Campbell and Bert A. Rockman, eds., *The Clinton Legacy* (Chatham House, 2000).

Colin Campbell and Bert A. Rockman, eds., *The Clinton Presidency: First Appraisals* (Chatham House, 1996).

Christopher Caplinger, "The Politics of Trustee Governance: Jimmy Carter's Fight for a Standby Gasoline Rationing Plan," *Presidential Studies Quarterly*, vol. 26, no. 3 (Summer 1996), pp. 778–94.

Jimmy Carter, *Keeping Faith* (Bantam, 1982).

Jimmy Carter, *Why Not the Best?* (Broadman Press, 1975).

Bill Clinton, *My Life* (Alfred A. Knopf, 2004).

Richard E. Cohen, *Changing Course in Washington: Clinton and the New Congress* (Macmillan, 1994).

Thomas E. Cronin, "A Resurgent Congress and the Imperial Presidency," *Political Science Quarterly*, vol. 95, no. 2 (Summer 1980), pp. 209–37.

Eric L. Davis, "Legislative Liaison in the Carter Administration," *Political Science Quarterly*, vol. 94, no. 2 (Summer 1979), pp. 287–301.

Eric L. Davis, "Legislative Reform and the Decline of Presidential Influence on Capitol Hill," *British Journal of Political Science*, vol. 9, no. 4 (October 1979), pp. 465–79.

Robert E. Denton Jr. and Rachel L. Holloway, eds., *The Clinton Presidency: Images, Issues, and Communication Strategies* (Praeger, 1996).

E. J. Dionne Jr., *They Only Look Dead: Why Progressives Will Dominate the Next Political Era* (Simon & Schuster, 1996).

E. J. Dionne Jr., *Why Americans Hate Politics* (Simon & Schuster, 1991).

Elizabeth Drew, *American Journal: The Events of 1976* (Random House, 1977).

Elizabeth Drew, *On the Edge: The Clinton Presidency* (Simon & Schuster, 1994).

Elizabeth Drew, *Showdown: The Struggle Between the Gingrich Congress and the Clinton White House* (Simon & Schuster, 1996).

James Fallows, "The Passionless Presidency: The Trouble with Jimmy Carter's Adminstration," *Atlantic*, vol. 243, no. 5 (May 1979), pp. 33–48.

James Fallows, "The Passionless Presidency II: More from Inside Jimmy Carter's White House," *Atlantic*, vol. 243, no. 6 (June 1979), pp. 75–81.

Richard F. Fenno Jr., *Learning to Govern: An Institutional View of the 104th Congress* (Brookings Institution, 1997).

Thomas Ferguson and Joel Rogers, *Right Turn: The Decline of the Democrats and the Future of American Politics* (Hill and Wang, 1986).

Gary M. Fink, *Prelude to the Presidency: The Political Character and Legislative Leadership Style of Governor Jimmy Carter* (Greenwood Press, 1980).

Gary M. Fink and Hugh Davis Graham, eds., *The Carter Presidency: Policy Choices in the Post–New Deal Era* (University Press of Kansas, 1998).

William Galston and Elaine Ciulla Kamarck, "The Politics of Evasion: Democrats and the Presidency" (Progressive Policy Institute, September 1989). http://www.ppionline.org, downloaded in Adobe PDF.

Michael A. Genovese, *The Presidency in an Age of Limits* (Greenwood Press, 1993), ch. 3.

Steven M. Gillon, *The Democrats' Dilemma: Walter F. Mondale and the Liberal Legacy* (Columbia University Press, 1992).

Newt Gingrich, *Lessons Learned the Hard Way* (HarperCollins, 1998).

Betty Glad, *Jimmy Carter: In Search of the Great White House* (W. W. Norton, 1980).

William F. Grover, *The President as Prisoner: A Structural Critique of the Carter and Reagan Years* (State University of New York Press, 1989).

Garland A. Haas, *Jimmy Carter and the Politics of Frustration* (McFarland, 1992).

Jacob S. Hacker, *The Road to Nowhere: The Genesis of President Clinton's Plan for Health Security* (Princeton University Press, 1997).

Jon F. Hale, "The Making of the New Democrats," *Political Science Quarterly*, vol. 110, no. 2 (Summer 1995), pp. 207–32.

Dan F. Hahn, "The Rhetoric of Jimmy Carter, 1976–1980," *Presidential Studies Quarterly*, vol. 14 (Spring 1984), pp. 265–88.

Erwin C. Hargrove, *Jimmy Carter as President: Leadership and the Politics of the Public Good* (Louisiana State University Press, 1988).

John F. Harris, *The Survivor: Bill Clinton in the White House* (Random House, 2005).

Paul R. Henggeler, *The Kennedy Persuasion: The Politics of Style Since JFK* (Ivan R. Dee, 1995), chs. 5–6, 11.

Paul S. Herrnson and Dilys M. Hill, eds., *The Clinton Presidency: The First Term, 1992–96* (St. Martin's Press, 1999).

John Hohenberg, *Reelecting Bill Clinton: Why America Chose a "New" Democrat* (Syracuse University Press, 1997).

Daniel Horowitz, ed., *Jimmy Carter and the Energy Crisis of the 1970s: The "Crisis of Confidence" Speech of July 15, 1979* (Bedford/St. Martin's, 2005).

Lawrence R. Jacobs et al., "Poll Trends: Medical Care in the United States—An Update," *Public Opinion Quarterly*, vol. 57, no. 3 (Autumn 1993), pp. 394–427.

Haynes Johnson and David S. Broder, *The System: The American Way of Politics at the Breaking Point* (Little, Brown, 1996).

Bryan D. Jones, ed., *The New American Politics: Reflections on Political Change and the Clinton Administration* (Westview Press, 1995).

Charles O. Jones, *Clinton and Congress, 1993–1996: Risk, Restoration, and Reelection* (University of Oklahoma Press, 1999).

Charles O. Jones, *The Trusteeship Presidency: Jimmy Carter and the United States Congress* (Louisiana State University Press, 1988).

Craig Allan Kaplowitz, "Struggles of the First 'New Democrat': Jimmy Carter, Youth Employment, and the Great Society Legacy," *Presidential Studies Quarterly*, vol. 28, no. 1 (Winter 1998), pp. 186–206.

Burton I. Kaufman, *The Presidency of James Earl Carter, Jr.* (University Press of Kansas, 1993).

Barbara Kellerman, *The Political Presidency: Practice of Leadership* (Oxford University Press, 1984), ch. 10.

John H. Kessel, "The Structures of the Carter White House," *American Journal of Political Science*, vol. 27, no. 3 (August 1983), pp. 431–63.

Douglas L. Koopman, *Hostile Takeover: The House Republican Party, 1980–1995* (Rowman & Littlefield, 1996).

Robert Kuttner, "Reaganism, Liberalism, and the Democrats," in Sidney Blumenthal and Thomas Byrne Edsall, eds., *The Reagan Legacy* (Pantheon, 1988), pp. 99–133.

Nicholas Lemann, "Jordan, Georgia, and the Establishment," *Washington Monthly*, vol. 10, no. 2 (April 1978), pp. 36–47.

Nicholas Lemann, "Why Carter Fails: Taking the Politics Out of Government," *Washington Monthly*, vol. 10, no. 6 (September 1978), pp. 12–23.

William E. Leuchtenburg, *In the Shadow of FDR: From Harry Truman to George W. Bush*, 3rd ed. (Cornell University Press, 2001), ch. 6.

Michael Lind, "Mapquest.Dem," *American Prospect*, vol. 16, no. 1 (January 2005), pp. 18–22.

Seymour Martin Lipset, "The Significance of the 1992 Election," *PS*, vol. 26, no. 1 (March 1993), pp. 7–16.

Laurence E. Lynn Jr. and David deF. Whitman, *The President as Policymaker: Jimmy Carter and Welfare Reform* (Temple University Press, 1981).

L. Sandy Maisel, "The Platform-Writing Process: Candidate-Centered Platforms in 1992," *Political Science Quarterly*, vol. 108, no. 4 (Winter 1993-94), pp. 671–98.

L. Sandy Maisel, ed., *The Parties Respond: Changes in American Parties and Campaigns*, 3rd ed. (Westview Press, 1998).

Michael J. Malbin, "Rhetoric and Leadership: A Look Backward at the Carter National Energy Plan," in Anthony King, ed., *Both Ends of the Avenue: The Presidency, the Executive Branch, and Congress in the 1980s* (American Enterprise Institute, 1983), pp. 212–45.

Thomas E. Mann and Norman J. Ornstein, eds., *Intensive Care: How Congress Shapes Health Policy* (American Enterprise Institute/Brookings Institution, 1995).

David Maraniss, *First in His Class: A Biography of Bill Clinton* (Simon & Schuster, 1995).

David Maraniss and Michael Weisskopf, *"Tell Newt To Shut Up!"* (Touchstone, 1996).

David McKay, *Domestic Policy and Ideology: Presidents and the American State, 1964–1987* (Cambridge University Press, 1989), ch. 5.

David Mervin, *Ronald Reagan and the American Presidency* (Longman, 1990), ch. 3.

Harold Meyerson, "Conflicted President, Undefined Presidency," *Dissent*, vol. 40, no. 4 (Fall 1993), pp. 438–46.

Harold Meyerson, "Why the Democrats Keep Losing: The Abandonment of Economic Populism," *Dissent*, vol. 36, no. 3 (Summer 1989), pp. 305–10.

William Lee Miller, *Yankee from Georgia: The Emergence of Jimmy Carter* (Times Books, 1978).

Alexander Moens, *Foreign Policy Under Carter: Testing Multiple Advocacy Decision Making* (Westview Press, 1990).

Iwan W. Morgan, *Beyond the Liberal Consensus: A Political History of the United States Since 1965* (St. Martin's Press, 1994), ch. 6.

James A. Morone, "Neglected Institutions: Politics, Administration, and Health Reform," *PS*, vol. 27, no. 2 (June 1994), pp. 220–23.

Kenneth E. Morris, *Jimmy Carter: American Moralist* (University of Georgia Press, 1996).

Daniel P. Moynihan, *Miles to Go: A Personal History of Social Policy* (Harvard University Press, 1996).

Joshua Muravchik, *The Uncertain Crusade: Jimmy Carter and the Dilemmas of Human Rights Policy* (Hamilton Press, 1986).

Tip O'Neill, *Man of the House* (Random House, 1987), ch. 13.

Norman J. Ornstein and Amy L. Schenkenberg, "The 1995 Congress: The First Hundred Days and Beyond," *Political Science Quarterly*, vol. 110, no. 2 (Summer 1995), pp. 183–206.

John H. Patton, "A Government as Good as Its People: Jimmy Carter and the Restoration of Transcendence to Politics," *Quarterly Journal of Speech*, vol. 63, no. 3 (October 1977), pp. 249–57.

Gillian Peele et al., eds., *Developments in American Politics 2* (Chatham House, 1995).

Mark A. Peterson, "The Politics of Health Care Policy: Overreaching in an Age of Polarization," in Margaret Weir, ed., *The Social Divide: Political Parties and the Future of Activist Government* (Brookings Institution/Russell Sage, 1998), pp. 181–229.

James P. Pfiffner, *The Strategic Presidency: Hitting the Ground Running*, 2nd ed. (University Press of Kansas, 1996), ch. 8.

James P. Pfiffner and Marcia Lynn Whicker, eds., "The Clinton Presidency in Crisis," *Presidential Studies Quarterly*, vol. 28, no. 4 (Fall 1998).

Nelson W. Polsby, *Consequences of Party Reform* (Oxford University Press, 1983).

Gerald M. Pomper et al., *The Election of 1980* (Chatham House, 1981).

Gerald M. Pomper et al., *The Election of 1992* (Chatham House, 1993).

Gerald M. Pomper et al., *The Election of 1996* (Chatham House, 1997).

The Presidential Campaign, 1976, 3 vols. (U. S. Government Printing Office, 1978).

Austin Ranney, ed., *The American Elections of 1980* (American Enterprise Institute, 1981).

Howard L. Reiter, "Intra-Party Cleavages in the United States Today," *Western Political Quarterly*, vol. 34, no. 2 (June 1981), pp. 287–300.

Stanley A. Renshon, *High Hopes: The Clinton Presidency and the Politics of Ambition* (New York University Press, 1996).

Stanley A. Renshon, ed., *The Clinton Presidency: Campaigning, Governing, and the Psychology of Leadership* (Westview Press, 1995).

Russell L. Riley, "Party Government and the Contract with America," *PS*, vol. 28, no. 4 (December 1995), pp. 703–707.

Paula Vaillancourt Rosenau, ed., *Health Care Reform in the Nineties* (Sage, 1994).

Herbert D. Rosenbaum and Alexej Ugrinsky, eds., *Jimmy Carter: Foreign Policy and Post-Presidential Years* (Greenwood Press, 1994).

Herbert D. Rosenbaum and Alexej Ugrinsky, eds., *The Presidency and Domestic Policies of Jimmy Carter* (Greenwood Press, 1994).

Mark J. Rozell, *The Press and the Carter Presidency* (Westview Press, 1989).

Mark E. Rushefsky and Kant Patel, *Politics, Power & Policy Making: The Case of Health-Care Reform in the 1990s* (M. E. Sharpe, 1998).

Ellis Sandoz and Cecil V. Crabb Jr., eds., *A Tide of Discontent: The 1980 Elections and Their Meaning* (Congressional Quarterly Press, 1981).

Harvey L. Schantz, ed., *Politics in an Era of Divided Government: Elections and Governance in the Second Clinton Administration* (Routledge, 2001).

Steven E. Schier, ed., *The Postmodern Presidency: Bill Clinton's Legacy in U. S. Politics* (University of Pittsburgh Press, 2000).

William Schneider, "JFK's Children: The Class of '74," *Atlantic*, vol. 263, no. 3 (March 1989), pp. 35–58.

Martin Schram, *Running for President, 1976: The Carter Campaign* (Stein and Day, 1977).

Byron E. Shafer, *Quiet Revolution: The Struggle for the Democratic Party and the Shaping of Post-Reform Politics* (Russell Sage, 1983).

Laurence H. Shoup, *The Carter Presidency and Beyond: Power and Politics in the 1980s* (Ramparts Press, 1980).

Theda Skocpol, *Boomerang: Clinton's Health Security Effort and the Turn Against Government in U. S. Politics* (W. W. Norton, 1996).

Stephen Skowronek, *The Politics Presidents Make: Leadership from John Adams to George Bush* (Belknap Press, 1993), esp. pp. 361–406.

Stephen Skowronek, "President Clinton and the Risks of 'Third-Way' Politics," *Extensions* (Spring 1996), pp. 10–15.

Gaddis Smith, *Morality, Reason, and Power: American Diplomacy in the Carter Years* (Hill and Wang, 1986).

Paul Starr, *The Logic of Health-Care Reform* (Grand Rounds Press, 1992).

James L. Sundquist, "The Crisis of Competence in Our National Government," *Political Science Quarterly*, vol. 95, no. 2 (Summer 1980), pp. 183–208.

Martin Walker, *The President We Deserve: Bill Clinton, His Rise, Falls, and Comebacks* (Crown, 1996).

Shirley Anne Warshaw, *Powersharing: White House–Cabinet Relations in the Modern Presidency* (State University of New York Press, 1996), ch. 5.

M. Stephen Weatherford and Lorraine M. McDonnell, "Clinton and the Economy: The Paradox of Policy Success and Political Mishap," *Political Science Quarterly*, vol. 111, no. 3 (Autumn 1996), pp. 403–36.

R. Kent Weaver, *Ending Welfare as We Know It* (Brookings Institution, 2000).

Aaron Wildavsky, *The Beleaguered Presidency* (Transaction, 1991), ch. 11.

Jules Witcover, *Marathon: The Pursuit of the Presidency, 1972–1976* (Viking, 1977).

Patricia Dennis Witherspoon, *Within These Walls: A Study of Communication Between Presidents and Their Senior Staffs* (Praeger, 1991).

Bob Woodward, *The Agenda: Inside the Clinton White House* (Simon & Schuster, 1994).

119 [Author's interview with Carter] : see James MacGregor Burns, "Jimmy Carter's Strategy for 1980: Leader or Born-Again Broker?," *Atlantic*, vol. 243, no. 3 (March 1979), pp. 41–46.

120 ["More complicated"] : *Atlanta Constitution*, June 14, 1966, quoted in Fink, *Prelude*, p. 4.

120 ["Tried to assess"] : Carter, *Why Not the Best?*, p. 99.

121 ["Strongest feeling"] : quoted in Witcover, p. 111.

122 ["Kennedy smile"] : Gerald Rafshoon, quoted in Schram, p. 25.

122 ["Get the country moving"] : quoted in Henggeler, p. 138.

122 ["Fusing contradictions"] : Woodward, "The Best?," *New York Review of Books*, vol. 27, no. 5 (April 3, 1980), pp. 9–11, quoted at p. 10.

122 ["Not an ideologue"] : interview with Robert Scheer, *Playboy*, November 1976, reprinted in G. Barry Golson, ed., *The Playboy Interview* (Playboy Press, 1981), pp. 466–88, quoted at p. 467.

123 ["Never lie"] : quoted in Drew, *American Journal*, p. 43.

123 ["Government as good"] : quoted in David Broder, "Falling Short After the 4th," *Washington Post*, December 29, 1976, p. A23.

123 ["Division between"] : Helen Dewar, "Carter Dubs Himself Washington 'Outsider,'" ibid., February 20, 1976, p. A4.

123 ["Maintain at all costs"] : quoted in Anthony Lewis, "In Search of Jimmy Carter," *New York Times*, May 31, 1976, p. 11.

123 ["Always been a Democrat"] : Acceptance Speech, July 15, 1976, in *Presidential Campaign, 1976*, vol. 1, part 1, pp. 347–52, quoted at pp. 348, 349.

124 ["Wait a minute"] : quoted in Lemann, "Why Carter Fails," p. 22.

125 ["Moral equivalent"] : Address to the Nation: The Energy Problem, April 18, 1977, in Carter, *Public Papers* (U. S. Government Printing Office, 1977–82), vol. 1977, part 1, pp. 656–62, quoted at p. 656.

125 ["I don't know"] : News Conference, February 23, 1977, in ibid., vol. 1977, part 1, pp. 216–26, quoted at p. 223.

125 ["Vintage Jimmy Carter"] : quoted in Jones, *Trusteeship Presidency*, p. 139.

125 ["Toughest fight"] : quoted in Kellerman, p. 191.

126 ["Right thing"] : quoted in O'Neill, p. 320.

126 ["Deep and serious trouble"] : quoted in Kaufman, p. 139.

126 ["Passionless presidency"] : Fallows, "Passionless Presidency," quoted at pp. 43, 42, respectively.

127 ["Small-picture soul"] : Lemann, "Why Carter Fails," p. 23.

127 ["Why does it always"] : quoted in ibid., p. 22.

127 ["Highly personal"] : Meg Greenfield, "A Government in Exile," *Newsweek*, vol. 94, no. 4 (July 23, 1979), p. 26.

127 ["Country was waiting"] : Carter, *Keeping Faith*, p. 119.

127 ["All the legislation"] : Address to the Nation: Energy and National Goals, July 15, 1979, in Carter, *Public Papers*, vol. 1979, part 2, pp. 1235–41, quoted at pp. 1236, 1237, 1238.

128 ["Events dominate us"] : Pat Caddell, quoted in Kaufman, p. 149.

128 ["Traditional Democrats"] : quoted in William E. Leuchtenburg, "Jimmy Carter and the Post–New Deal Presidency," in Fink and Graham, *The Carter Presidency*, pp. 7–28, at p. 12.

128 [Election results, 1980] : Gerald M. Pomper, "The Presidential Election," in Pomper et al., *Election of 1980*, pp. 65–96, esp. pp. 67, 72–73 (table 3.2); for the evangelical Christian vote, 1976 and 1980, see Dionne, *Why Americans Hate Politics*, p. 227.

129 ["A lot of working Democrats"] : Pat Caddell, quoted in Kaufman, p. 207.

130 ["Politics of Evasion"] : Galston and Kamarck, quoted at p. 12.

130 ["Moral and cultural values"] : quoted in Baer, p. 181.

131 ["Most attractive"] : Michael Steinhardt, quoted in ibid., p. 163.

132 ["A core"] : quoted in Walker, p. 77.

132 ["Best organization"] : John Robert Starr, quoted in ibid., p. 87.

133 ["New generation"] : quoted in F. Christopher Arterton, "Campaign '92: Strategies and Tactics of the Candidates," in Pomper et al., *Election of 1992*, pp. 74–109, at p. 99.

133 [1992 election results] : Richard B. Morris and Jeffrey B. Morris, *Encyclopedia of American History*, 7th ed. (HarperCollins, 1996), p. 550.

134 ["Where are all the Democrats?"] : quoted in Woodward, p. 165.

135 ["President's finest hour"] : quoted in Baer, p. 218.

135 [Uninsured and underinsured Americans] : Rushefsky and Patel, p. 29 (table 2.3); Starr, p. 19.

136 ["National system"] : quoted in Skocpol, p. 45.

136 ["Magic moment"] : Address to a Joint Session of the Congress on Health Care Reform, September 22, 1993, in Clinton, *Public Papers* (U. S. Government Printing Office, 1994–2002), vol. 1993, part 2, pp. 1556–65, quoted at p. 1558.

137 ["Health care that's always there"] : ibid., p. 1557.

138 ["Core family issues"] : quoted in Skocpol, p. 155.

138 ["Great innovations"] : letter to Thaddeus Kosciusko, May 2, 1808, in Jefferson, *Writings*, Andrew A. Lipscomb, ed. (Thomas Jefferson Memorial Association, 1905), vol. 12, pp. 44–46, quoted at p. 45.

138 [1994 election results] : see Jones, *Clinton and Congress*, pp. 95–115, esp. p. 96.

139 ["Bill Clinton won"] : Phil Gramm, quoted in Walker, p. 329.

139 ["Transformational figure"] : Dan Balz, "The Whip Who Would Be Speaker," *Washington Post*, October 20, 1994, pp. A1, A26–27, quoted at p. A1.

139 ["Genuine revolution"] : quoted in Fenno, p. 19.

139 ["Renew American civilization"] : Gingrich, "Beyond the 100 Days," *New York Times*, February 22, 1995, p. A19.

140 ["Our government operates"] : quoted in David Broder, "GOP House Party," *Washington Post*, September 28, 1994, p. A23.

140 ["Invisible foot"] : Armey, *The Freedom Revolution* (Regnery, 1995), p. 316.

141 ["President is relevant"] : News Conference, April 18, 1995, in Clinton, *Public Papers*, vol. 1995, part 1, pp. 541–49, quoted at p. 547.

141 ["If you want to pass"] : quoted in Maraniss and Weisskopf, p. 148.

142 ["Not about moving left"] : Address to the Nation on the Middle Class Bill of Rights, December 15, 1994, in Clinton, *Public Papers*, vol. 1994, part 2, pp. 2182–84, quoted at p. 2184.

142 ["Bridge to the 21st Century"] : Remarks Accepting the Presidential Nomination, Chicago, August 29, 1996, in ibid., vol. 1996, part 2, pp. 1409–17, quoted at p. 1410, and passim.

143 [1996 election results] : Paul R. Abramson et al., *Change and Continuity in the 1996 Elections* (CQ Press, 1998), pp. 44–45 (table 3-1), 46 (figure 3-1), and 195; Harold W. Stanley and Richard G. Niemi, eds., *Vital Statistics on American Politics, 2005–2006* (CQ Press, 2006), pp. 12-13 (table 1-1).

144 ["They're for the powerful"] : "Gore to Delegates and Nation: 'My Focus Will Be on Working Families,'" *New York Times*, August 18, 2000, pp. A21–22.

144 ["New Deal political philosophy"] : Al From, quoted in Charles Babington, "Democrats Split On What Went Wrong," *Washington Post,* January 25, 2001, p. A6.

144 ["Successfully defined Bush"] : Stanley Greenberg, quoted in Thomas B. Edsall, "Fissures Widening Among Democrats After Gore's Loss," ibid., December 16, 2000, p. A20.

CHAPTER 7 — THE BUSHES: STANDING TOGETHER ALONE

Alan I. Abramowitz and Walter J. Stone, "The Bush Effect: Polarization, Turnout, and Activism in the 2004 Presidential Election," *Presidential Studies Quarterly,* vol. 36, no. 2 (June 2006), pp. 141–54.

Paul R. Abramson et al., *Change and Continuity in the 2000 and 2002 Elections* (CQ Press, 2003).

Mike Allen and David Broder, "Bush's Leadership Style Another Question," *Washington Post,* August 30, 2004. http://web.lexis-nexis.com/universe, accessed November 21, 2005.

Eric Alterman, *When Presidents Lie: A History of Official Deception and Its Consequences* (Viking, 2004).

Daniel Altman, *Neoconomy: George Bush's Revolutionary Gamble with America's Future* (PublicAffairs, 2004).

James A. Barnes, "Bush's Insiders," *National Journal,* vol. 33, no. 25 (June 23, 2001), pp. 1866–72.

James A. Barnes, "The Company He Keeps," *National Journal,* vol. 31, no. 32 (August 7, 1999), pp. 2284–85.

Bruce R. Bartlett, *Impostor: How George W. Bush Bankrupted America and Betrayed the Reagan Legacy* (Doubleday, 2006).

William C. Berman, *America's Right Turn: From Nixon to Clinton,* 2nd ed. (Johns Hopkins University Press, 1998).

Sidney Blumenthal, *Pledging Allegiance: The Last Campaign of the Cold War* (HarperCollins, 1990).

Jon R. Bond and Richard Fleisher, eds., *Polarized Politics: Congress and the President in a Partisan Era* (CQ Press, 2000).

Meena Bose and Rosanna Perotti, eds., *From Cold War to New World Order: The Foreign Policy of George H. W. Bush* (Greenwood Press, 2002).

James Bovard, *Terrorism and Tyranny: Trampling Freedom, Justice, and Peace to Rid the World of Evil* (Palgrave, 2003).

Mary C. Brennan, *Turning Right in the Sixties: The Conservative Capture of the GOP* (University of North Carolina Press, 1995).

Richard Brookhiser, "Gravedigger of the Revolution," *Atlantic*, vol. 270, no. 4 (October 1992), pp. 70–78.

Richard Brookhiser, "The Mind of George W. Bush," *Atlantic*, vol. 291, no. 3 (April 2003), pp. 56–69.

John P. Burke, *Becoming President: The Bush Transition, 2000–2003* (Lynne Rienner, 2004).

George Bush and Brent Scowcroft, *A World Transformed* (Alfred A. Knopf, 1998).

Colin Campbell and Bert A. Rockman, eds., *The Bush Presidency: First Appraisals* (Chatham House, 1991).

Colin Campbell and Bert A. Rockman, eds., *The George W. Bush Presidency: Appraisals and Prospects* (CQ Press, 2004).

Carl M. Cannon, "Bush and God," *National Journal*, vol. 36, no. 1 (January 3, 2004), pp. 12–18.

James W. Ceaser and Andrew E. Busch, *The Perfect Tie: The True Story of the 2000 Presidential Election* (Rowman & Littlefield, 2001).

James W. Ceaser and Andrew E. Busch, *Red Over Blue: The 2004 Elections and American Politics* (Rowman & Littlefield, 2005).

Jonathan Chait, "Mad About You: The Case for Bush Hatred," *New Republic*, vol. 229, no. 13 (September 29, 2003), pp. 20–24.

Citizens for Tax Justice, "Year-By-Year Analysis of the Bush Tax Cuts Shows Growing Tilt to the Very Rich," June 12, 2002. http://www.ctj.org/pdf/gwb0602.pdf.

"The Contradictory Conservative," *Economist*, vol. 372 (August 28, 2004), pp. 22–26.

Corey Cook, "The Permanence of the 'Permanent Campaign': George W. Bush's Public Presidency," *Presidential Studies Quarterly*, vol. 32, no. 4 (December 2002), pp. 753–64.

David Corn, *The Lies of George W. Bush: Mastering the Politics of Deception* (Crown, 2003).

William Crotty, ed., *America's Choice 2000* (Westview Press, 2001).

William Crotty, ed., *The Politics of Terror: The U. S. Response to 9/11* (Northeastern University Press, 2004).

Ivo H. Daalder and James M. Lindsay, *America Unbound: The Bush Revolution in Foreign Policy*, rev. ed. (John Wiley & Sons, 2005).

Richard Darman, *Who's in Control?: Polar Politics and the Sensible Center* (Simon & Schuster, 1996).

Sara Diamond, *Roads to Dominion: Right-Wing Movements and Political Power in the United States* (Guilford Press, 1995).

Michael Duffy and Dan Goodgame, *Marching in Place: The Status Quo Presidency of George Bush* (Simon & Schuster, 1992).

George C. Edwards III and Philip John Davies, eds., *New Challenges for the American Presidency* (Pearson/Longman, 2004).

Leslie D. Feldman and Rosanna Perotti, eds., *Honor and Loyalty: Inside the Politics of the George H. W. Bush White House* (Greenwood Press, 2002).

Thomas Ferguson and Joel Rogers, *Right Turn: The Decline of the Democrats and the Future of American Politics* (Hill and Wang, 1986).

Jo Renee Formicola et al., *Faith-Based Initiatives and the Bush Administration: The Good, the Bad, and the Ugly* (Rowman & Littlefield, 2003).

Lawrence Freedman and Efraim Karsh, *The Gulf Conflict, 1990–1991: Diplomacy and War in the New World Order* (Princeton University Press, 1993).

Michael A. Genovese, *The Presidency in an Age of Limits* (Greenwood Press, 1993), ch. 5.

Jack W. Germond and Jules Witcover, *Mad as Hell: Revolt at the Ballot Box, 1992* (Warner Books, 1993).

Betty Glad, "How George Bush Lost the Presidential Election of 1992," in Stanley A. Renshon, ed., *The Clinton Presidency: Campaigning, Governing, and the Psychology of Leadership* (Westview Press, 1995), pp. 11–35.

Stephen R. Graubard, *Mr. Bush's War: Adventures in the Politics of Illusion* (Hill and Wang, 1992).

John C. Green et al., *Religion and the Culture Wars: Dispatches from the Front* (Rowman & Littlefield, 1996).

Joshua Green, "The Other War Room: President Bush Doesn't Believe in Polling—Just Ask His Pollsters," *Washington Monthly*, vol. 34, no. 4 (April 2002), pp. 11–16.

John Robert Greene, *The Presidency of George Bush* (University Press of Kansas, 2000).

Fred I. Greenstein, ed., *The George W. Bush Presidency: An Early Assessment* (Johns Hopkins University Press, 2003).

Gary L. Gregg II and Mark J. Rozell, eds., *Considering the Bush Presidency* (Oxford University Press, 2004).

Jacob S. Hacker and Paul Pierson, *Off Center: The Republican Revolution and the Erosion of American Democracy* (Yale University Press, 2005).

Lori Cox Han and Diane J. Heith, eds., *In the Public Domain: Presidents and the Challenges of Public Leadership* (State University of New York Press, 2005).

J. H. Hatfield, *Fortunate Son: George W. Bush and the Making of an American President* (St. Martin's Press, 2000).

Gary R. Hess, *Presidential Decisions for War: Korea, Vietnam, and the Persian Gulf* (Johns Hopkins University Press, 2001), chs. 5–6.

Richard Himelfarb and Rosanna Perotti, eds., *Principle over Politics?: The Domestic Policy of the George H. W. Bush Presidency* (Praeger, 2004).

Jerome L. Himmelstein, *To the Right: The Transformation of American Conservatism* (University of California Press, 1990).

Godfrey Hodgson, *The World Turned Right Side Up: A History of the Conservative Ascendancy in America* (Houghton Mifflin, 1996).

Jack Huberman, *The Bush-Hater's Handbook* (Nation Books, 2003).

Kathleen Hall Jamieson, ed., *Electing the President, 2004* (University of Pennsylvania Press, 2006).

Bill Keller, "Reagan's Son: The Radical Presidency of George W. Bush," *New York Times Magazine*, January 26, 2003, pp. 26–31, 42–44, 62.

Douglas Kellner, *From 9/11 to Terror War: The Dangers of the Bush Legacy* (Rowman & Littlefield, 2003).

Donald F. Kettl, *Team Bush: Leadership Lessons from the Bush White House* (McGraw-Hill, 2003).

Charles Kolb, *White House Daze: The Unmaking of Domestic Policy in the Bush Years* (Free Press, 1994).

Jon Kraus et al., eds., *Transformed by Crisis: The Presidency of George W. Bush and American Politics* (Palgrave, 2004).

Paul Krugman, *The Great Unraveling* (W. W. Norton, 2003).

David C. Leege et al., *The Politics of Cultural Differences: Social Change and Voter Mobilization Strategies in the Post–New Deal Period* (Princeton University Press, 2002).

Nicholas Lemann, "The Controller: Karl Rove," *New Yorker*, vol. 79, no. 11 (May 12, 2003), pp. 68–83.

Nicholas Lemann, "The Quiet Man: Dick Cheney's Discreet Rise to Unprecedented Power," *New Yorker*, vol. 77, no. 10 (May 7, 2001), pp. 56–71.

Michael Lienesch, *Redeeming America: Piety and Politics in the New Christian Right* (University of North Carolina Press, 1993).

Joel Lieske, "Cultural Issues and Images in the 1988 Presidential Campaign: Why the Democrats Lost—Again!," *PS*, vol. 24, no. 2 (June 1991), pp. 180–87.

Michael Lind, *Made in Texas: George W. Bush and the Southern Takeover of American Politics* (Basic Books, 2003).

Michael Lind, *Up From Conservatism: Why the Right Is Wrong for America* (Free Press, 1996).

James Mann, *Rise of the Vulcans: The History of Bush's War Cabinet* (Viking, 2004).

Kevin Mattson, "Goodbye to All That," *American Prospect*, vol. 16, no. 4 (April 2005), pp. 32–38.

David Mervin, *George Bush and the Guardianship Presidency* (St. Martin's Press, 1996).

John Micklethwait and Adrian Wooldridge, *The Right Nation: Conservative Power in America* (Penguin, 2004).

Mark Crispin Miller, *Cruel and Unusual: Bush/Cheney's New World Order* (W. W. Norton, 2004).

Bill Minutaglio, *First Son: George W. Bush and the Bush Family Dynasty* (Times Books, 1999).

Elizabeth Mitchell, *W: Revenge of the Bush Dynasty* (Hyperion, 2000).

James Moore and Wayne Slater, *Bush's Brain: How Karl Rove Made George W. Bush Presidential* (John Wiley & Sons, 2003).

Kerry Mullins and Aaron Wildavsky, "The Procedural Presidency of George Bush," *Political Science Quarterly*, vol. 107, no. 1 (Spring 1992), pp. 31–62.

Michael Nelson, ed., *The Elections of 2000* (CQ Press, 2001).

Michael Nelson, ed., *The Elections of 2004* (CQ Press, 2005).

George Packer, *The Assassins' Gate: America in Iraq* (Farrar, Straus and Giroux, 2005).

Herbert S. Parmet, "The Bush Vice Presidency: Getting Right with the Right," in Eric J. Schmertz et al., eds., *Ronald Reagan's America* (Greenwood Press, 1997), vol. 2, pp. 623–32.

Herbert S. Parmet, *George Bush: The Life of a Lone Star Yankee* (Lisa Drew/Scribner, 1997).

Pew Forum on Religion and Public Life, "Religion and Public Life: A Faith-Based Partisan Divide" (2005).

James P. Pfiffner, "Presidential Lies," *Presidential Studies Quarterly*, vol. 29, no. 4 (December 1999), pp. 903–17.

Kevin Phillips, *American Dynasty: Aristocracy, Fortune, and the Politics of Deceit in the House of Bush* (Viking, 2004).

James Pinkerton, "Life in Bush Hell," *New Republic*, vol. 207, no. 25 (December 14, 1992), pp. 22–27.

John Podhoretz, *Hell of a Ride: Backstage at the White House Follies, 1989–1993* (Simon & Schuster, 1993).

Gerald M. Pomper et al., *The Election of 1988* (Chatham House, 1989).

Gerald M. Pomper et al., *The Election of 2000* (Chatham House, 2001).

Jack N. Rakove, ed., *The Unfinished Election of 2000* (Basic Books, 2001).

Stanley A. Renshon, *In His Father's Shadow: The Transformations of George W. Bush* (Palgrave, 2004).

Richard Rose, *The Postmodern President: George Bush Meets the World*, 2nd ed. (Chatham House, 1991).

Mark J. Rozell, "Executive Privilege Revived?: Secrecy and Conflict During the Bush Presidency," *Duke Law Journal*, vol. 52, no. 2 (November 2002), pp. 403–21.

Andrew Rudalevige, *The New Imperial Presidency: Renewing Presidential Power After Watergate* (University of Michigan Press, 2005).

Christopher Scheer et al., *The Five Biggest Lies Bush Told Us About Iraq* (Seven Stories/Akashic, 2003).

Steven E. Schier, ed., *High Risk and Big Ambition: The Presidency of George W. Bush* (University of Pittsburgh Press, 2004).

William Schneider, "The In-Box President," *Atlantic*, vol. 265, no. 1 (January 1990), pp. 34–43.

Peter Schweizer and Rochelle Schweizer, *The Bushes: Portrait of a Dynasty* (Anchor, 2005).

J. Merrill Shanks and Warren E. Miller, "Partisanship, Policy and Performance: The Reagan Legacy in the 1988 Election," *British Journal of Political Science*, vol. 21, no. 2 (April 1991), pp. 129–97.

Micah L. Sifry and Christopher Cerf, eds., *The Gulf War Reader* (Times Books, 1991).

Alexis Simendinger, "Power of One," *National Journal*, vol. 34, no. 4 (January 26, 2002), pp. 230–35.

Alexis Simendinger, "Power Plays," *National Journal*, vol. 36, no. 16 (April 17, 2004), pp. 1166–72.

Jean Edward Smith, *George Bush's War* (Henry Holt, 1992).

Jean Stefancic and Richard Delgado, *No Mercy: How Conservative Think Tanks and Foundations Changed America's Social Agenda* (Temple University Press, 1996).

Ron Suskind, "Why Are These Men Laughing?," *Esquire*, vol. 139, no. 1 (January 2003), pp. 96–105.

Kathryn Dunn Tenpas, "Words vs. Deeds: President George W. Bush and Polling," *Brookings Review*, vol. 21, no. 3 (Summer 2003), pp. 32–35.

Evan Thomas et al., *Election 2004* (PublicAffairs, 2005).

Charles Tiefer, *The Semi-Sovereign Presidency: The Bush Administration's Strategy for Governing without Congress* (Westview Press, 1994).

Charles Tiefer, *Veering Right: How the Bush Administration Subverts the Law for Conservative Causes* (University of California Press, 2004).

Stephen J. Wayne and Clyde Wilcox, eds., *The Election of the Century* (M. E. Sharpe, 2002).

Marcia Lynn Whicker et al., eds., *The Presidency and the Persian Gulf War* (Praeger, 1993).

Clyde Wilcox, *Onward Christian Soldiers?: The Religious Right in American Politics* (Westview Press, 1996).

148   [Bush family relations to presidents] : see Schweizer and Schweizer, p. xvi.

148   ["Really irks me" and "you were judged apart"] : R. W. Apple Jr., "Dad Was President (but Please, No Dynasty Talk)," *New York Times*, January 31, 2000, pp. A1, A20.

149   ["You can find everything"] : quoted in "Cactus-Nasty Campaign," *Time*, vol. 84, no. 16 (October 16, 1964), p. 39.

149   ["Some of the far right positions"] : quoted in Mervin, p. 222.

150   ["Procedural presidency"] : Mullins and Wildavsky.

150   ["Man of no discernible"] : quoted in Parmet, *George Bush*, p. 300.

150   ["Congress will push"] : Acceptance Speech, August 18, 1988, quoted at p. 7, George Bush Presidential Library. http://bushlibrary.tamu.edu/research/pdfs/rnc.pdf.

151   ["More like Ronald Reagan"] : quoted in Parmet, *George Bush*, p. 339.

151   ["Kinder, gentler"] : Acceptance Speech, p. 8.

151   ["Harvard Yard's boutique"] : quoted in Maureen Dowd, "Bush Paints Rival as Elitist, With 'Harvard Yard' Views," *New York Times*, June 10, 1988, p. B6.

151   [Poll on Americans' wishes for alternative candidates] : W. Lance Bennett, *The Governing Crisis: Media, Money, and Marketing in American Elections*, 2nd ed. (St. Martin's Press, 1996), p. 29.

151   [Election results, 1988] : see Gerald M. Pomper, "The Presidential Election," in Pomper et al., *Election of 1988*, pp. 129–52.

152   ["Anathema"] : quoted in Parmet, *George Bush*, p. 430.

152   ["You want a strategy"] : quoted in Mervin, pp. 72–73.

152   [READ MY LIPS] : see News Conference, June 29, 1990, in Bush, *Public Papers* (U. S. Government Printing Office, 1990–93), vol. 1990, part 1, pp. 880–89, esp. p. 883.

152   [Quayle on best Republican issue] : Quayle, *Standing Firm* (HarperCollins, 1994), pp. 192–93.

152   ["More supportive"] : quoted in Parmet, *George Bush*, p. 440.

153 ["Bush League"] : "Bush League," *Newsweek*, vol. 116, no. 17 (October 22, 1990), p. 20.

154 ["Kuwait is liberated"] : February 27, 1991, in Bush, *Public Papers*, vol. 1991, part 1, pp. 187–88, quoted at p. 187.

154 ["No second thoughts"] : quoted in Schweizer and Schweizer, p. 399.

154 [Bush on sending troops without congressional authorization] : Bush and Scowcroft, p. 446.

154 [Bush's approval rating after war] : Phillips, p. 310.

154 ["No clear idea"] : quoted in Kolb, p. 123.

155 ["Politics drives some things"] : quoted in Mervin, p. 222.

155 [Poll on country's direction, spring 1992] : see Greene, p. 164.

155 ["Religious war"] : 1992 Republican National Convention Speech, August 17, 1992. http://www.buchanan.org/pa-92-0817-rnc.html.

155 [Study on religious faith in Texas] : quoted in Phillips, p. 221.

156 ["Vision thing"] : quoted in Parmet, *George Bush*, p. 379.

156 ["Message: I care"] : Remarks and a Question-and-Answer Session at a Town-Hall Meeting, Exeter, New Hampshire, January 15, 1992, in Bush, *Public Papers*, vol. 1992–93, part 1, pp. 94–99, quoted at p. 99.

156 [Bush I's drop in support, 1988 to 1992] : see Phillips, pp. 74–75.

156 ["Messenger was unable"] : quoted in Minutaglio, p. 273; see also Hatfield, pp. 112–13.

157 ["Damn thing"] : quoted in Schweizer and Schweizer, p. 166.

157 ["Thought they could create"] : quoted in Skip Hollandsworth, "Born to Run," *Texas Monthly*, vol. 22, no. 5 (May 1994). General Reference Center Gold, Thomson Gale, accessed at Williams College Library, April 21, 2006.

158 ["What his father wanted"] : Fred Malek, quoted in Minutaglio, p. 253.

158 ["You'll be astounded"] : quoted in Fred Barnes, "Sore Winners," *New Republic*, vol. 199, no. 23 (December 5, 1988), pp. 16–18, at p. 16.

159 ["I might embarrass"] : quoted in Minutaglio, p. 210.

159 ["Renewal of faith"] : quoted in Cannon, "Bush and God," p. 16.

159 ["Wrong father"] : quoted in Bob Woodward, *Plan of Attack* (Simon & Schuster, 2004), p. 421.

159 [Government spending and poverty in Texas under Bush II] : see Hatfield, p. 207.

159 [Dent on Bush II] : quoted in ibid., p. 261.

160 ["Different candidate"] : quoted in Schweizer and Schweizer, p. 461.

160 ["Slaughterhouse politics"] : Moore and Slater, p. 256.

160 [McCain's plea] : quoted in Alison Mitchell and Frank Bruni, "Spotlight Turns on Ugly Side of Politicking," *New York Times*, February 11, 2000, p. A26.

160 [Conservative and evangelical vote in 2000 primaries] : Stephen J. Wayne, "It's Party Time," in Wayne and Wilcox, pp. 125–39, esp. pp. 127–28.

161 ["Uniter, not a divider"] : quoted in Dana Milbank, "W. Is for Warm and Fuzzy," *Washington Post*, March 20, 2000, pp. C1–C3, at p. C1.

161 ["Say anything"] : quoted in Terry M. Neal and Ceci Connolly, "Bush, Gore Grab for Reform Mantle," ibid., March 13, 2000, p. A4.

162 [Poll on Bush as moderate] : Kathleen A. Frankovic and Monika L. McDermott, "Public Opinion in the 2000 Election: The Ambivalent Electorate," in Pomper et al., *Election of 2000*, pp. 73–91, esp. p. 81.

162 [2000 election results] : Gerald M. Pomper, "The Presidential Election," in ibid., pp. 125–54; Clyde Wilcox, "Wither the Christian Right? The Elections and Beyond," in Wayne and Wilcox, pp. 107–22, esp. p. 116.

162 ["Believe I'm standing here"] : quoted in Patty Reinert, "Bush Plans Education, Tax Cut First: Takes His Case to the Hill," *Houston Chronicle*, December 19, 2000, p. A1. http://web.lexis-nexis.com/universe, accessed November 21, 2005.

162 ["Complete lack"] : quoted in Suskind, p. 99.

163 ["Hard-working people"] : "The First Gore-Bush Presidential Debate" (transcript), October 3, 2000. http://www.debates.org/pages/trans2000a.html.

163 ["Heck of a lot bigger"] : quoted in Dana Milbank, "Tax Cut Compromise Close Enough, Bush Says," *Washington Post*, April 7, 2001, p. A11.

163 ["Our strategy"] : Nicholas E. Calio, quoted in Alan K. Ota, "Calio's Assertive Style Moves Legislation," *Congressional Quarterly Weekly*, vol. 60, no. 48 (December 14, 2002), pp. 3251–54, at p. 3253.

164 ["One-term president"] : quoted in John Lancaster, "Senate Republicans Try to Regroup," *Washington Post*, May 26, 2001, p. A18.

164 [Bush on his new presidency, post-9/11] : David E. Sanger and Elisabeth Bumiller, "In One Month, a Presidency Transformed," *New York Times*, October 11, 2001, pp. B1, B11, esp. p. B1.

164 ["Rid the world"] : Remarks at the National Day of Prayer and Remembrance Service, September 14, 2001, in Bush, *Public Papers* (U. S. Government Printing Office, 2003–), vol. 2001, part 2, pp. 1108–1109, quoted at p. 1108.

164 [Bush as "decider"] : see Burke, p. 120; see also David S. Cloud, "Here's Donny! In His Defense, a Show Is Born," *New York Times*, April 19, 2006, pp. A1, A15.

165 ["Very tight team"] : quoted in Todd S. Purdum, "Mr. Heat Shield Keeps Boss Happy," *New York Times*, December 6, 2001, p. B7.

165 ["Go to the country"] : quoted in Thomas B. Edsall, "GOP Touts War as Campaign Issue," *Washington Post*, January 19, 2002, p. A2.

165 [Election results, 2002] : Abramson et al., ch. 11, esp. p. 260; Howard Fineman, "How Bush Did It," *Newsweek*, vol. 140, no. 21 (November 18, 2002), pp. 28–35.

165 [Rove on "fundamental" shift] : quoted in Michael Janofsky, "Rove Declares Nation Is Tilting to Republicans," *New York Times*, November 14, 2002, p. A33.

166 ["Got his mandate"] : Tony Coehlo, quoted in Dana Milbank and Mike Allen, "White House Claims Election Is Broad Mandate," *Washington Post*, November 7, 2002, pp. A27, A33, at p. A33.

166 [GOP "micro-targeting"] : Jamieson, pp. 26–27.

167 ["Even when we don't agree"] : "Bush Accepts," *New York Times*, September 3, 2004, p. P4.

167 ["Strong leader"] : Gerald M. Pomper, "The Presidential Election: The Ills of American Politics After 9/11," in Nelson, *Elections of 2004*, pp. 42–68, quoted at p. 56 (table 3-6).

167 [Election results, 2004] : ibid.; Ceaser and Busch, *Red Over Blue*, esp. ch. 5.

168 [Bush's support in Congress] : Stephen J. Wayne, "Bush and Congress: Old Problems and New Challenges," in Edwards and Davies, pp. 101–22, esp. p. 119 (table 6.10).

168 ["Gone far past"] : Lemann, "The Quiet Man," p. 67.

169 ["A hard-liner"] : quoted in Todd S. Purdum, "A Face Only a President Could Love," *Vanity Fair*, no. 550 (June 2006), pp. 124–29, 174–79, at p. 176.

169 ["Earned capital"] : President Holds News Conference, November 4, 2004. http://www.whitehouse.gov/news/releases/2004/11/20041104-5.html.

169 ["Permanent majority"] : quoted in John F. Harris and Jim VandeHei, "Doubts About Mandate for Bush, GOP," *Washington Post*, May 2, 2005, p. A1. http://web.lexis-nexis.com/universe, accessed June 30, 2005.

170 [Bush's isolation] : see Evan Thomas and Richard Wolffe, "Bush in the Bubble," *Newsweek*, vol. 146, no. 25 (December 19, 2005), pp. 30–39; see also Nancy Gibbs and Mike Allen, "One Thousand and Sixty-Five Days To Go," *Time*, vol. 167, no. 9 (February 19, 2006), pp. 24–30.

170 ["Erosion of the powers"] : quoted in Dana Milbank, "Cheney Refuses Records' Release," *Washington Post*, January 28, 2002, pp. A1, A12, at p. A1.

170 ["Protect the executive branch"] : News Conference, March 13, 2002, in Bush, *Public Papers*, vol. 2002, part 1, pp. 394–407, quoted at p. 399.

170 ["Not a monarchy"] : quoted in Bruce Shapiro, "Executive Obstruction," *The Nation* (Web only), posted December 19, 2001. http://www.thenation.com/doc/20011231/shapiro20011219.

171 ["President's determinations"] : John C. Yoo, "The President's Constitutional Authority to Conduct Military Operations Against Terrorists and Nations Supporting Them," September 25, 2001. http://www.usdoj.gov/olc/warpowers925.htm.

171 [Cheney on presidential power] : Vice President's Remarks to the Traveling Press, December 20, 2005. http://www.whitehouse.gov/news/releases/2005/12/20051220-9.html.

172 ["Make Nixon jealous"] : Hugh Davis Graham, quoted in Carl M. Cannon, "For the Record," *National Journal*, vol. 34, no. 2 (January 12, 2002), pp. 90–96, at p. 96.

172 ["Little cabal"] : Lawrence Wilkerson, "Weighing the Uniqueness of the Bush Administration's National Security Decision-Making Process: Boon or Danger to American Democracy?," remarks to the American Strategy Program Policy Forum, New America Foundation, October 19, 2005. http://www.thewashingtonnote.com/archives/Wilkerson%20Speech%20—%20WEB.htm.

173 ["Prime mover"] : "The Prison Puzzle" (editorial), *New York Times*, November 3, 2005, p. A26.

173 [January 2001 survey on national priorities] : Wayne, "Bush and Congress," p. 103 (tables 6.1, 6.2).

174 ["Just ignoring"] : quoted in David D. Kirkpatrick, "Christian Groups Warn G.O.P. That Inaction Could Be Costly," *New York Times*, May 15, 2006, pp. A1, A18, at p. A18.

174 ["How quickly"] : Bush, *A Charge To Keep* (William Morrow, 1999), p. 218.

175 [Bush as "impostor"] : see Bartlett, ch. 8, and passim.

175 [Rove on 2006 and Democratic party] : quoted in Dan Balz, "Rove Offers Republicans a Battle Plan for Elections," *Washington Post*, January 21, 2006. http://web.lexis-nexis.com/universe, accessed February 19, 2006.

CHAPTER 8 — NEEDED: PARTY POLARIZATION

Alan I. Abramowitz and Kyle L. Saunders, "Ideological Realignment in the U. S. Electorate," *Journal of Politics*, vol. 60, no. 3 (August 1998), pp. 634–62.

John H. Aldrich, *Why Parties?: The Origin and Transformation of Political Parties in America* (University of Chicago Press, 1995).

American Political Science Association, *Toward a More Responsible Two-Party System* (Rinehart, 1950).

Kenneth S. Baer, *Reinventing Democrats: The Politics of Liberalism from Reagan to Clinton* (University Press of Kansas, 2000).

Matt Bai, "The Framing Wars," *New York Times Magazine*, July 17, 2005, pp. 39–45, 68–71.

Matt Bai, "Notion Building," *New York Times Magazine*, October 12, 2003, pp. 82–87.

W. Lance Bennett, *The Governing Crisis: Media, Money, and Marketing in American Elections*, 2nd ed. (St. Martin's Press, 1996).

Jeffrey M. Berry, *The New Liberalism: The Rising Power of Citizen Groups* (Brookings Institution, 1999).

Robert L. Borosage and Roger Hickey, eds., *The Next Agenda: Blueprint for a New Progressive Movement* (Westview Press, 2001).

David W. Brady and Craig Volden, *Revolving Gridlock: Politics and Policy from Jimmy Carter to George W. Bush,* 2nd ed. (Westview Press, 2006).

James MacGregor Burns, *Leadership* (Harper & Row, 1978).

James MacGregor Burns et al., eds., *The Democrats Must Lead: The Case for a Progressive Democratic Party* (Westview Press, 1992).

James W. Ceaser, "Direct Participation in Politics," *Proceedings of the American Academy of Political Science*, vol. 34, no. 2 (1981), pp. 121–37.

James W. Ceaser, "Political Parties and Presidential Ambition," *Journal of Politics*, vol. 40, no. 3 (August 1978), pp. 708–39.

Jonathan Chait, "The Case Against New Ideas," *New Republic*, vol. 233, nos. 2–3 (July 11 and 18, 2005), pp. 19–23.

Matthew A. Crenson and Benjamin Ginsberg, *Downsizing Democracy: How America Sidelined Its Citizens and Privatized Its Public* (Johns Hopkins University Press, 2002).

William Crotty, ed., *The State of Democracy in America* (Georgetown University Press, 2001).

George Crowder, *Liberalism and Value Pluralism* (Continuum, 2002).

E. J. Dionne Jr., *Stand Up Fight Back: Republican Toughs, Democratic Wimps, and the Politics of Revenge* (Simon & Schuster, 2004).

E. J. Dionne Jr., *They Only Look Dead: Why Progressives Will Dominate the Next Political Era* (Simon & Schuster, 1996).

E. J. Dionne Jr., *Why Americans Hate Politics* (Simon & Schuster, 1991).

Jeff Faux, *The Party's Not Over: A New Vision for the Democrats* (Basic Books, 1996).

Thomas Frank, *What's the Matter with Kansas?: How Conservatives Won the Heart of America* (Metropolitan Books/Henry Holt, 2004).

Thomas Frank, "What's the Matter with Liberals?," *New York Review of Books*, vol. 52, no. 8 (May 12, 2005), pp. 46–51.

Marshall Ganz, "Voters in the Crosshairs: How Technology and the Market Are Destroying Politics," *American Prospect*, vol. 5, no. 16 (Winter 1994), pp. 100–109.

John G. Geer, "New Deal Issues and the American Electorate, 1952–1988," *Political Behavior*, vol. 14, no. 1 (March 1992), pp. 45–65.

Paul Glastris, "Why Can't Democrats Get Tough?," *Washington Monthly*, vol. 34, no. 3 (March 2002), pp. 38–44.

John C. Green and Rick Farmer, eds., *The State of the Parties: The Changing Role of Contemporary American Parties*, 4th ed. (Rowman & Littlefield, 2003).

Philip Green, *Equality and Democracy* (New Press, 1998).

Stanley B. Greenberg, "The Revolt Against Politics," *The New Democrat*, vol. 7, no. 1 (January-February 1995), pp. 7–14.

Stanley B. Greenberg, *The Two Americas: Our Current Political Deadlock and How to Break It* (St. Martin's Press, 2004).

Stanley B. Greenberg and Theda Skocpol, eds., *The New Majority: Toward a Popular Progressive Politics* (Yale University Press, 1997).

John A. Hall and Charles Lindholm, *Is America Breaking Apart?* (Princeton University Press, 1999).

John F. Harris, "In '04, GOP Is Missed Target," *Washington Post*, October 31, 2004, p. A17.

Ronald Hayduk and Kevin Mattson, eds., *Democracy's Moment: Reforming the American Political System for the 21st Century* (Rowman & Littlefield, 2002).

John R. Hibbing and Elizabeth Theiss-Morse, *Stealth Democracy: Americans' Beliefs About How Government Should Work* (Cambridge University Press, 2002).

James Davison Hunter, *Culture Wars: The Struggle to Define America* (Basic Books, 1991).

"Inequality and American Democracy: A Symposium," *PS*, vol. 39, no. 1 (January 2006).

Lesley A. Jacobs, *Pursuing Equal Opportunities: The Theory and Practice of Egalitarian Justice* (Cambridge University Press, 2004).

John B. Judis, *The Paradox of American Democracy: Elites, Special Interests, and the Betrayal of the Public Trust* (Pantheon, 2000).

John B. Judis and Ruy Teixeira, *The Emerging Democratic Majority* (Lisa Drew/Scribner, 2002).

Evron M. Kirkpatrick, "'Toward a More Responsible Party System': Political Science, Policy Science, or Pseudo-Science?," *American Political Science Review*, vol. 65, no. 4 (December 1971), pp. 965–90.

James R. Kluegel and Eliot R. Smith, *Beliefs About Inequality: Americans' Views of What Is and What Ought to Be* (Aldine de Gruyter, 1986).

Peter Knapp et al., *The Assault on Equality* (Praeger, 1996).

David Kusnet, *Speaking American: How the Democrats Can Win in the Nineties* (Thunder's Mouth Press, 1992).

David G. Lawrence, *The Collapse of the Democratic Presidential Majority: Realignment, Dealignment, and Electoral Change from Franklin Roosevelt to Bill Clinton* (Westview Press, 1996).

David C. Leege et al., *The Politics of Cultural Differences: Social Change and Voter Mobilization Strategies in the Post–New Deal Period* (Princeton University Press, 2002).

William E. Leuchtenburg, *In the Shadow of FDR: From Harry Truman to George W. Bush*, 3rd ed. (Cornell University Press, 2001).

L. Sandy Maisel, "The Platform-Writing Process: Candidate-Centered Platforms in 1992," *Political Science Quarterly*, vol. 108, no. 4 (Winter 1993-94), pp. 671–98.

L. Sandy Maisel, ed., *The Parties Respond: Changes in American Parties and Campaigns*, 4th ed. (Westview Press, 2002).

William G. Mayer, *The Divided Democrats: Ideological Unity, Party Reform, and Presidential Elections* (Westview Press, 1996).

David Menefee-Libey, *The Triumph of Campaign-Centered Politics* (Chatham House, 2000).

Sidney M. Milkis, *The President and the Parties: The Transformation of the American Party System Since the New Deal* (Oxford University Press, 1993).

Michael Nelson, ed., *The Elections of 2004* (CQ Press, 2005).

Michael Nelson, ed., *The Presidency and the Political System*, 7th ed. (CQ Press, 2003).

Richard E. Neustadt, *Presidential Power and the Modern Presidents: The Politics of Leadership from Roosevelt to Reagan* (Free Press, 1991).

Charles Noble, *The Collapse of Liberalism: Why America Needs a New Left* (Rowman & Littlefield, 2004).

George Packer, ed., *The Fight Is for Democracy: Winning the War of Ideas in America and the World* (Perennial, 2003).

Thomas E. Patterson, *The Vanishing Voter: Public Involvement in an Age of Uncertainty* (Alfred A. Knopf, 2002).

Robert D. Putnam, *Bowling Alone: The Collapse and Revival of American Community* (Simon & Schuster, 2000).

Marcus G. Raskin, *Liberalism: The Genius of American Ideals* (Rowman & Littlefield, 2004).

H. Mark Roelofs, *The Poverty of American Politics*, 2nd ed. (Temple University Press, 1998).

Stephen A. Salmore and Barbara G. Salmore, "Candidate-Centered Parties: Politics Without Intermediaries," in Richard A. Harris and Sidney M. Milkis, eds., *Remaking American Politics* (Westview Press, 1989), pp. 215–38.

Steven E. Schier, *You Call This an Election?: America's Peculiar Democracy* (Georgetown University Press, 2003).

David Sirota, "The Democrats' Da Vinci Code," *American Prospect Online*, December 8, 2004. http://www.prospect.org/web/page.ww?section=root&name=ViewWeb& articleId=8917.

Neil J. Smelser and Jeffrey C. Alexander, eds., *Diversity and Its Discontents: Cultural Conflict and Common Ground in Contemporary American Society* (Princeton University Press, 1999).

James L. Sundquist, "Has America Lost Its Social Conscience—and How Will It Get It Back?," *Political Science Quarterly*, vol. 101, no. 4 (1986), pp. 513–33.

Ruy Teixeira and Joel Rogers, *America's Forgotten Majority: Why the White Working Class Still Matters* (New Republic/Basic Books, 2000).

Julius Turner, "Responsible Parties: A Dissent from the Floor," *American Political Science Review*, vol. 45, no. 1 (March 1951), pp. 143–52.

Martin P. Wattenberg, *The Rise of Candidate-Centered Politics: Presidential Elections of the 1980s* (Harvard University Press, 1991).

Martin P. Wattenberg, "Turnout in the 2004 Presidential Election," *Presidential Studies Quarterly*, vol. 35, no. 1 (March 2005), pp. 138–46.

Stephen J. Wayne, ed., *Is This Any Way to Run a Democratic Government?* (Georgetown University Press, 2004).

Margaret Weir, ed., *The Social Divide: Political Parties and the Future of Activist Government* (Brookings Institution/Russell Sage, 1998).

John Kenneth White and Jerome M. Mileur, eds., *Challenges to Party Government* (Southern Illinois University Press, 1992).

Jules Witcover, *Party of the People: A History of the Democrats* (Random House, 2003).

Daniel Yankelovich, "How Changes in the Economy Are Reshaping American Values," in Henry J. Aaron et al., eds., *Values and Public Policy* (Brookings Institution, 1994), pp. 16–53.

178 [2004 election and scholarly explanations for Democratic decline] : see Nicole Mellow, "Voting Behavior: The 2004 Election and the Roots of Republican Success," in Nelson, *Elections of 2004*, pp. 69–87.

180 ["Democrats Must Lead"] : Burns et al., *Democrats Must Lead*.

180 ["Appear to be related"] : quoted in Burns and Sorenson, *Dead Center: Clinton-Gore Leadership and the Perils of Moderation* (Lisa Drew/Scribner, 1999), pp. 342, 344.

181 ["Unheard of in Europe"] : Patterson, p. 46.

181 [Turnout, 2004] : see Wattenberg, "Turnout," esp. p. 140.

182 ["Once I received"] : Schier, p. 12.

183 [African American registration in the South, 1960s] : William C. Havard, "The South: A Shifting Perspective," in Havard, ed., *The Changing Politics of the South* (Louisiana State University Press, 1972), pp. 3–36, esp. pp. 20, 21 (tables 3, 4).

183 ["Forever forming associations"] : Tocqueville, *Democracy in America*, George Lawrence, trans. (Harper & Row, 1966), p. 485 (vol. 2, part 2, ch. 5).

183 [Putnam on participation] : Putnam, esp. chs. 2, 21.

184 [Patterson survey] : Patterson, p. 59 (table 2.2).

185 ["Fairly egalitarian"] : Bartels, "Is the Water Rising? Reflections on Inequality and American Democracy," *PS*, vol. 39, no. 1 (January 2006), pp. 39–42, quoted at p. 41.

185 [Poverty under Clinton and Bush II] : U. S. Census Bureau, "Historical Poverty Tables" (table 2). http://www.census.gov/hhes/www/poverty/histpov/hstpov2.html; and Bartels, p. 41 fn. 3.

185 ["Substantial decline"] : Hacker, "Inequality, American Democracy, and American Political Science: The Need for Cumulative Research," *PS*, vol. 39, no. 1 (January 2006), pp. 47–49, quoted at p. 47.

185 [FDR on Tweedledum and Tweedledee] : "Introduction: The Continuing Struggle for Liberalism," in Roosevelt, *Public Papers and Addresses*, Samuel I. Rosenman, comp. (Random House, 1938–50), vol. 7, pp. xxi–xxxiii, esp. p. xxxii.

187 ["They are unanimous"] : Campaign Address at Madison Square Garden, New York City, October 31, 1936, in ibid., vol. 5, pp. 566–71, quoted at p. 568.

CHAPTER 9 — EMPOWERING FOLLOWERS

American Political Science Association, *Toward a More Responsible Two-Party System* (Rinehart, 1950).

Wayne Baker, *America's Crisis of Values: Reality and Perception* (Princeton University Press, 2005).

Jeffrey M. Berry, *The New Liberalism: The Rising Power of Citizen Groups* (Brookings Institution, 1999).

Sarah A. Binder, *Stalemate: Causes and Consequences of Legislative Gridlock* (Brookings Institution, 2003).

Jon R. Bond and Richard Fleisher, eds., *Polarized Politics: Congress and the President in a Partisan Era* (CQ Press, 2000).

Robert L. Borosage and Roger Hickey, eds., *The Next Agenda: Blueprint for a New Progressive Movement* (Westview Press, 2001).

David W. Brady and Craig Volden, *Revolving Gridlock: Politics and Policy from Jimmy Carter to George W. Bush,* 2nd ed. (Westview Press, 2006).

James MacGregor Burns, *Congress on Trial: The Legislative Process and the Administrative State* (Harper & Brothers, 1949).

James MacGregor Burns, *The Deadlock of Democracy: Four-Party Politics in America* (Prentice-Hall, 1963).

James MacGregor Burns, *Leadership* (Harper & Row, 1978).

James MacGregor Burns, *The Power to Lead: The Crisis of the American Presidency* (Simon and Schuster, 1984).

James MacGregor Burns, *Presidential Government: The Crucible of Leadership* (Houghton Mifflin, 1966).

James MacGregor Burns, *Transforming Leadership: A New Pursuit of Happiness* (Atlantic Monthly Press, 2003).

Colin Campbell, *The U. S. Presidency in Crisis: A Comparative Perspective* (Oxford University Press, 1998).

Richard S. Conley, *The Presidency, Congress, and Divided Government: A Postwar Assessment* (Texas A&M University Press, 2003).

George Crowder, *Liberalism and Value Pluralism* (Continuum, 2002).

E. J. Dionne Jr., *They Only Look Dead: Why Progressives Will Dominate the Next Political Era* (Simon & Schuster, 1996).

Lawrence C. Dodd and Bruce I. Oppenheimer, eds., *Congress Reconsidered*, 7th ed. (CQ Press, 2001).

Paul Frymer, "Ideological Consensus within Divided Party Government," *Political Science Quarterly*, vol. 109, no. 2 (Summer 1994), pp. 287–311.

Robert A. Goldwin and Art Kaufman, eds., *Separation of Powers—Does It Still Work?* (American Enterprise Institute, 1986).

Philip Green, *Equality and Democracy* (New Press, 1998).

Stanley B. Greenberg, *The Two Americas: Our Current Political Deadlock and How to Break It* (St. Martin's Press, 2004).

Stanley B. Greenberg and Theda Skocpol, eds., *The New Majority: Toward a Popular Progressive Politics* (Yale University Press, 1997).

Ronald Hayduk and Kevin Mattson, eds., *Democracy's Moment: Reforming the American Political System for the 21st Century* (Rowman & Littlefield, 2002).

Hugh Heclo and Lester M. Salamon, eds., *The Illusion of Presidential Government* (Westview Press, 1981).

Stephen Holmes and Cass R. Sunstein, *The Cost of Rights: Why Liberty Depends on Taxes* (W. W. Norton, 1999).

James Davison Hunter, *Culture Wars: The Struggle to Define America* (Basic Books, 1991).

"Inequality and American Democracy: A Symposium," *PS*, vol. 39, no. 1 (January 2006).

Charles O. Jones, *The Presidency in a Separated System*, 2nd ed. (Brookings Institution, 2005).

Charles O. Jones, *Separate But Equal Branches: Congress and the Presidency* (Chatham House, 1995).

Evron M. Kirkpatrick, "'Toward a More Responsible Party System': Political Science, Policy Science, or Pseudo-Science?," *American Political Science Review*, vol. 65, no. 4 (December 1971), pp. 965–90.

Peter Knapp et al., *The Assault on Equality* (Praeger, 1996).

Michael J. Korzi, *A Seat of Popular Leadership: The Presidency, Political Parties, and Democratic Government* (University of Massachusetts Press, 2004).

James M. Kouzes and Barry Z. Posner, "Follower-Oriented Leadership," in George R. Goethals and Georgia J. Sorenson, eds., *Encyclopedia of Leadership* (Sage, 2004), vol. 2, pp. 494–99.

George Lakoff, *Moral Politics: How Liberals and Conservatives Think*, 2nd ed. (University of Chicago Press, 2002).

Marc Landy and Sidney M. Milkis, *Presidential Greatness* (University Press of Kansas, 2000).

William E. Leuchtenburg, *In the Shadow of FDR: From Harry Truman to George W. Bush*, 3rd ed. (Cornell University Press, 2001).

Andrew Levine, *The American Ideology* (Routledge, 2004).

Lawrence D. Longley and Neil R. Peirce, *The Electoral College Primer 2000* (Yale University Press, 1999).

Theodore J. Lowi, "Presidential Democracy in America: Toward the Homogenized Regime," *Political Science Quarterly*, vol. 109, no. 3 (Summer 1994), pp. 401–15.

Sidney M. Milkis, "The Presidency, Democratic Reform, and Constitutional Change," *PS*, vol. 20, no. 3 (Summer 1987), pp. 628–36.

Sidney M. Milkis, *The President and the Parties: The Transformation of the American Party System Since the New Deal* (Oxford University Press, 1993).

Michael Nelson, ed., *The Presidency and the Political System*, 7th ed. (CQ Press, 2003).

Richard E. Neustadt, *Presidential Power and the Modern Presidents: The Politics of Leadership from Roosevelt to Reagan* (Free Press, 1991).

Charles Noble, *The Collapse of Liberalism: Why America Needs a New Left* (Rowman & Littlefield, 2004).

George Packer, ed., *The Fight Is for Democracy: Winning the War of Ideas in America and the World* (Perennial, 2003).

Mark P. Petracca et al., "Proposals for Constitutional Reform: An Evaluation of the Committee on the Constitutional System," *Presidential Studies Quarterly*, vol. 20 (Summer 1990), pp. 503–32.

Austin Ranney, "The President and His Party," in Anthony King, ed., *Both Ends of the Avenue: The Presidency, the Executive Branch, and Congress in the 1980s* (American Enterprise Institute, 1983), pp. 131–53.

Marcus G. Raskin, *Liberalism: The Genius of American Ideals* (Rowman & Littlefield, 2004).

Donald L. Robinson, ed., *Reforming American Government: The Bicentennial Papers of the Committee on the Constitutional System* (Westview Press, 1985).

H. Mark Roelofs, *The Poverty of American Politics*, 2nd ed. (Temple University Press, 1998).

John E. Schwarz, *Freedom Reclaimed: Rediscovering the American Vision* (Johns Hopkins University Press, 2005).

Boas Shamir, "Motivation of Followers," in Goethals and Sorenson, vol. 2, pp. 499–504.

David Sirota, "The Democrats' Da Vinci Code," *American Prospect Online*, December 8, 2004. http://www.prospect.org/web/page.ww?section=root&name=ViewWeb&articleId=8917.

Neil J. Smelser and Jeffrey C. Alexander, eds., *Diversity and Its Discontents: Cultural Conflict and Common Ground in Contemporary American Society* (Princeton University Press, 1999).

Robert J. Spitzer, *President and Congress: Executive Hegemony at the Crossroads of American Government* (Temple University Press, 1993).

James L. Sundquist, *Constitutional Reform and Effective Government*, rev. ed. (Brookings Institution, 1992).

James L. Sundquist, "Has America Lost Its Social Conscience—and How Will It Get It Back?," *Political Science Quarterly*, vol. 101, no. 4 (1986), pp. 513–33.

James L. Sundquist, ed., *Back to Gridlock?: Governance in the Clinton Years* (Brookings Institution, 1995).

James L. Sundquist, ed., *Beyond Gridlock?: Prospects for Governance in the Clinton Years—and After* (Brookings Institution, 1993).

Raymond Tatalovich and Thomas S. Engeman, *The Presidency and Political Science: Two Hundred Years of Constitutional Debate* (Johns Hopkins University Press, 2003).

James A. Thurber, ed., *Divided Democracy: Cooperation and Conflict Between the President and Congress* (CQ Press, 1991).

James A. Thurber, ed., *Rivals for Power: Presidential-Congressional Relations*, 2nd ed. (Rowman & Littlefield, 2002).

James A. Thurber, ed., *Rivals for Power: Presidential-Congressional Relations,* 3rd ed. (Rowman & Littlefield, 2006).

Kurt von Mettenheim, ed., *Presidential Institutions and Democratic Politics: Comparing Regional and National Contexts* (Johns Hopkins University Press, 1997).

Alan Ware, "Divided Government in the United States," in Robert Elgie, ed., *Divided Government in Comparative Perspective* (Oxford University Press, 2001), pp. 21–39.

Richard W. Waterman, ed., *The Presidency Reconsidered* (F. E. Peacock, 1993).

Ben J. Wattenberg, *Values Matter Most* (Free Press, 1995).

Martin P. Wattenberg, *The Rise of Candidate-Centered Politics: Presidential Elections of the 1980s* (Harvard University Press, 1991).

Stephen J. Wayne, ed., *Is This Any Way to Run a Democratic Government?* (Georgetown University Press, 2004).

John Kenneth White, *The Values Divide: American Politics and Culture in Transition* (Chatham House/Seven Bridges Press, 2003).

Aaron Wildavsky, *The Beleaguered Presidency* (Transaction, 1991).

Aaron Wildavsky, ed., *The Presidency* (Little, Brown, 1969).

Daniel Yankelovich, "How Changes in the Economy Are Reshaping American Values," in Henry J. Aaron et al., eds., *Values and Public Policy* (Brookings Institution, 1994), pp. 16–53.

189 [Presidential ratings] : Arthur M. Schlesinger Jr., "The Ultimate Approval Rating," *New York Times Magazine*, December 15, 1996, pp. 46–51, Kennedy quoted at p. 46; see also Schlesinger, *A Thousand Days: John F. Kennedy in the White House* (Houghton Mifflin, 1965), pp. 674–76.

190 [Gergen on expectations] : Gergen, *Eyewitness to Power: The Essence of Leadership, Nixon to Clinton* (Simon & Schuster, 2000), p. 344.

191 [CCS] : see Robinson; Sundquist, *Constitutional Reform.*

193 ["Too brief"] : quoted in Sundquist, *Constitutional Reform*, p. 70.

193 ["Proved himself"] : Rufus King, echoing an earlier remark by Roger Sherman, July 19, 1787, in Max Farrand, ed., *The Records of the Federal Convention of 1787*, rev. ed. (Yale University Press, 1937), vol. 2, p. 55.

193 ["One of the strengths"] : Lyn Nofziger, quoted in Ken Bode, "Reagan Runs Ahead," *New Republic*, vol. 178, no. 7 (February 18, 1978), pp. 8–14, at p. 14.

193 [Reagan's support in Congress] : *Congressional Quarterly Weekly*, vol. 48, no. 51 (December 22, 1990), p. 4208 (table).

195 ["Values" in 2004 vote] : see Gerald M. Pomper, "The Presidential Election: The Ills of American Politics After 9/11," in Michael Nelson, ed., *The Elections of 2004* (CQ Press, 2005), pp. 42–68, esp. pp. 59–61.

196 ["Greatest degree of happiness"] : letter to Francis Adrian van der Kemp, August 22, 1812, in Jefferson, *Works*, H. A. Washington, ed. (Townsend Mac Coun, 1884), vol. 6, pp. 44–46, quoted at p. 45.

197 [Jefferson's advice to American travelers] : Jefferson, "Hints to Americans Travelling in Europe" (1788), in Jefferson, *Papers*, Julian P. Boyd, ed. (Princeton University Press, 1950–), vol. 13, pp. 264–75, esp. p. 269.

197 [Four Freedoms and second Bill of Rights] : Annual Message to the Congress, January 6, 1941, in Roosevelt, *Public Papers and Addresses*, Samuel I. Rosenman, comp. (Random House, 1938–50), vol. 9, pp. 663–72, esp. p. 672; and Message to the Congress on the State of the Union, January 11, 1944, in ibid., vol. 13, pp. 32–42, quoted at p. 41.

197 ["Liberation of the diverse energies"] : Address in Berkeley at the University of California, March 23, 1962, in Kennedy, *Public Papers* (U. S. Government Printing Office, 1962–64), vol. 1962, pp. 263–66, quoted at p. 265.

198 [American expectations for leadership] : see Kouzes and Posner, p. 495 (table 1).

Acknowledgments

Susan Dunn's review of the first version of *Running Alone* was both inspiring and exacting. The participation of Milton Djuric in all aspects of this work was generous, creative, and indispensable. I am grateful to my agent, Ike Williams, for his major role in helping to launch this book to publication. I thank Lara Heimert at Basic Books for her long and devoted editorial contribution. Also at Basic Books, production editor Marco Pavia and copyeditor Jessica Hoffmann efficiently sped the manuscript to print. Irwin F. Gellman provided a review of the chapters. The "second generation"—Deborah and Mecca, Stewart and David—helped in many diverse ways.

Robin Keller and the Faculty Secretarial Office at Williams College helped mightily with communication between author and publisher. The staff of Sawyer Library at Williams and of the John F. Kennedy Presidential Library in Boston were generous in making their skills and resources available.

An earlier version of chapters eight and nine appeared in *Working Papers*, edited by Barbara Kellerman and published by the John F. Kennedy School of Government at Harvard University, Spring 2006.

Index